Lesbian Identity and Contemporary Psychotherapy

Lesbian Identity and Contemporary Psychotherapy
A Framework for Clinical Practice

Eda G. Goldstein

Lois C. Horowitz

THE ANALYTIC PRESS

2003   Hillsdale, NJ   London

Published by
The Analytic Press, Inc., Publishers
101 West Street, Hillsdale, NJ 07642
www.analyticpress.com

Book Antiqua 10/12
Designed and typeset by
Christopher Jaworski, Bloomfield, NJ
qualitext@verizon.net

Index by
Leonard S. Rosenbaum, Washington, DC

Library of Congress
Cataloging-in-Publication Data

Goldstein, Eda G.
Lesbian identity and contemporary psychotherapy : a framework for clinical
  practice / Eda G. Goldstein and Lois C. Horowitz.
p. cm.
Includes bibliographical references and index.

ISBN 0–88163–349–6

1. Lesbian — Mental health.
2. Psychodynamic psychotherapy.
3. Psychoanalysis.
I. Horowitz, Lois C., 1953–.
II. Title.

RC558.5.G653   2003
616.89′14′086643 — dc21
2003041778

Printed in the United States of America
10 9 8 7 6 5 4 3 2 1

To Our Partners
Patricia A. Petrocelli
Patricia K. Norton

Contents

Acknowledgments

Our desire to write a clinical book about lesbian identity and psychotherapy developed gradually over many years. We wanted to describe a treatment approach that is affirmative for lesbians. This book presents a synthesis of our personal and professional experiences, clinical practice, and theoretical interests that include a broad range of psychoanalytic literature. There are many wonderful individuals and psychoanalytic writers who have influenced our thinking. We hope that sharing our ideas about the treatment process for lesbians will be useful to clinicians.

This book was both a professional undertaking and a personal journey. Writing it gave us the opportunity to reflect on our life transitions and transformations and on the clinical process work in which we have been engaged for many years. Writing a book is arduous, but our collaboration lightened the work. When we began, we did not know that our task would provide such intellectual stimulation as well as opportunities to share our own life challenges and triumphs, become friends, and have fun. We believe that the book is much richer than it would have been had each of us written on her own.

We thank those, especially John Kerr of The Analytic Press, who encouraged our efforts and provided valuable assistance. Numerous family members, friends, and colleagues were particularly supportive during the writing of this book.

Individually, we thank several people.

E. G. G.: I am grateful to the faculty of the New York University and Shirley M. Ehrenkranz School of Social Work; my partner, Patricia A. Petrocelli; and my good friends Enid Ain, Dick Rizzo, Lucille Spira, Hannalynn and Frank Wilkens, Norma Hakusa, and Robert Counts. They have all been a source of encouragement. I regret that my late brother, Mervyn F. Goldstein, who died in February 2002, is not able to share the moment.

L. C. H.: I am deeply grateful to my partner, Patricia Norton, and to my sister, Jayne Horowitz, for their unconditional love and encouragement. I also thank my parents, Annette and Arthur Horowitz, and my good friends and colleagues, Ellen Paul, John LaValle, Arleen Bergen, Ken Sommer, Sal Licata, and the late Alvin Finkelstein, for their inspiration and support. Finally, I am thankful to Margaret Black for her valuable guidance.

We profoundly appreciate the patients who allowed us to enter their lives and who shared their narratives with us. Their life experiences have affected us deeply. Last, we are grateful to all those lesbians who came before us and paved the way.

Introduction

This book is about clinical work with lesbians. It is based on both our personal and professional experiences. Our keen interest in applying relational concepts and treatment principles and new perspectives on gender and sexuality have provided the impetus for our writing. We shall try to describe and illustrate how contemporary psychoanalytic psychotherapy can provide women with the opportunity to explore the often difficult and complex process by which they have come to identify as lesbians, to understand the unique meaning that being a lesbian has to their self-concept and lives, and to validate their personal struggles and journey.

We are not proposing a unique approach or a set of rigid techniques for the psychotherapy of lesbians nor do we focus on the treatment of lesbianism itself. Rather, we are interested in articulating a way of working with lesbians that takes into consideration the special issues that they have confronted in the course of their lives and that affirms their sense of self and sexual identity. Our approach relies heavily on the therapist–patient bond and on the flexible use of a range of techniques that include interpretation, support, and therapeutic responsiveness to selected patient needs. Clinicians may differ with respect to where they place our approach on the continuum between psychoanalysis and psychoanalytic psychotherapy. We agree with those who have argued that there is not a clear dividing line between these two types of treatment and that they are more similar than different (Fosshage, 1991; Miller, 1991). Moreover, since Wallerstein's (1986) research, which led him to conclude that supportive techniques and other types of therapeutic activity are found in psychoanalysis as well as in psychoanalytic psychotherapy, psychoanalysis has evolved greatly. It encompasses the intersubjective and relational context and the "ever-present, fluctuating, mutual influence of patient and analysand on each other" (Miller, 1991, p. 46).

Unlike most psychoanalytic authors, we do not focus on why a woman becomes a lesbian nor do we view lesbianism as a pathological development that reflects a rejection of femininity and the adoption of a masculine gender identity. Since the Kinsey et al. (1948) seminal study of sexual behavior, mounting evidence has shown that there is a broad continuum of normal sexuality and that the development of a core gender identity proceeds separately from the sexual object choice. Numerous writers, such as Stoller (1968, 1976, 1985), Benjamin (1988), Schwartz (1998), Goldner (1991), Mitchell (1993), and Aron (1996), have argued that lesbianism is a normal variant of sexuality. Like women who identify as heterosexual, lesbians show the full gamut of psychosexual, ego, self, and object relations development and do not necessarily suffer from developmental arrests. Several decades of research on lesbianism have not reliably differentiated homosexual and heterosexual women with respect to their personality characteristics, family background, psychopathology, and social adjustment (Gonsiorek, 1982a, b; Reiter, 1989; Falco, 1991; Gonsiorek and Weinrich, 1991; Tully, 1992, 1995; O'Connor and Ryan, 1993; Glassgold and Iasenza, 1995; Magee and Miller, 1997).

The Nature of Lesbian Identity

As noted by Burch (1993, pp. 23–24), until recently, psychoanalytic theory was preoccupied with understanding the reasons for same-sex object choice rather than with the broader concept of sexual identity. A lesbian sexual identity encompasses emotional bonds, social connections, and sometimes political attitudes and actions, as well as sexual and romantic interests and behavior. There are women who identify as lesbians who do not engage in same-sex sexual behavior and there are those who have sexual encounters with other women, and some who even engage in long-term relationships, who do not identify as lesbians (Falco, 1991; Burch, 1993).

Sexual and gender identities evolve through an often complex and lengthy process and are based on a range of complex and ongoing identifications with early caretakers and internalization of relational patterns. From a cultural perspective, lesbianism is a stigmatized sexual identity even in today's more tolerant social climate. Whether it is determined early in life and remains fixed (the essentialist position) or stays more fluid, malleable, and responsive to environmental circumstances (the constructivist position) is a matter of debate. What is true, however, is that lesbianism is laden with highly charged meanings and may have negative as well as positive consequences.

The Diversity of Lesbian Experience

Lesbians are a diverse group with respect to their self-definition, coming-out process, gender-role behavior, personality characteristics, family and cultural background, life experiences, and environmental supports. Although many women are "primary" lesbians, having identified their same-sex interests at an early age, others evolve a lesbian identity later in life, often after having relationships with men, marrying, and having children (Burch, 1993, pp. 19–23). This distinction, however, is not always valid because some members of the latter group may have felt "different" with respect to their emotional attachments and sexual interests from childhood or adolescence. Still other women have romantic partners of either gender at different times in their lives and see themselves as bisexual. These common variations do not include those women who identify as heterosexual but have sexual encounters with other women at times.

In contrast to prevalent stereotypes that view lesbians as being more masculine and rejecting of femininity, most lesbians have s strong sense of being female in their core gender identity. Like women who identify as heterosexual, however, they differ in their gender-role behavior. Many exhibit traditionally feminine behavior, whereas others may appear androgynous. Some have engaged in cross-gender behavior from childhood or have adopted some traditionally masculine traits (Saghir and Robbins, 1973; Bernard, 1992). Older lesbians who came out in a more repressive and intolerant period may have taken on masculine characteristics and roles less because of a sense of being like a man but more because of a lack of visible role models.

The Process of Identifying as a Lesbian

In spite of their diversity, women who identify as lesbians confront similar types of internal and external challenges with which they must cope. An important shared feature of their lives is their ongoing struggle with feelings of being different in a hostile environment. Being a member of a stigmatized and marginalized group has devastating effects that shape the nature and process of lesbian identity formation and all aspects of personality development (Malyon, 1982a, b).

Numerous writers have described the lesbian coming-out process (Cass, 1979; Coleman, 1982; Lewis, 1984; Falco, 1991). This developmental achievement refers to two distinct but interrelated constellations of experience (Horowitz, 1998). The first, identity formation, involves the awareness and interpretation of sexual and romantic attachments to others of the same gender. In a second stage, coming out proper, a woman acknowledges her lesbian identity to herself and begins to disclose it to others. Coleman (1982, p. 32) describes these steps as pre–coming out, coming out, exploration, first relationships, and identity integration. Each has its own issues and poses crucial tasks although not all women go through each stage.

In the discovery period, a person becomes more or less aware of same-sex feelings but may feel alienated, alone, and stigmatized. Denial, repression of sexual feelings, or other defensive reactions, low self-esteem, and serious symptoms may result. Although marked by a great deal of confusion, coming out proper begins the task of self-acceptance. During this period, the person tends to seek out validation from the external environment; and in the exploration stage, she likely experiments with new behaviors. In the first-relationship stage, she looks for an intimate partner. The integration of a lesbian identity often is a lengthy, evolving, and complex development. It goes beyond acceptance to include pride and sometimes community involvement and political activism. Clearly, the outcome of all of these stages is affected by the presence or absence of peer, family, and social supports, positive role models, gratifying relationships, and societal attitudes and policies (Hetrick and Martin, 1988).

Psychoanalytic writings are beginning to incorporate knowledge about how women process their early feelings of difference and integrate them into their self-concepts. They recognize the shifts in sexual identity that some women undergo over time in response to the different relational, social, and historical contexts in which they find themselves (Schwartz, 1998; Horowitz, 2000).

Because many lesbians, particularly those of earlier generations, were socialized into a society that viewed heterosexuality as normal and compulsory (Rich, 1980) and homosexuality as undesirable, their healthy narcissism and self-acceptance may have been seriously compromised. Often lacking positive reflections of herself in family, friends, media images, and society (Buloff and Osterman, 1995), a lesbian's core identity went unmirrored and her true self was hidden (Gair, 1995, p. 111). Parents and other close relatives who were shaming, rejecting, or devaluing may have compounded the struggle to achieve a positive self-concept. Many lesbians remained in the closet and hid their sexual identity from family and coworkers out of fear of disapproval or more serious negative consequences should it become known. Those who were more openly lesbian may have experienced actual threats to their sense of security and safety. It was difficult for many lesbians to escape the development of internalized homophobia themselves. "These negative feelings about sexual orientation may be overgeneralized to encompass the entire self" (Appleby and Anastas, 1998, p. 30).

Lesbians do differ, however, in their degree of and manner of coping with internalized homophobia. Some may recognize their own negative attitudes and lack of self-acceptance, whereas others may think and act in ways that are connected to deep-seated antihomosexual sentiments of which they are not fully aware. Participation in a gay or lesbian subculture buffers and helps to overcome the sense of difference and alienation and creates "a separate space that allows a sense of community and naturalness" (Appleby and Anastas, 1998, p. 29). Yet there are those who continue to hide their sexual identity. Some open lesbians who experience social acceptance in the "straight world" and who achieve career success may shun association with the so-called lesbian community, minimize their difference from their heterosexual counterparts, or show a lack of interest in lesbian organizations and causes. At the opposite end of the spectrum, many lesbians are politically active in the gay movement. In recent years, some lesbians have embraced the term queer to define themselves. They identify as members of a broad grouping of nonheterosexuals (gay men and lesbians, bisexuals, transsexuals, and transgender persons).

Factors such as age, geographic location, socioeconomic status, education, and religion influence the ways in which lesbians view themselves. For example, middle-aged and older women, who grew up prior to the gay rights movement in the 1970s, and those who have been raised outside large urban centers may have lacked positive role models and parental and peer supports. Because of the invisibility of lesbians in their world, they experienced isolation and it was necessary for them to interpret what it meant to be a lesbian on their own (Parks, 1999). They searched for themselves in the limited resources that were available. Some read novels, such as *The Well of Loneliness* (Hall, 1928), in which the main character suffers disappointment and despair, or viewed films, such as *The Children's Hour* (1961), in which the protagonist, who fears she is a lesbian, commits suicide. Others may have studied religious texts that viewed homosexuality as a sin or psychoanalytic journals that equate lesbianism with mental illness.

Younger lesbians live in a time in which there is increasing tolerance of homosexuality and in which successful gays are more visible in society and the media than previously. Many women today have experienced more family and social supports than previously and may be more self-accepting regarding their lesbianism than were lesbians of earlier generations. They have access to a vast literature and even prime-time television programs, such as *Ellen, Will and Grace,* and *Queer as Folk,* that provide more positive images of gays and lesbians. They also can locate resources on lesbian life on the Internet and access organizations that offer help with the psychological and social consequences of coming out as well as opportunities for peer support and socialization. Some states recognize lesbian marriages or other domestic partnership arrangements. Increasingly, single and coupled lesbians are raising biological, foster, or adopted children and are struggling with parenting issues that are sometimes similar to those of heterosexuals and sometimes unique to lesbians (Baptiste, 1987).

In spite of the greater visibility and acceptance of lesbians and the presence of social supports, today's generation of lesbians still struggle with complex identity issues and continuing stigmatization and discrimination. Moreover, they confront new challenges as they take on roles and pursue options that were previously off limits. Family members, friends, coworkers, and the community regard them in considerably variable ways (Herek, 1984, 1995; Nava and Davidoff, 1994). Likewise, the legal, health care, and other significant societal systems reflect heterosexist policies and practices. The media's current portrayal of lesbianism as a fashionable, conflict-free, and exciting lifestyle is nearly as skewed as its previous preoccupation with lesbians who were suicidal, obsessed, or insane. The advertising industry's discovery of gays and lesbians as a group that has discretionary income has not led to economic parity with respect to income tax and inheritance laws.

Nevertheless, women who identify as lesbians are able to have successful and fulfilling lives. Many achieve considerable satisfaction over the life cycle in their work and personal lives and advance educationally, occupationally, and economically (Tully, 1995; Kertzner and Sved, 1996). No objective evidence exists that justifies the stereotype of aging lesbians as lonely and isolated women who lack longstanding committed relationships, close family ties, or good friends. Studies of aging lesbians have shown that they share many of the same concerns as older heterosexuals (Berger and Kelly, 1986; Berger, 1992; Tully, 1992).

Psychotherapy and Lesbian Identity

Women who have romantic attachments to other women sometimes enter psychotherapy because of issues related to their lesbianism, for example, how to deal with their emerging feelings of attraction to other women or whether and how to disclose their sexual orientation to family, friends, coworkers, or children. It is more likely, however, that lesbians seek treatment for the same reasons as do individuals who identify as heterosexual. It is important for clinicians to recognize that whatever propels lesbians to enter psychotherapy, they have had to face common stresses and acquire special coping mechanisms that may be affecting their self-concept, self-esteem regulation, day-to-day lives, and future goals. For example, a woman's relationship problems with her female partner may stem from her reticence to socialize publicly together and her refusal to include her in family gatherings because of her fear of disapproval and rejection. Or a lesbian's repeated failure to move up professionally may stem from wanting to remain aloof and distant from associates in order to protect her personal life. Likewise, a woman's depression may be caused by her attempts to deny recognition of her own wishes and needs to be with other women, leading her to try unsuccessfully to have relationships with men that are unfulfilling. Similarly, a young lesbian's alcohol abuse and feelings of isolation may result from her conflict over having moved away from the small Midwestern town in which she was raised, in order to avoid bringing shame to her family as a result of her sexual identity. Thus, therapy should help lesbians understand the subjective meaning of their sexual identity and its impact on their lives.

More important, therapy can provide some lesbians with the opportunity to identify both the conscious and unrecognized components of their self-concept and understand how they have organized and constructed their self-experience. It can foster an appreciation of their unique struggles, developmental accomplishments, and life achievements and can validate aspects of their identity that family and culture have not supported.

The Limitations of Traditional Theory and Practice

As chapter 2 discusses in more detail, classical Freudian theory and psychoanalytic ego psychology embodied a culturally based anti-homosexual bias (Irigaray, 1985; Mereck, 1986; Friedman, 1988; Harris, 1991; O'Connor and Ryan, 1993; DeLauretis, 1994; Fuss, 1995). Although Freud favored society's acceptance of homosexuals and did not condemn their behavior, his followers based their clinical approach on his theoretical writings that presented male and female homosexuality as grossly abnormal (Freud, 1905, 1920; Lewes, 1988; Magee and Miller, 1997).

- They viewed lesbianism as a form of severe psychopathology, for example, a defensive regression or developmental arrest.

- They used male development as a model for understanding female development, thus reflecting the patriarchal attitudes that were prevalent in the culture.
- They failed to differentiate between lesbians in treatment who suffered from severe psychopathology or early trauma and lesbians who were higher functioning.
- They collapsed the concepts of gender identity, gender-role behavior, object choice or sexual orientation, and level of personality development, so that they viewed lesbians as rejecting of femininity, masculine-identified, and preoedipal or immature in their object relations.
- They did not make a distinction between male and female homosexuality and ignored the normative and special issues that lesbians confront during the life cycle.
- They neglected the effects of environment and culture, particularly with respect to the impact of negative attitudes, stigma, oppression, and social change on personality development.
- They minimized the impact of actual traumatic events or experiences on personality development and thus tended to blame sexual orientation for any psychopathology that lesbians displayed.

In traditional psychoanalytically oriented treatment, the analyst attempted to help the lesbian patient to understand and resolve the conflicts involved in her perverse sexual object choice and regression to preoedipal sexuality, to overcome her rejection of femininity, and to achieve a heterosexual adaptation. Later, psychoanalytic ego psychologists tried to enable lesbians to repair their developmental arrests. Clinicians took the correctness of their theories for granted rather than recognizing that they embodied personal and cultural bias.

The older psychoanalytic treatment model encouraged the therapist to assume the role of an expert whose view of what the patient needed, thought, and felt took precedence over the patient's own subjective experience and reality. It admonished therapists to examine their own countertransference reactions but these did not appear to include their personal views and anxiety about homosexuality. It urged therapists to interpret their patients' unconscious conflicts, the reasons for their developmental arrests, the nature of their resistance, and their transference manifestations rather than to employ more supportive interventions. Even when therapists used ego-building or reparative techniques, their goal was to help patients achieve a higher developmental level. It was customary to regard patients who did not go along with their approach as resistant or as too damaged to benefit from treatment. Viewing lesbianism as always symptomatic of pathology and seeing lesbians as disturbed human beings tended to foreclose exploration or affirmation of the positive or healthy aspects of a lesbian's identity. Most therapists did not see their role as one of helping lesbians to modify their internalized homophobia, increase their ability to cope with being stigmatized and experiencing environmental hostility, and advocate for their rights.

Prior to the gay liberation movement in the 1970s, personal horror stories about the negative effects of psychotherapy were prevalent among gays and lesbians. In spite of the good intentions of many clinicians, it was common for lesbian patients to experience psychotherapy as hurtful, if not traumatizing and oppressive. Many lesbians felt judged and misunderstood or confirmed in their negative self-concept. Equating normality and cure with becoming heterosexual, some tried to alter their sexual orientation, or adopted a strange type of self-acceptance based on learning to live with a deviant sexual identity. There was little, if anything, in traditional forms of psychotherapy that was empowering. Anticlinical sentiments ran high in the gay and lesbian community and potential consumers of psychotherapy showed understandable distrust of the so-called experts. Even more recently, research findings show that gays and lesbians are largely dissatisfied with past treatment experiences. For example, in numerous studies, 25 to 66 percent of the respondents indicated that they received poor or inappropriate care because of their sexual orientation (Rudolph, 1988; Schatz and O'Hanlan, 1994; Nystrom, 1997).

New Directions in Theory and Practice

Three major interrelated factors are contributing to making psychoanalytic practice more responsive to the needs of lesbians: the emergence of relational and postmodern theoretical frameworks; the effects of societal changes brought about by the feminist and gay rights movements; and the impact of the writings of lesbian theorists and clinicians.

Relational and Postmodern Theories

Psychoanalytic thinking has expanded far beyond classical Freudian theory and psychoanalytic ego psychology. It encompasses British and American object relations theories, self psychology, and contemporary relational theory, which reflects postmodernist thinking. Object relations theories view human beings as social animals and see interpersonal relationships as having a major impact on development (Aron, 1996). Self psychology, which many writers classify as a relational theory, focuses on the self as an innate and enduring structure of the personality that has its own needs for an attuned and empathic selfobject environment and separate developmental track (Goldstein, 2001). Postmodernist thinking, which rejects the philosophical stance of logical positivism, "can be thought of as a group of approaches that hold that there is no fixed reality, only constructed versions of reality determined by the perspective of the one doing the describing" (DeLaCour, 1996, p. 214). It challenges the correctness or truth of any particular paradigm because all personality theories are merely ways of thinking about individuals and are embedded in social, political, and moral contexts.

Unlike psychoanalysis, which addresses the personal dimension of experience, postmodernism focuses on the influence of the social context. Some clinicians are trying to integrate postmodernist and psychoanalytic perspectives. When applied to the clinical situation, postmodernism alerts clinicians to the impact of a therapist's personality, attitudes, beliefs, and cultural background on his or her understanding of a patient (Hoffman, 1991, p. 77). More important, it shifts the psychotherapeutic focus away from the therapist's so-called objective view of the patient to the patient's subjective experience and to the personal meaning of events and relationships in his or her life.

Robert Stolorow's theory of intersubjectivity, one of the current relational approaches, is an overarching framework that views all human behavior as codetermined by two interacting and mutually influencing worlds of experience. Each individual develops a unique set of organizing principles that both influence and are affected by ongoing life experiences and interactions with others (Stolorow and Lachmann, 1980; Stolorow and Atwood, 1992; Stolorow, Atwood, and Brandchaft, 1994). Likewise, Stephen Mitchell's (1988, 1993) relational-conflict model originally brought together a wide variety of alternative (nonclassical) analytic schools. Greatly influenced by social constructivist and feminist thinking, Mitchell began to call his theory relational constructivism, which is concerned with the interaction between the intrapsychic, interpersonal, and social dimensions of life.

As a result of these theoretical developments, a revised and expanded clinical repertoire exists that reflects at least 10 important changes (Ornstein and Ganzer, 1997; Goldstein, 2001).

1. The therapist strives to be collaborative rather than authoritarian in the treatment relationship.

2. Therapists show empathy, involvement, realness, and genuineness rather than detached observation; neutrality in their interventions; a strict abstinence with respect to gratifying some of the patients' needs; and anonymity in terms of revealing personal information.

3. The therapist elicits the patient's personal narrative and accepts the truth of his or her subjective experience rather than making experience-distant interpretations.

4. The therapist's understanding of the patient and the clinical situation contains elements of uncertainty and may change over time.

5. Treatment focuses on the intersubjective nature of the clinical situation and on both the patient's and the therapist's contributions to the therapeutic interaction.

6. The therapist relies on theoretical revisions and expansions as well as emerging ways of thinking about the developmental process.

7. The therapist recognizes that transference reactions encompass developmental repetition, attempts to move forward, and here-and-now aspects of the therapist–patient relationship.

8. The therapist understands that countertransference reactions encompass not only the therapist's reactions that stem from unresolved unconscious conflicts and other developmental issues but also those that stem from the impact of the patient's personality on the therapist. The therapist also recognizes that he or she always brings his or her own personality and organizing principles to the treatment relationship and this affects his or her perceptions and interactions with the patient.

9. The repertoire of treatment interventions includes not only insight-oriented techniques but also a broad range of developmentally attuned interventions.

10. The therapist uses the therapeutic relationship as a curative force in the treatment process rather than relying solely on traditional verbal and insight-oriented techniques.

The Feminist and Gay Rights Movements

Concurrent with the theoretical and practice developments discussed so far, the feminist and gay rights movements began to have a major impact on society and the mental health community. A watershed development occurred when the American Psychiatric Association bowed to political pressure and removed homosexuality and, later, ego-dystonic homosexuality from its official description of mental disorders in 1973 and 1987, respectively (Krajeski, 1996). It is noteworthy, however, that these changes occurred amid considerable controversy and outright opposition (Bayer, 1981). They came about more because of the gay liberation movement's success in drawing attention to the widespread nature and debilitating effects of discrimination against homosexuals than because of psychiatrists' theoretical convictions. Many psychoanalysts and psychotherapists did become more accepting of their gay and lesbian patients but they did not necessarily revise their basic attitudes and stereotypes, theoretical stance, or treatment approach. In spite of the increasing visibility of gays and lesbians, clinicians continued to remain uninformed about gay and lesbian experience (Forstein, 1988).

Lesbian Theorists and Clinicians

In this changing atmosphere, the professional literature reflected revisionist thinking. Feminist writers drew attention to the inadequacy and male bias in psychoanalytic theory, introduced new ways of thinking about gender and sexuality, challenged the ways in which women were diagnosed or labeled, identified the impact of environment and culture and the process of socialization on personality development, and emphasized the importance of empowering and affirmative interventions. Nevertheless, the early feminist literature gave short shrift to lesbianism perhaps because feminists did not want their cause to be weakened by its association with a stigmatized population. Likewise, the burgeoning gay literature paid more attention to male rather than female homosexuality until recently, so much so that lesbians were referred to as an invisible or unseen minority (Potter and Darty, 1981). Psychoanalytic writings did not fare any better initially, perhaps because there were few open lesbian theorists and analysts, who often were excluded from or at risk for dismissal in American psychotherapy training institutes (Burch, 1993; Glassgold and Iasenza, 1995; Magee and Miller, 1997; Drescher, 1998; Schwartz, 1998). The thrust for change achieved more momentum when lesbian feminist psychoanalytic writers and clinicians became more visible. Their increased presence also was accompanied by their applying postmodernist ideas to discourse on lesbianism.

- They reconceptualized lesbianism as a normal rather than pathological variant of sexuality.
- They redefined the concepts of gender identity, gender-role behavior, and sexual identity.
- They differentiated between male and female homosexuality and considered the normative and special issues that lesbians confront during the life cycle.

- They considered the impact of society and culture on personality development and drew attention to the effects of discrimination against, negative attitudes toward, and stereotyping of gays and lesbians.
- They advocated for a more affirmative treatment process with lesbians.

The Current State of Clinical Practice

The integration into clinical practice of newer ideas that are more user-friendly to lesbians, however, has been uneven and still is at an early stage in the mainstream psychotherapy community. Gays and lesbians may be more favorable in their assessment of psychotherapy than previously (Jones and Gabriel, 1999). In spite of their good intentions toward and greater acceptance of lesbians, clinicians still lack knowledge about lesbian life and are unaware of deeply embedded homophobic attitudes and practices (Moses and Hawkins, 1982; DeCrescenzo, 1984; American Psychological Association, 1991; Gould, 1995).

The Plan of the Book

This book focuses on the clinical situation in work with lesbians who enter psychotherapy for a host of reasons and at different times in their lives. We have attempted to write in a user-friendly style and to illustrate the main components of our therapeutic approach with case vignettes and examples of treatment process that are based on our clinical and supervisory experiences. We have edited the illustrations for reasons of confidentiality, clarity, and space. In some instances, we have condensed session material and utilized composite examples of similar cases.

Chapter 1 presents an overview of the nature and diversity of lesbian experience and the role of psychotherapy with lesbians. It discusses the limitations of traditional theoretical frameworks and treatment models and deals with changes in theory and society with respect to lesbians and their treatment needs.

Chapter 2 traces the evolution of traditional and current trends in psychoanalytic thinking on lesbian identity and discusses new perspectives on gender and sexuality.

Chapter 3 describes the major components of the book's approach to clinical work with lesbians.

Chapter 4 demonstrates how therapists elicit and work with patients' personal narratives about their self-identification as lesbians and their coming-out experiences.

Chapter 5 illustrates the process of working with the lesbian patient's transference reactions.

Chapter 6 shows the process of working with the therapist's counter-transference.

Chapter 7 discusses some of the clinical issues that arise when lesbians date and initiate romantic relationships.

Chapter 8 describes some of the clinical issues that arise in midlife and later life when relationship problems emerge, or when a lesbian becomes a parent, develops physical illness, becomes a caretaker for aging parents, or becomes dependent.

Chapter 9 addresses some of the issues that arise when lesbian therapists treat lesbian patients.

We hope that this book will serve as a guide to practitioners and trainees. Our approach requires that clinicians overcome their view of lesbianism as inherently pathological, their tendency to practice along traditional lines, and their lack of familiarity with lesbian life. It necessitates shifts in the therapist's stance, use of self, demands for self-scrutiny, and ways of conveying acceptance and support of diversity. It encourages clinicians to be genuine, creative, and spontaneous in the therapeutic process. We urge practitioners to try out some of the ideas presented in the book, and we feel confident that the experience will be liberating and rewarding.

Chapter 2

Psychoanalytic Theory and Lesbianism

The Changing Landscape

After discussing the ways in which traditional psychoanalytic theory viewed lesbians and their treatment, this chapter considers the impact of relational theories and early and postmodern feminist perspectives on gender and sexual identity.

Nineteenth-Century Writers

Nineteenth-century theorists emphasized the congenital nature of homosexuality. It is noteworthy that prominent German gay (male) activists of the day, such as Ulrich, Hirshfeld, and Benkert, hoped that the country would be more likely to enact social reforms if people viewed homosexuality, like gender, as biologically inherited (Greenberg, 1988). Ulrich, who viewed sexual preferences as inborn, described homosexuals as the third sex (Kennedy, 1980/1981).

The term lesbian was not evident in the medical literature until the 19th century. The first published case study of a lesbian (Westphal, 1869), described a woman who was hospitalized for hysteria. The author, a German psychiatrist, associated lesbianism with masculine behavior and described his lesbian patient as being a "man trapped in a woman's body." Chevalier (1883) elaborated on Westphal's idea, describing lesbianism as a congenital problem resulting from a combination of female and male "organic elements." Other 19th-century psychologists, such as Charcot, Morel, Magnan, Tarnowsky, and Moll (Greenberg, 1988), echoed this view, as did Ellis (1897) in his case studies of lesbians. Havelock Ellis was among those who believed that homosexuality was biologically determined and argued for social tolerance for homosexuals. Nevertheless, he described lesbians in negative terms, referring to them as sloppy, attracted to rough masculine games, competitive, and inclined toward the sciences.

Freud and Lesbianism

Influenced by the prevailing views of the times in which Freud lived, Freudian theory laid the underpinnings for subsequent psychoanalytic theories of lesbianism. Freud appeared to be sympathetic to homosexuals as a group and to the movement for the enactment of social reforms regarding homosexuality (Freud, 1935, pp. 423–424). Nevertheless, he acknowledged his lack of direct psychoanalytic experience with homosexuals. In fact, he relied on case studies published by Kraft-Ebing, Ellis, and other distinguished physicians in generating his views and his writings are contradictory and confusing. For example, in one of his major papers, Freud observed that too little was known about homosexuality to draw definite conclusions and, in the same work, stated his beliefs in the universality of bisexual urges and the capacity for all human beings to make a homosexual object choice (1905, pp. 185–243). In other writings, however, he described homosexuality as a perversion and this latter view prevailed among his followers.

It is important to place Freud's views on lesbianism within the context of his general theorizing about women and his emphasis on the oedipal complex in determining gender identity and sexual object choice (Freud, 1931, 1933). Freud believed that women are anatomically inferior to men, blame their mothers for castrating them, and turn their love away from their mothers toward their fathers. Their biologically based sense of inadequacy leads to penis envy. He further argued that a woman optimally resolves her oedipal stage by identifying with her mother, toward whom she remains ambivalent, and by wishing thereby to attract a man like her father. She remains strongly attached to her father but tempers her sexual interest in him and eventually transfers her sexual feelings to other men. In later life, bearing a child, particularly a son, enables her to compensate for her sense of deficiency. Freud concluded that successful resolution of the oedipal period leads to the consolidation of gender identity, heterosexual object choice, and adoption of a traditional maternal role. In addition to his view of women as biologically deficient, Freud wrote that women, in comparison to men, are less ethical, possess less of a sense of social justice and social interest, and are more envious, vain, narcissistic, secretive, insincere, masochistic, childlike, and incomplete.

Compared to the four separate theories Freud developed on male homosexuality, he addressed lesbianism in only two of his publications, "Three Essays on the Theory of Sexuality" (1905) and "Psychogenesis of a Case of Homosexuality in a Woman" (1920). Freud wrote that lesbians either reject heterosexuality because of penis envy and severe disappointment in men or repudiate their femininity as a result of envy or devaluation of their mothers. He saw female homosexuality as a failure to resolve the normal oedipal stage and believed that if a girl is destined to become a lesbian, she develops a negative oedipal complex, taking her mother rather than her father as a love object and using her father instead of her mother as an object of identification. He argued that a woman who loves other women develops a masculinity complex that reflects her rebellion against her own femaleness, her wishes to be a man, her rejection of heterosexuality, and her adoption of masculine traits.

In his only case study of a lesbian (Freud, 1920), Freud explained the dynamics of his adolescent lesbian's same-sex object choice as a defensive turning of her repressed disappointment in her father and as the repudiation of all men for her father's impregnating her mother with another baby. He saw her damaged femininity as driving her into an active masculine identification (masculinity complex). After he traced the possible contributions to the girl's acquired homosexuality, however, he made a contradictory comment, suggesting that the girl might actually have an inborn (biological) homosexual inclination (DeLauretis, 1994). Thus, Freud left his readers confused as to what he truly thought. At the end of the case, Freud (1920) wrote that female homosexuals are "not less common than men . . . [yet are] ignored by law . . . [and] also neglected by psychoanalytic research" (p. 133).

In addition to his negative and phallocentric portrayal of women's development generally and his confusion about whether lesbianism was innate or acquired, Freud erroneously saw gender identity, sexual object choice, and level of psychosexual development as interconnected. He offered "a condensed way of thinking about sex and gender" that later observations and research challenged (Friedman, 1988, p. 52).

Early Dissent

Not all the psychoanalysts during Freud's time wholly embraced his views of women generally and lesbians specifically. Theorists, including Jones, Deutsch, Horney, Klein, and others, challenged some of his formulations on female development in a series of articles in the early 1920s and 1930s and in professional debates. They thought that existing theoretical constructs marginalized women, including lesbians, and questioned some of Freud's ideas. Nevertheless, they continued to adopt a pathological view of lesbianism.

For example, Ernest Jones (1927), an ardent follower and biographer of Freud, believed that male analysts harbored phallocentric views in regard to female development. He argued that theories should differentiate female from male development, and rejected Freud's concept of inherent bisexuality. Yet, he maintained a pathological interpretation of lesbianism and believed that a lesbian replaced her sexual desire for her father with sexual interest in another woman in order to protect herself from a fear of heterosexual incest.

Helene Deutsch (1932, 1944), who, like Jones, also had a classical orientation, based her distinctive ideas about female homosexuality on a wide variety of cases. Deutsch's writings reflected her relatedness to her patients and were unusual in drawing attention to their subjective experience. Unlike Jones, she retained Freud's notion of bisexuality but she argued that complex psychogenic motivations rather than a male gender identity are responsible for adoption of the female homosexual position. In fact, she refuted the idea that lesbians all took on masculine traits and thought it was erroneous to interpret any masculine features that they may show as evidence of masculine desire.

Deutsch emphasized the preoedipal mother–child relationship and problematic daughter–father dynamics as causing a retrogressive return to the mother and speculated that an increased fear of the father during puberty can set off the defense of identification with the aggressor. She actually acknowledged some of the positive aspects of lesbian love relationships and put forth an idea that was a harbinger of later developments when she wrote that part of the "powerful motives" in many lesbian relationships is the oscillation between roles. "The differences and similarities, non-identity and yet identity, the quasi double experience of oneself, the simultaneous liberation from one part of one's ego and its preservation and security in the possession of the other, are among the 'attractions of the homosexual experience'" (p. 267). Nevertheless, many of Deutsch's descriptions of and comments about her lesbian patients emphasized the infantile nature of their relationships and reflected her ambivalence about them (O'Connor and Ryan, 1993, p. 273).

Karen Horney (1924, 1926, 1934), who rejected Freudian drive theory and drew attention to the interpersonal and cultural determinants of personality development, was a prominent early critic of Freud's phallocentric theorizing. She argued that the true nature of women was eclipsed by masculine narcissism, and she was one of the first analysts to dispute the centrality of penis envy in female development. Countering Freud's position on women's deficiencies, she argued that men's dread and envy of female reproductive capacities accounted for the presumption that females experience genital inferiority. Moreover, she thought that women's envy of men was influenced by societal attitudes toward men and treatment of men as more powerful and important than women.

Despite her revisionist views, Horney (1924) assumed that a girl's inborn pleasure-driven capacities, via the clitoris and the vagina, along with her loving attachment to her father, turn her toward men and motherhood. She hypothesized that the fantasy of having been castrated, not being given a baby by her father, and envy of her mother drive a female child to an identification with her father. "We know that in every case in which the castration complex predominates there is without exception a more or less marked tendency to homosexuality . . . to play the father's part, always amount[ing] also to desiring the mother in some sense" (p. 48). Thus, she interpreted female homosexuality as solely resulting from a father's rejection of his daughter's love.

Like Horney, Clara Thompson (1942, 1947) broke with classical thinking and was influential in shaping the interpersonal approach to psychoanalysis. She gave voice to some of the problems with prevailing theories of homosexuality. In "Changing Concepts of Homosexuality in Psychoanalysis" (Thompson, 1947, p. 3), she commented on how the term homosexual had come to be used in psychoanalysis as "a kind of wastebasket into which are dumped all forms of relationships with one's own sex." She also drew attention to the fact that many psychoanalytic theories confused a homosexual's object choice with his or her level of personality development, further suggesting that becoming a homosexual did not mean that an individual possessed an infantile personality. Thompson further argued that homosexuality, like heterosexuality, cuts across persons of diverse character structures and that it is these character structures that determine the level of success adapting to the stresses associated with being a member of a sexual minority.

Ego Psychology and American Object Relations Theory

As theoretical attention shifted away from the vicissitudes of the drives to the nature of ego development and the separation-individuation process, ego psychology and American object relations theory held out promise for substantial revisions in the ways that psychoanalytic thinking regarded male and female homosexuality. Instead, these theories continued to reflect a pathological perspective on male homosexuality and lesbianism, seeing lesbians as suffering from preoedipal pathology and developmental arrests. It was thought that they exhibited an anaclitic form of love that searched for reparation in the earliest mother–daughter relationship (Bergmann, 1973; McDougall, 1979, 1980, 1995; Eisenbud, 1982; Siegel, 1988; Socarides, 1988; Suchet, 1995).

Charles Socarides (1988), who was instrumental in supporting the American Psychiatric Association's former classification of homosexuality as a psychiatric diagnosis, became a primary spokesman for post-Freudian antigay theorists. He viewed lesbianism as reflecting a pathological sexual object choice, a disturbance of gender identity, and a developmental arrest. He argued that lesbianism is a preoedipal gender identity disorder resulting from difficulties in negotiating the separation-individuation stages. His treatment approach aimed at repairing the abnormality of the patient's ego structure and reworking a patient's arrested development in order to move the patient toward heterosexual functioning.

Like Socarides, Elaine Siegel's (1988) view of lesbianism is filled with references to its pathological nature. She maintained that lesbianism is a serious disturbance derived from early failures in the differentiation and practicing subphases of separation-individuation. Siegel viewed her lesbian patients as suffering from incomplete differentiation from the mother and deep feelings of castration and genital loss. She argued that lesbians cannot achieve full womanhood and mature psychological health (stable and appropriate object relations) because they have psychically failed to "take full possession of their vaginas" (p. 22), emphasizing an unconscious denial of sexual differentiation (p. 5). She believed that lesbian relationships function as a restorative compromise to correct both partners' failure to incorporate their vaginas into their self-representations. It is through identification with each other's genitals that lesbians attempt to repair their psychic body defects that were the consequence of their mother's failure to give them "unconscious and conscious approval" (p. 23).

Basing her ideas on her clinical experience with lesbians who appear to have suffered from borderline and narcissistic personality disorders, Joyce McDougall (1979, 1980) provided some of the most extensive writing on lesbianism. Her early writings adhered to earlier ways of thinking about female homosexuality although she later revised some of her views. She first understood lesbianism as a developmental failure, a "fictitious sexual identity" that maintains "psychic survival" through a girl's unconscious identification with the father and allows her to develop a "subjective identity" that guards against the "dangerous forbidding aspects" of the "maternal imago" (1979, p. 87). She thought that the girl's entire body becomes invested with the symbolic significance of the penis in order that she may engage in heterosexual fantasy (1979, p. 133). Thus, McDougall believed that the image of womanhood is rigidly split into two extremes, the inaccessible highly idealized and the castrated. To guard against further psychic chaos, the girl must disguise her femininity at all costs (p. 135). The parental couples of McDougall's female homosexuals are comprised of mothers who are dangerous, manipulative, and idealized, whereas fathers are ineffectual, devalued by their narcissistic wives, and they fail to serve as an adequate separating object from the omnipotent mother.

In a more recent work, McDougall (1995) admitted that her former findings lack the generalizability she once believed, acknowledged the existence of the "homosexualities," and limited her conclusions to those patients with whom she has worked. Moreover, in her later works, she differentiates between disturbed homosexuals and those who are creative and functional. Nevertheless, she articulated the view that sexual deviations or the "neosexualities" result from constructions that children make to deal with the psychic pain of early life for psychic survival.

Ruth Jean Eisenbud's views were rooted in the beliefs of this period but she showed more awareness of the impact of homophobia on lesbians than did earlier analysts. In some ways, her writings provided a bridge to more contemporary perspectives on lesbianism. Eisenbud subscribed to a developmental model that privileged heterosexuality as the natural outcome of healthy development. Consequently, she saw lesbianism as a reparative effort to deal with early deficits. In her article, "The Early and Later Determinants of Lesbian Choice" (Eisenbud, 1982), however, she acknowledged that lesbianism could be an acceptable compromise for some women. Moreover, she grasped the impact of parental and societal rejection on lesbians' personality development.

The Expansion of Relational Theories

Diverse object relations and self-psychological formulations put forth different views of early development that emphasized attachment behavior, patterns of relatedness, the importance of infant–mother attunement, the presence of a nuclear self, and the significance of selfobject self-needs (Greenberg and Mitchell, 1993; Goldstein, 2001). Despite their distinctive emphases, all object relations formulations are relational and describe the process by which the infant takes in (internalizes) the outside world, thereby acquiring basic perceptions of and attitudes toward the self and others and patterns of relating. They share the view that human beings are social animals whose early interpersonal relationships create intrapsychic structures that become the building blocks of personality development (Aron, 1996).

A major psychoanalytic innovator, Heinz Kohut placed the self at the core of his developmental theory (Kohut, 1971, 1977, 1984). He envisioned the self as innately intact, creative, organized, and self-regulating although requiring an attuned caretaking environment or empathic selfobjects to facilitate and nurture its unfolding development. Kohut identified three main types of early selfobject needs, the gratification of which enables the child to develop a cohesive self: (1) the need for mirroring that confirms the child's sense of vigor, greatness, and perfection; (2) the need for an idealization of others whose strength and calmness soothe the child; and (3) the need for a twin or alter ego who provides the child with a sense of humanness, likeness to, and partnership with others (Wolf, 1988).

The self-psychological therapist prizes nondestructive self-expression in all its forms rather than a maturity morality in which the patient is encouraged to live his or her life in accordance with the society's or therapist's values and expectations regarding what is normal and appropriate. Being different is not equated with being pathological. Enabling patients to develop "a sense of inner freedom, of joyful search, and the courageous ability to go one's own way" (Kohut, 1984, p. 169) takes precedence over helping them to conform to societal expectations.

In addition to generating new treatment approaches, object relations theory and self psychology provided some of the underpinnings to a different view of lesbian development. In addition to reflecting more acceptance of diverse normal developmental pathways, relational thinking emphasized the importance of early relationships in personality development and showed how gratifying affective experiences can result in loving bonds between members of the same as well as the opposite sex. They also lead to an appreciation of the varied internalizations that help to shape a person's gender identity and behavior. Recent research supports the view that for many women lesbian object relations and self-development arise as variants of positive developmental experiences, in contrast to the traditional belief that they reflect arrested, immature, narcissistic, and undifferentiated object relations (Spaulding, 1993). A more affirmative view of female homosexuality is possible, given that the term lesbianism can connote "a special affinity and special feeling" toward other women and represents "a special capacity and need to love and express one's love for people of the same gender in all the meanings of the term" (Woodman and Lenna, 1980, p. 11). This does not mean that, like their heterosexual counterparts, many women who identify as lesbians do not have conflicts surrounding their sexuality or gender identity or do not experience serious emotional problems. It does mean that their loving and sexual feelings toward other women are not pathological in themselves.

Early and Postmodernist Feminist Revisions

As noted earlier, some female psychoanalysts during Freud's time, like Horney and Thompson, challenged the masculine bias and basic assumptions of classical formulations. It was not until the success of the feminist movement in the 1970s, however, that theorists addressed female development more systematically. Many of the early feminists embraced relational theories. Although they gave little direct attention to lesbianism, their views of women's development provided the foundations for a more affirmative view of lesbianism as a variant of normal sexual identity and of gender identity as being multifaceted.

Nancy Chodorow (1978, 1989) and Carol Gilligan (1982) were early feminist pioneers who challenged the masculine bias implied in Freudian and other early developmental theories. They moved away from drive theory and advanced object-relations–based interpretation of female development, which they regarded as largely influenced by early mother–child interactions. Chodorow and Gilligan argued that all females have a different individuation process than males because of their primary connection to a same-sex rather than opposite-sex parent. They described girls, in contrast to boys, as sharing a greater sense of identification and merger with one another and believed that the consolidation of their psychological growth does not require distancing from or rejection of their mothers. They suggested that girls, instead of separating from their mothers, experience a prolonged closeness and diffuse individuation process. Moreover, they thought that girls' ego strengths develop through connection rather than separation and autonomy. Alternatively, they thought that boys go through a process of defensive autonomy and denial of their identification with the mother. These two writers also observed that for females, unlike males, self-development involves more permeable rather than rigid boundaries and a greater capacity for empathy, caring, and intuition. Like Chodorow and Gilligan, a group of feminist theorists at the Stone Center, Wellesley College, also noted the importance of connection and "mutual empathy" in women's "self in relation" development (Jordan et al., 1991).

Expanding this line of thought, some writers have suggested that because empathic relatedness is a significant subjective component of all women's development, same-sex sexual desire among women can be viewed as a natural outgrowth of their relational needs and early positive attachments rather than a regression from the oedipal father or fixation on the preoedipal mother. In this vein, Weille (1993) and Suchet (1995) proposed that the girl's lingering close tie to her mother and attachment to her father results in a normal "bisexual relational triangle" during her oedipal phase. This triangle leads to mature connections to both parents. They concluded that love between women later in life usually is as likely to be based on mature object relations and a solid identification with the mother rather than on regressive preoedipal and oedipal bonds.

Recent research findings have supported the view that many lesbians have a history of positive relationships with both parents. For example, in a study of 24 lesbian college graduates who received high scores on a psychological stability test and who displayed "evidence of highly evolved, differentiated and integrated levels of object relatedness," the subjects' perceptions of their parents did not follow common stereotypes. Instead, both parents were perceived as supportive, competent, and nurturing role models (Spaulding, 1993, p. 17).

It is possible that a girl's early and continuous attachments to both parents may account for the fluidity and variability of some women's sexual expression over the life cycle. This helps to explain why lesbians often show a strong sense of femaleness and why many women are secondary or bisexual lesbians who come out later in life after having had significant relationships with men, or why they move back and forth between men and women in their love relationships, thus showing a longstanding bisexual orientation. Because of the consequences of living with a stigmatized identity, however, women who self-identify as lesbians early in their lives have had different challenges than those who identified as heterosexual before coming out later in life (Burch, 1993).

It must be noted that despite their innovative thrust, the writings cited here embodied a traditional view of gender roles. In contrast, Jessica Benjamin (1988, 1995) emphasized the importance of the balance between oneness and separateness, merging and differentiation, in both men and women. In her view, true independence involves self-assertion and mutuality, separateness, and sharing, and she holds that the individual's inability to reconcile dependence and independence leads to patterns of domination and submission.

Benjamin also drew attention to the lack of attention to the role of the preoedipal father in early development. She proposed that normally girls display an identificatory love with their fathers, who often represent excitement and freedom from dependence on the powerful mother. Benjamin did not account for the development of lesbianism per se. She recognized, however, that those lesbians who find traditional feminine roles alien to their nature and are predominantly masculine-identified are not the products of developmental failure.

Among the second generation of feminists, Judith Butler (1990), a postmodernist thinker and philosopher by training, put forth a more radical view of gender and sexual identity that has particular significance for understanding the nature of nonheterosexual identities. She emphasized the social construction of gender and sexual identity and rejected the notion that gender and sexual identity are derived from biology or become fixed as a result of early experiences. Butler also believed that gender identity and sexual desire are variable and that cultural conditions restrict self-expression and prevent women and men from discovering and expressing themselves in different ways on the basis of a person's relational and environmental contexts. Moreover, cultural norms reinforce the labeling of nonconforming behavior as deviant.

Butler advanced the possibility for a nonpathological theory of lesbian identity and experience. Moreover, she shed new light on the gender roles that some lesbians adopt in their romantic relationships and sexual behavior. Rather than viewing butch and femme roles as reflective of core gender identities, she believed that they permit women to express and enact different parts of themselves at different times instead of conforming to rigid and culturally prescribed gender expectations. For example, a woman can play out a butch role in which she dresses like and enjoys acting like a man or can adopt a femme role that allows her to experience what it is like to be a particular type of female.

Butler did not try to bridge her views on the social construction of gender and sexuality with how individuals personally experience and internalize outside influences in the process of development. In a critique of Butler, Benjamin (1994) wrote, "Butler collapses self and subject as if political, epistomological positions, such as identity of women as a unified political subject, fully correspond to the psychological concept of the self" (p. 223). In order to make Butler's thinking useful in understanding the unique meaning of a lesbian's sexual identity and in guiding treatment, it is necessary to look at how social and cultural attitudes influence the personal dimension of a lesbian's experience.

Applying Butler's thinking, Beverly Burch (1993, 1997), one of the most prolific postmodern lesbian clinical writers, focused on the psychological experience and clinical implications of a woman's identifying as a lesbian and living with a stigmatized identity. Like other contemporary lesbian and gay clinicians, such as Isay and Frommer, Burch believed that the lingering psychological effects of societal disapproval and stigmatization are significant for those individuals who identify as a lesbian. She was one of the first psychoanalysts to write extensively on the differences in the paths that lesbians follow in evolving a sexual identity and in the psychological consequences of identifying as a lesbian.

Although mainly known for his writings on gay men, Richard Isay (1989, 1996) espoused views that are applicable to lesbians. An analyst by training, he emphasized the impact of social stigma, negative stereotyping, fear of parental and peer rejection, and the lack of positive homosexual role models on the development and emergence of sexual identity. In writing about feelings of difference related to gender behavior and homosexual desire, Stephan Martin Frommer (1994) echoed Isay's thinking. He observed, "There is no other developmental circumstance that is fully comparable to the experience of the child who senses this difference but lacks the cognitive perspective to understand it and the emotional support to cope with it" (p. 222). Before the child or adolescent even comprehends the nature of his or her gender, he or she may feel alienated and must contend with family members' conscious and unconscious disapproval. Both Isay and Frommer point out that negative self-representations form in the context of a hostile and homophobic environment and may delay the coming-out process. Other factors in this delay may be attributable to the lack of visible nonheterosexual role models, opportunities for positive mirroring, and peer and social supports. Isay also noted that failed attempts at heterosexual experiences can be traumatizing for the adolescent who has not consolidated his or her sexual identity and can result in internalized homophobia.

More recently, Adria Schwartz (1998), a relational theorist who incorporated postmodernist ideas, focused on how lesbians experience their gendered selves as outside socially constituted female roles, and on how they express feelings of difference from female role models, especially their mothers. Applying Isay's (1989) observation that homophobic fathers often withdraw from their sons who exhibit feminine traits or whom they perceive as exhibiting homosexual tendencies, Schwartz described how mothers of childhood lesbians may engage in distancing behaviors that the girls experience as rejecting. Drawing on Winnicott, she noted that false self-states emerge in the girl in an effort to gain positive attention from the mother.

Research on Lesbian Identity

A significant focus of the research conducted in the last two decades of the 20th century was on the complex cultural and subjective processes that are active in the construction of a lesbian identity. For example, the sociologist Barbara Ponse (1978) studied the subjective process of lesbian identity formation in 75 women who ranged in age from 16 to 75. She concluded that a number of paths could lead a woman toward a lesbian lifestyle. The gay trajectory for these women began at any number of points and the chronological order of events varied. She identified five events as providing the conditions leading women through the process of acknowledging lesbian sexual identity: the subjective feeling of being different; attraction to the same sex; the acceptance of lesbian feelings and the significance of a lesbian identity; involvement in a lesbian relationship; and finding a lesbian community.

Vivian Cass's (1979) work on the coming-out process is another important example of attempts to describe the subjective experience of lesbian identity formation. At the heart of her model is the assumption that this process involves the girl's or woman's attempts to resolve the conflict between her desires and messages from her environment. As a result of her research, Cass concluded that a young lesbian's ability to accept her feelings of being different has a crucial impact on how she manages the coming-out process, which involves identity confusion, identity comparison, identity tolerance, identity acceptance, identity pride, and identity synthesis. At each step of this process, the lesbian must accept certain aspects of her self-experience in the midst of an often rejecting and disapproving interpersonal or social reality.

By examining the mean ages at which lesbians experienced the different stages of the coming-out process, Riddle and Morin (1977) also attempted to develop a time-specific understanding of the stages lesbians pass through. In their study of women who began to identify as lesbians in their teens, they found that women reported recognition of lesbian feelings on average at age 14, that comprehension of the word homosexual followed two years later, and that the first sexual experience occurred at approximately 20 years of age. They observed that women develop their first lesbian romantic relationship at 23 years of age. Although an acceptance of being a lesbian occurs at this time, a positive and more integrated lesbian identity is not usually established until age 30. Schafer's (1976) study of West German lesbians showed a similar trajectory. She examined additional variables such as attraction to women, suspicion of lesbianism, perception of self as lesbian, and sexual relations with women. She noted that identity formation usually occurs before a lesbian enters the gay community and that 80 percent of those studied engaged in sexual activity with men as a defensive maneuver against self-awareness.

Bridging Theoretical and Clinical Realms

Contemporary psychoanalytic theories are gradually incorporating postmodernist and contemporary feminist thought about gender and sexuality in order to make them more relevant to clinical work. For example, some of the followers of differing relational frameworks, such as self psychology, intersubjectivity, relational constructivism, and modern Kleinian theory, are adopting the following ideas into their clinical approach.

1. Rather than viewing gender identity and sexual desire as solely biologically driven, they regard these as influenced by interpersonal experience and cultural constructions. Gender identity and sexual desire develop in a complex way as a result of the interaction between an individual's potentialities and past and ongoing relational experiences.

2. They posit a broad range of normative developmental possibilities. Heterosexuality is not privileged over homosexual or bisexual desire, and many forms of gender expression exist that are not restricted by one's biologic sex.

3. They question whether the attainment of a singular and cohesive identity generally and a gender and sexual identity specifically is the hallmark of healthy development. They allow for the existence of multiple selves rather than one core self, and for changing gender expression and sexual identity over time in response to different relational contexts.

4. They observe that nonconforming gender and sexual behavior that may begin early in life provokes disapproving and rejecting homophobic attitudes, which are then internalized in the developmental process. This results in struggles between a person's desires and the stigmatizing attitudes of others and can result in deep-seated feelings of inadequacy and self-depreciation. Delays in the coming-out process and certain symptoms and problematic functioning may be the consequence of internalized homophobia.

These four main ideas can be integrated into treatment based on relational theories that stress the intersubjective nature of treatment and the importance of exploring the patient's subjective experience. The psychotherapy literature is at an early stage, however, in showing how a relational treatment process proceeds when it is based on these new perspectives on gender and sexuality.

Chapter 3

A Framework for Clinical Practice

This chapter provides an overview of the components of our approach to clinical work with lesbians. It reflects contemporary views on the nature of psychoanalytic psychotherapy and newer perspectives on sexual and gender identity. It is intended as a guide to treatment rather than as a rigid set of techniques.

Viewing the Process of Lesbian Identity Formation as a Positive Developmental Achievement

Lesbianism is a normal variant of sexuality and lesbian identity formation is a creative interpretive process that emerges out of a relational context. The awareness of same-sex attractions in the context of a non-supportive environment prompts women to find ways of understanding and coping with their emerging sexual identity. This process takes considerable psychic energy and poses challenges that most heterosexual women do not have to address. Self-identifying as a lesbian often reflects strengths and the ability to engage in introspection. It can be an integrative and consolidating process.

Like women who identify as heterosexual, lesbians are subject to developmental stressors that have a profound impact on their personalities. Becoming aware of same-sex feelings and taking on a stigmatized identity in the course of development usually has considerable intrapsychic consequences. Consequently, certain personality characteristics, defensive constellations, interpersonal patterns of relating, vulnerabilities of self-structures, and symptomatic syndromes may be related to how a woman has coped with her feelings of difference both early and even later in her life. For example, coming out, although often liberating, may have dramatic and unsettling effects and lead to an outbreak of symptoms or to ongoing dysfunction, which can be misdiagnosed as reflecting more severe personality pathology.

Holding a positive view of lesbian identity enables therapists to be attuned to and to validate their patients' unique struggles, developmental accomplishments, strengths, and life achievements. This positive view is especially important because many lesbians have taken in negative attitudes about their sexual identity that affect their self-acceptance, self-esteem, and other aspects of their functioning. They may not be fully aware of their own internalized homophobia, which may be masked by politically correct or seemingly self-accepting attitudes. Therapists need to identify and help the patient reflect on the overt and sometimes subtle ways in which patients' homophobia appears in their personal narratives.

Demonstrating Knowledge of Lesbian Life and Culture

Clinicians who work with lesbians in psychotherapy must be knowledgeable about many aspects of lesbians' sexuality and romantic relationships, lifestyle and subculture, coming-out process, and life-stage issues. It also is important for therapists to be aware of societal attitudes and policies that affect lesbians and to be familiar with available community resources. This knowledge fosters the therapist's attunement to lesbian experience, which, in turn, facilitates the therapeutic alliance and contributes to the building of an affirmative collaborative clinical process. It also deepens the therapeutic encounter and fosters the goals of treatment.

The clinician's sensitivity to the diversity of lesbians' life experiences and the complexity of their gender and sexual identities helps patients to recount their personal narratives, to explore the meaning of significant life events, and to reflect on the ways in which they have constructed their identities. Likewise, the clinician's familiarity with the ways in which lesbians come out, express affection and sexuality, and manage their romantic attachments and friendships helps lesbian patients to be more open in sharing important aspects of their life experiences. Additionally, the therapist's awareness of the impact of societal stigma and family disapproval, the risks of being openly lesbian, and the social, economic, and legal policies that discriminate against lesbians enables patients to appreciate their unique frustrations and strengths.

A clinician's lack of knowledge of lesbian life can result in a serious lack of attunement or incorrect assessment. The therapist may misinterpret a patient's reaction in a specific situation as a result of a defense or an intrapsychic conflict rather than as a realistic response to an external threat. For example, a therapist might interpret a patient's anxiety after disclosing her lesbianism to a coworker as an example of the patient's low self-esteem and need for approval rather than as reality-based concern.

Creating a Collaborative Treatment Process

It is essential that the clinician engage in a collaborative process in which both therapist and patient are coparticipants in the clinical work. This means that the therapist should try to create an atmosphere in which patients feel free to express their subjective reality and life stories and in which they feel encouraged to think about different ways of understanding the meaning and significance of their life experiences. The therapist must pay close attention to and value the patient's truths and must offer his or her own ideas in a tentative and spontaneous manner. He or she should not automatically consider the patient's dismissal or rejection of the therapist's interpretations as indicative of resistance.

A collaborative approach is particularly important in beginning clinical work with lesbian patients, many of whom have not felt safe in disclosing significant aspects of their sexual identity and lifestyle to others or may be wary in revealing themselves in new situations. Moreover, such a stance communicates respect and validates the patient's own experience and goes a long way in preventing a nontherapeutic interaction in which the lesbian is placed in a diminished position in relationship to authority.

Engaging in Experience-Near Empathy

Kohut, self psychology's originator, described empathy as "a fundamental mode of human relatedness, the recognition of the self in the other; it is the accepting, confirming and understanding human echo" (Kohut and Wolf, 1978, pp. 704–705). Likewise, Schafer defined empathy as "the inner experience of sharing in and comprehending the momentary psychological state of another person based to a great extent on remembered, corresponding, affective states of one's own" (Schafer, 1959, p. 385).

In self-psychological treatment, the therapist's empathy or ability to place himself or herself in the shoes of the patient and to see the world through the patient's eyes is a crucial part of the treatment process. Therapists must convey that they appreciate what the patient thinks and feels. Empathy fosters the patient's sharing her personal narrative. Together the therapist and patient coconstruct a shared tentative account of the patient's experiences and feelings that are conscious or in the process of becoming more available. Newly emerging affect-laden past and present relational experiences become reconstructed and mediated within the therapeutic dyad in an atmosphere of trust.

A reliance on empathy contrasts with the use of experience-distant comments and interpretations that the therapist imposes on a patient even if they do not appear to fit with the patient's experience. Such interventions tend to place priority on the therapist's view of reality rather than on the patient's subjectivity and personal narrative. For example, a therapist was working with a woman who was previously in therapy with a seemingly homophobic therapist and who was currently expressing doubts about whether treatment could help her. She questioned the therapist about her own attitudes toward lesbians. An example of experience-near empathic comments might be, "Your concern about my attitudes and ability to help you is understandable given your past disturbing experiences and the fact that some therapists are judgmental of gays and lesbians. Is there something specific that you would like to know?" In contrast, an experience-distant interpretation might be, "I think it is likely that your concern reflects your own ambivalence about seeking treatment." Although it is possible that the patient might be feeling conflicted about entering therapy, the latter comment ignores the reality basis of the patient's concerns and is not attuned to what the patient may be feeling.

Most practitioners are likely to see themselves as reasonably empathic people, but, regrettably, it is often difficult for therapists to understand and accept others' life experiences when they differ greatly from their own. Although gay clinicians are not free from blind spots that place constraints on their empathy, they have been extensively exposed to the mainstream culture. In contrast, many nongay therapists, who have been socialized and trained in a heterosexist society and lack familiarity with gay and lesbian life, face special challenges in clinical work with this population.

Displaying Genuineness, Realness, and Spontaneity

It is important for therapists to display genuineness, realness, and spontaneity in the therapeutic relationship, rather than to adhere to the traditional stance of neutrality, abstinence, and anonymity. These personal qualities encourage a bond of mutual identification that permits the therapeutic work to go forward. Researchers on psychotherapeutic outcome confirm that when the therapist demonstrates kindness, understanding, and warmth, the therapeutic outcome is usually more positive (Whiston and Sexton, 1993).

It may be beneficial for therapists to engage in self-disclosure rather than viewing it as detrimental to the treatment and a form of countertransference acting-out (Gorkin, 1987; Gerson, 1996). Self-disclosure involves the therapist's sharing conscious thoughts, feelings, attitudes, or information about the therapist and others and about events in the therapist's life to the patient (Goldstein, 1994, p. 419). It may enable some patients to feel that their needs are understood, to risk relating, to diminish their feelings of shame and aloneness, to explore their experiences, and to feel validated in their very existence. Writers such as Hoffman (1991), Aron (1992, 1996), Goldstein (1994), Maroda (1994, 1999), Ehrenberg (1995), Renik (1995), and Shane, Shane, and Gales (1997) consider therapist self-disclosure to be an essential part of therapeutic work.

From a more general perspective, therapist self-disclosure takes many forms and ranges from sharing superficial to more intimate and revealing personal information, thoughts, and feelings. It may include disclosing, unavoidably, the way the therapist dresses or decorates; sharing his or her birth date, marital status, astrological sign, children's ages, or vacation and weekend location; commenting on good restaurants, politics, and personal interests; discussing events in the therapist's life, such as marriage, pregnancy, illness, hospitalization, speaking engagements, or professional achievements; revealing feelings, experiences, or problems that are similar to those of the patient; talking about how the therapist has solved problems, coped with stress, or thought about life; and communicating the nature of countertransference feelings or the reasons for mistakes or empathic failures. Extratherapeutic encounters may also occur, in which the therapist may accidentally meet a patient at an event or place outside the treatment setting, where it is impossible not to reveal aspects of one's personal self. Or the patient may learn about the therapist from others.

In clinical work with lesbians, who have often lived without family and cultural supports, it is impossible to overstate the value to patients of therapists' self-disclosure of their gay or straight sexual orientation. A therapist's sharing of his or her own gay or lesbian identity or, in the case of a nongay therapist, an honest discussion of his or her lack of knowledge and possible bias about sexual-identity issues, can create a positive collaborative process. Moreover, such discussion may be necessary to counteract the negative effects of the patient's previous life experiences on her self-concept and may be a validating and empowering tool in therapy.

Some of the caveats and problems associated with the therapist's deliberate use of self-disclosure, particularly of the therapist's counter-transference, are discussed later in this chapter, but other considerations exist as well. For some lesbian patients, however, gaining knowledge about the therapist's personal life can also lead to boundary concerns and potential negative consequences, particularly when the therapist is a lesbian. Because of the relatively small circles in which lesbians travel, especially outside large metropolitan areas but even within them, and the lack of privacy that ensues, it may be useful for some lesbian patients to have a therapist who is safe, that is, not a part of the patient's world. This is a complicated issue because it often is not possible for a lesbian therapist to remain anonymous even if she does not self-disclose or does not frequent events and places that are advertised as openly lesbian. She still may be known in the community, and it is possible that situations will arise in which patients may be friends with or physically and romantically involved with people in the therapist's life. Chapter 9 discusses some of the special challenges of being a lesbian therapist.

Exploring the Personal Meaning of Lesbian Identity

A major focus of treatment is the facilitation and development of pa-tients' personal narratives, which encompass what they think and feel about many different facets of their self-experience and relationships with others and the world. In clinical work with lesbians, exploring how they have evolved their sexual identity and have integrated it into their lives is crucial. Focusing on the lesbian narrative is important because evolving and living with a stigmatized identity is such a core aspect of most lesbians' self-organization and experience. Moreover, lesbians have had to face special developmental challenges, often without family, environmental, and cultural supports. Many women have had to find their way by themselves, have not been able to share and validate their experiences with others, and may have lacked a way of thinking about their own developmental achievements and struggles. The clinical ex-ploration of lesbian narratives can be a powerful self-organizing experi-ence for the patient. The clinician may be able to forge ties between incongruous and disconnected aspects of lesbians' past and present experiences and enable them to identify the conscious and unrecognized components of their self-concepts. Additionally, the therapeutic relation-ship may provide a secure atmosphere in which old patterns of feelings and behaviors can emerge and in which opportunities emerge for new object experiences.

It is important for the therapist to listen to a particular lesbian's narrative as a multilayered communication that contains complex conscious and unconscious dimensions of experience. The narrative often may contain repetitive themes that reflect the ways in which a patient views herself, others, and the world. The same patient may relate different narratives that give expression to a variety of experiences of the self that, depending on the context, reveal developmental, gender, coming-out, abandonment, self-esteem–regulation, and narcissistic issues. It often is the case that narratives contain significant fantasies and reflect major defensive constellations. The therapist's ability to tease out the emotional complexity of such narratives can be useful in enabling the patient to gain access to and make sense of experiences that were previously not readily understood or grasped.

As with other narrative material explored in treatment, the therapist should refrain from interfering with the patient's spontaneous elaboration of her own narrative and imposing the therapist's point of view. Moreover, the therapeutic exploration of lesbian narrative requires a collaborative framework in which the therapist helps patients to consider the ways in which their lesbian identity has influenced and continues to shape their personality and life experiences. The timing of this investigation into the subjective meaning of the patient's sexual identity is dependent on the bond of trust that has been established in the therapeutic relationship. It does not occur all at once but may arise at many points when the patient is recounting significant events or emotional responses in her life.

In eliciting the patient's narrative, it is useful for the clinician to be attuned to:

1. The age when same-sex affectionate, romantic, and sexual feelings emerged, how they were interpreted, and how they were manifested and responded to.
2. Feelings of sameness or difference with respect to other girls and women, the nature of gender feelings and behavior, and the ways in which others reacted to her.
3. The history of her self-identification and coming-out process and others' reactions to it, particularly family members.
4. The degree of openness in disclosing her sexual identity and the contexts in which this does or does not occur.
5. A history of significant romantic and sexual experiences and relationships.

6. The availability of family and peer support at different life stages in regard to her lesbianism.
7. The meaning of being a member of a sexual minority with respect to self-regard, self-concept, friendships, family life, occupational and career achievement, parenting, and other major life roles.
8. Changes in the ways in which significant others have reacted over time.
9. Contemporary situations that create stress or problems, for example, adoption, parenting, medical care, or inheritance.
10. Experiences with oppression and hate crimes.

Although lesbian narratives are quite diverse, they often reveal that many aspects of a lesbian's experience that may not have been acknowledged and appreciated by family, friends, and the culture. Moreover, she may have had to evolve an identity on her own without a clear road map or models for her development and may have disguised or disowned aspects of her identity. Consequently, merely helping the patient to share her narratives in an accepting and respectful atmosphere may have therapeutic benefits. Additionally, therapists can work with the patient's narrative in a variety of ways. The therapist may engage in an in-depth exploration of the lesbian experience in order to strengthen her personal integration of her past and present, to help her appreciate her unique struggles and strengths, and to foster a more positive or cohesive self-concept.

Even lesbians who have achieved a relatively solid sense of themselves and are comfortable in their relations with others and the world around them may benefit from revisiting their identity development and past coming-out experiences. It is possible that they will come to understand old problems and current life challenges in a new light. Whatever the specific focus of the clinical work, the treatment's integrative process may be emotionally empowering to the lesbian who comes to value herself as a woman among equals with respect to those who identify as heterosexual.

The type of process just described does not preclude working with the clinical material to shed light on the nature of other areas of difficulty that the patient displays that do not necessarily stem from their lesbianism. Whatever the specific focus, the therapist should draw on diverse theoretical frameworks in trying to understand the patient's core issues. Being wedded to a particular theoretical framework may not do justice to the patient's reality and may also reflect the values and biases of the clinician.

In order to achieve the goals of the treatment, it is useful for the therapeutic process to blend reflective, insight-oriented techniques with supportive techniques and the use of the therapist's self in the relationship. In addition to helping the patient to understand the nature of her developmental and life experiences, the therapist may need to validate aspects of the lesbian's experiences, to provide a framework for thinking about lesbianism, and to acknowledge and show respect for the lesbian's strivings to be herself. It also may be beneficial to help lesbians connect to available resources and support systems.

Reconceptualizing Transference

Although the concept of transference has different meanings depending on the particular school of psychoanalytic thinking, it always refers to the patient's conscious and unconscious attitudes about and responses to the therapist. In the classical psychoanalytic model, Freud emphasized the repetitive nature of transference, in which patients displace their infantile conflicts, wishes, and fears onto the therapist and consequently experience the therapist in distorted ways because of their early childhood relationships. Freud's followers admonished therapists to remain neutral, abstinent, and anonymous in the therapeutic relationship in order to encourage the development of transference and to employ interpretation in order to help the patients gain insight into the childhood origins of their conflicts. Ego psychology embraced this view but also drew attention to the manifestations of defenses in the transference and to the therapeutic alliance and the real relationship, both of which were considered to be outside of the transference. The therapeutic work expanded to focus on the analysis of defenses and the use of the non-transference elements of the relationship, including the role of the therapist as a new object (Greenson, 1967; Blanck and Blanck, 1974, 1979).

Early object relations theorists have tended to emphasize the repetition of early patterns of relating and the expression of internalized self-representations and object representations in the treatment, whereas self psychologists have stressed the emergence of frustrated early needs or what is termed the selfobject transferences in the therapeutic relationship. Both frameworks focus on the here-and-now therapist–patient interaction but differ in how they address transference reactions.

Object relations therapists have tended to focus on what the therapist is feeling and doing as well as on what the patient says and does and to rely heavily on reflective and interpretative techniques. The therapist tries to understand how the patient is replicating, enacting, actualizing, or projecting his or her past relational patterns or internalized object relations into the treatment relationship (Aron, 1996, pp. 189–220). Some object relations writers recognized the therapist's role as a container of the patient's feelings and as a provider of new kinds of relational experiences (Winnicott, 1947; Bion, 1962; Guntrip, 1973). In this connection, Winnicott (1971) also drew attention to the therapist's ability to be playful with the patient as a prelude to the deepening of the analytic process and as an activity that facilitates the patient's transference. "If the therapist cannot play, then he is not suitable for the work. If the patient cannot play, then something needs to be done to enable the patient to become able to play, after which psychotherapy may begin. The reason why playing is essential is that it is in playing that the patient is being creative" (p. 54).

Kohut's self-psychological approach is based on his discovery of what he called the selfobject transferences, which reflect the revival of frustrated early mirroring, idealization, and alter-ego or twinship needs in the new, more empathic and nonjudgmental context of treatment. Wolf (1988, pp. 124–135), a collaborator of Kohut, expanded the types of selfobject transferences to include the transference of creativity and the adversarial transference. All the selfobject transferences contain elements of merger, in which the patient experiences the therapist as an extension of himself or herself who is subject to the patient's wishes and needs and must be totally in tune with them. When patients defend against such merger experiences, they may maintain distance from the therapist in order to protect themselves from reexperiencing trauma at the hands of a disappointing or frustrating selfobject.

In this framework, the therapist must understand the appearance of a selfobject transference, however extreme, as an understandable, albeit dysfunctional outcome of the client's early caretaking experiences and as the patient's opportunity or second chance to complete his or her development. Thus, any signs of such a reaction should be allowed to flourish and should be welcomed rather than discouraged or confronted. Overcoming a patient's fear of developing a selfobject transference usually is accomplished by the therapist's conveying empathic understanding of the patient's anxiety about being let down or hurt and by moving at the patient's pace. Some patients, however, will require concrete evidence that their needs are understood, demonstrations of the therapist's active caring, genuineness and willingness to self-disclose, and responsiveness (Goldstein, 1994, 1997). Additionally, individuals who experience chronic feelings of rage, because of the severe and repeated assaults they experienced in early childhood, may be very provocative and tax the therapist's empathic abilities.

Disruptions of the selfobject transferences occur inevitably and commonly result from the therapist's lack of attunement to the patient's needs, failure to live up to the patient's expectations, or inevitable limitations. For example, a fragile lesbian patient who believed that her therapist completely understood her, without her having to explain herself, experienced a painful rupture in her mirror transference when the therapist asked her to clarify some of the details of her earlier coming-out process. Although many other patients might have interpreted this seemingly benign intervention as evidence of the therapist's interest and positive involvement, this particular patient found it jarring and disruptive. Turbulent reactions, setbacks, and impasses like this one often occur even when there are minor and transient lapses in the therapist's attunement. During such moments, it is necessary for the therapist to repair the break in the relationship in order to restore the transference. In order to achieve this, it usually is necessary for the therapist to recognize and acknowledge to the patient that something has gone wrong in the therapist–patient interaction. Then, it is useful for the therapist to explore the patient's perception of the therapist's possible insensitivity, mistakes, or failures that have led to the disruption. The therapist also might explore and explain how the current derailment resembles incidents in the patient's past when her significant selfobjects were disappointing and frustrating and how these early experiences have led to certain characteristic expectations of and responses to others in the patient's current life. It is important, however, for the therapist not to move too quickly into this type of approach, before having sufficiently acknowledged the patient's perception of the therapist's actual role in precipitating the disruption. It is not always easy to accomplish these tasks, particularly for those unaccustomed to using this approach. Well-meaning and empathic therapists may nevertheless make what are experienced by the patient as inadvertent and unintentional lapses or errors, even while thinking they are doing the right thing, or they may staunchly defend their point of view and actions. "There is a ubiquitous resistance to the acknowledgement that the truth we believe about ourselves is no more (though no less) real than the patient's view of us" (Schwaber, 1983, p. 389).

Expanding on these ideas, both intersubjective and contemporary relational theorists have added an important dimension to understanding transference. Criticizing most other approaches to transference as being based on a one-sided view of treatment, they view all therapeutic interactions as influenced by both therapist and patient, who exert a mutual impact on each other (Stolorow and Atwood, 1979; Mitchell, 1993; Stolorow, Atwood, and Brandchaft, 1994; Aron, 1996). The therapist is never merely an objective observer of the patient but is both an observer and a participant who shapes the process. Although patients may attempt to repeat their past early relationships in the therapeutic relationship, the therapist invariably plays a part in eliciting the patient's reactions. Thus, therapists must pay attention to the impact of their personality, cultural background, attitudes, beliefs, comments, and behavior on patients. The patient's so-called transference to the therapist may in part stem from her accurate reading of the therapist rather than from a distortion of the therapist's personality and participation. For example, a therapist's lack of knowledge of some of the unique experiences that lesbians have or a therapist's failure to disclose her sexual identity may stimulate an outsider transference in which the patient reexperiences in the present what she has often felt in the past. Likewise, a therapist's anxiety about discussing sexual practices may result in a lesbian patient's feeling that there is a barrier between her and the therapist. In either case, if the therapist fails to recognize her contribution to the patient's reaction and instead interprets it as the patient's problem, a therapeutic impasse can occur. In both instances, the therapists' acknowledgment of their uninformed or unattuned behavior may provide a dual opportunity to deepen the treatment relationship and facilitate the therapeutic work. Needless to say, therapists may not always be aware of their impact on the patient or may fail to acknowledge the reality of a patient's perceptions, tending to see the patient's reaction as stemming only from what she brings to the treatment relationship.

Because it is necessary for therapists to consider actively the ongoing impact of both therapist and patient in understanding and working with transference, it may be useful for the therapist to elicit the patient's ideas about what the therapist is thinking and feeling. For example, in working with a patient who expresses pride and excitement in her discovery of her sexual attractiveness to other women, the therapist might encourage the patient to share her thoughts and fantasies about how the therapist is reacting to the patient's communications. Whatever the patient says can reveal important information that might remain dormant to both members of the therapeutic dyad if the therapist does not raise the issue. The therapist can draw on various ways of working with what the patient says in this kind of situation. Rather than only exploring the content of what the patient expresses, it may be necessary for the therapist to validate or disconfirm the patient's ideas about the therapist's subjectivity.

Some clinicians maintain the view that although the therapist exerts an influence on the transference, patients do bring their past relational patterns into the treatment and these contribute to transference developments. Some patients display entrenched negative views of themselves and fears of human relationships as a result of early and persistent traumatic life experiences. They may have difficulty developing and sustaining a positive transference or may distort the therapist's intent, personal characteristics, or actions even when the therapist is basically attuned to them. In such cases, the therapist must recognize the patient's struggle and refrain from reacting in ways that aggravate the patient's vulnerability. For example, even with a therapist who has demonstrated repeatedly that she values and likes the patient, the latter may insist that the therapist is playing a role and just being nice so that she can get her fee or is secretly critical of the patient's lesbianism. In this instance, it would be important for the therapist to resist getting provoked by the patient's distrust and accusations and, instead, show her understanding of how difficult it is for the patient to believe that the therapist cares about her.

Because patients of this type show a tendency to enact rather than to verbalize about significant past relational experiences (Hoffman, 1991; Renik, 1995; Aron, 1996), their behavior may stimulate the therapist to participate or play a part in the enactment. When the therapist does get pulled into the interaction, the result is a collusion with or actualization of a patient's deeply entrenched pathological pattern of relating or negative expectations. This may prevent the therapist and patient from understanding what is transpiring and obstruct the therapist's ability to relate to the patient in a new and more positive way. It is essential that the therapist recognize that an enactment is taking place and intervene to extricate both himself or herself and the patient so that the repetition can be understood. As some current relational theorists point out (Aron, 1996), it is erroneous to view so-called enactments as stemming only from the therapist's participation in what is being induced in him or her by the patient (pp. 221–253). A therapist's strong feelings that arise in working with a patient may stem from his or her own issues, which are stimulated but not induced by the patient. As Maroda notes (1999, pp. 121–140), a therapist's own personality and past can get together with the patient's need for pathological forms of enactment, leading to a serious therapeutic problem that also makes it difficult to know who is doing what to whom. Natterson and Friedman (1995) suggest that "both patient and therapist [are] continuously living out in the relationship some fantasy of fundamental importance to each party" (p. 137). Thus, the therapist's blind spots or personality problems may lead to an unfortunate replay of the patient's past traumatic history. The therapist may be at risk for participating in a repetition or enactment of both the patient's and the therapist's earlier experiences without recognizing and understanding this. Consequently, the therapist may find it useful to share her uncertainty about how to understand what is happening between patient and therapist and to invite the patient to participate in the process of clarifying the therapist–patient interaction.

The following example illustrates a likely enactment and its management. In her work with a lesbian patient who was having trouble finding ways of meeting other lesbians, the lesbian therapist shared some of her knowledge and experience of the lesbian community in order to provide some guidance. Instead of appreciating the therapist's help and good intentions, the patient became angry with the therapist and accused her of being intrusive and domineering. The therapist recognized that she had made a mistake but was unsure why the patient reacted to her so negatively. Instead of becoming defensive, she asked the patient if she could talk about what had made her so angry. The patient responded sarcastically that she wasn't paying the therapist to be like her controlling mother. The therapist commented, "So my desire to help you to meet other lesbians actually made you feel like I was taking over. You have told me that your mother tried to take ownership of your life and had trouble letting you find your own way. Maybe I am acting like her even though I'm not trying to control you." In subsequent sessions, the therapist was able to move beyond her own countertransference and to extricate the therapeutic dyad from the enactment. The therapist realized that her mistake stemmed from an enactment of her countertransference desire for a twinship experience with the patient. She identified with the patient's struggle to connect with the lesbian community and wanted to rescue the patient from the suffering and torment that the therapist had experienced in her own youth. Unfortunately, the therapist stimulated the patient's negative maternal transference by creating a relational situation in which the patient's autonomy felt threatened.

Mutual enactments are an inevitable part of the treatment process (Renik, 1995). Even when they occur, however, the outcome can be positive if the therapist and patient are able to reflect on and process the meaning of the enactment in a growth-promoting way. Although processing an enactment is clearly indicated when a therapeutic impasse occurs, it also may be useful for the therapist and patient to have an ongoing dialogue about what transpires in the relationship.

Although the therapist must keep all these transference paradigms in mind in clinical work with lesbians, it is especially important to be attuned to lesbian patients' needs for a positive new selfobject or new types of relational experiences and to be mindful of their defenses against disappointment and rejection. This is so because of the far-reaching impact of lesbians' early sense of being different and their stigmatized identity. From a broader perspective, what gets expressed in the transference with lesbian patients also reflects societal attitudes and behavior. Some of what the patient exhibits in the treatment may be conditioned by her cultural experience as a lesbian and the expectations about how others will view her. Sometimes these feelings go far back into the patient's early childhood and adolescence and have led to adaptive strategies that have become integrated into her personality organization. For example, some lesbians grow up making sure that others do not learn of their sexual interest in women and may become secretive or socially isolated. Or in early stages of treatment, a lesbian patient might be reluctant to share information about her sexual and relational experiences and thus may appear guarded and rigid. She may have experienced rejection by her family or peers or she may have learned to keep the details of her personal life hidden in professional interactions. Alternatively, the therapist may be unwittingly recreating the patient's cultural experience by not asking direct questions or not exploring the patient's sexual experiences and relationships. A clinician who interprets the patient's behavior as reflecting purely intrapsychic struggles would be making a mistake.

Rethinking the Role and Nature of Countertransference

Countertransference is an inevitable part of the treatment process and the ways in which it is understood and addressed are crucial to successful treatment. Nevertheless, few psychoanalytic writings address countertransference reactions in clinical work with lesbian patients.

In Freudian theory, countertransference reflected the therapist's reactions to the patient that stem from the therapist's unresolved neurotic conflicts. It was commonly believed that analysis would enable therapists to eliminate or become aware of the conflicts that might interfere with the treatment. Fully analyzed, they would be able to evaluate the patient's personality and reality objectively.

In contrast to the traditional view, the totalistic conception of countertransference that arose in object relations circles emphasized all the therapist's conscious and unconscious reactions to the patient, including those that are induced by the patient's personality, psychopathology, and life situation (Hanna, 1993a, b). The totalistic view encompassed what Winnicott termed objective countertransference, which refers to natural or quite justifiable reactions of the therapist to extreme aspects of the patient's behavior and to both concordant and complementary identification (Racker, 1957). In concordant identification, the therapist identifies with the main emotion that the patient is feeling at a given time or with the feeling that the patient has put into the therapist by means of projective identification. For example, the therapist's empathic immersion in the patient's story may lead him or her to experience the patient's rage. Or the therapist's feelings of anger may stem from the patient's use of projective identification, in which the patient projects his or her aggressive, often disavowed, impulses into the therapist, who then is experienced as a hostile enemy who can be justifiably hated and controlled. In complementary identification, the therapist takes on a role in response to the patient's behavior. He or she may begin to feel like a harsh and controlling figure while the patient experiences fear of the therapist, who is perceived as being like the patient's authoritarian parent (Goldstein, 2001, pp. 104–109).

The main treatment implications of the totalistic conception of countertransference are that the therapist must contain the patient's projective identifications in his or her mind without acting on them. Therapists then use their feelings to understand the nature of the patient's internalized object relations as they appear in or are enacted in the transference–countertransference dynamics. They help the patient to reflect on these dynamics and to connect these transference reactions to difficulties in the patient's current and past life experiences.

More contemporary views of countertransference can be grouped into two major perspectives. The first continues to advise therapists to be self-scrutinizing about their countertransference and to try to regulate it. This perspective broadens the scope of the discussion, however, to include the therapist's conscious and unconscious attitudes and reactions to patients that arise from the therapist's personality, cultural background, values, theoretical beliefs, or unwitting need to express certain emotional needs in the treatment relationship. The implication of this view is that therapists must strive to overcome reactions that have the potential of disrupting the transference and repair those ruptures that do occur. For example, a lesbian patient entered treatment with a male therapist and discussed her female-centered world repeatedly in the treatment. The therapist began to feel annoyed and wanted to ask the patient if she ever had any male friends but refrained from doing so. In his supervision, in speaking about his view that the patient's world was very narrow, the supervisor picked up on the therapist's anger at the patient. The therapist, who was raised in a female-dominated family and felt alone as a boy among his numerous sisters, was able to recognize that his feeling of being devalued by his patient was a displacement from his own early life. In the treatment, the therapist was able to convey greater interest in the patient's friendship network.

Alternatively, countertransference can be thought of as an intersubjective process that results from the mutual interplay of two personalities in the here and now therapeutic interaction (Hanna, 1993a, b). In embracing what they consider to be a two-person rather than one-person psychology, numerous current relational and intersubjective theorists have launched some far-reaching criticisms of the ways in which self psychology and other developmental arrest models manage countertransference (Teicholz, 1999). They argue that the therapist cannot truly understand the nature of his or her countertransference without learning about the patient's perceptions of the therapist. Moreover, it is neither possible nor desirable for therapists to try to eliminate their reactions completely because this would deny them a subjective existence. Instead, therapists practicing within a so-called two-person model should actively consider the ongoing impact of the personalities of both the patient and the therapist on the treatment process and help the patient to think about both participants as separate people. Therapists should attempt to communicate what they think and feel about what is happening in the treatment and to encourage patients to explore their ideas about the therapist. It often may be necessary to validate or disconfirm the patient's views.

In the example cited above, although the therapist's annoyance with his patient had a basis in the therapist's early life experience, he might explore how the patient was feeling about being in treatment with a man, given her strong feelings of connections to women and the lack of men in her life. He might have said, "Sometimes when you speak about all the women in your life, I get an uneasy feeling and wonder how you feel about working with a male therapist." If the therapist does not have sufficient distance from his own reaction, it may be difficult to ask the patient this question in a nonthreatening way. Processing what is occurring in the interaction might or might not lead the patient to develop a different understanding of her communications.

Recently, numerous authors who adhere to a relational framework (Hoffman, 1983; Ehrenberg, 1995; Renik, 1995; Maroda, 1999) have advocated the use of countertransference disclosure, that is, the revealing of feelings that the therapist has about the patient or in interaction with the patient. They argue that this intervention opens up the discussion of potentially frightening and disruptive feelings, clarifies the nature of enactments, shows the patient that the therapist understands the patient's inner world, and enables the patient to experience the therapist as genuine and truthful. Nevertheless, Maroda (1999) cautions therapists not to disclose strong feelings at times when they feel on the verge of being out of control and expresses caution about revealing erotic countertransference because it is too stimulating and threatening generally. Moreover, it becomes difficult to understand the nature of the mutual enactment if the therapist's feelings about the patient are interfering with her therapeutic role. For example, a lesbian therapist revealed to her supervisor that she was attracted to a very seductive lesbian patient who wanted the therapist to terminate the therapeutic relationship and date the patient. Although the therapist did not acknowledge her feelings to the patient, the therapist felt that the patient could see through her silence. She felt ashamed and guilty for being so transparent. The therapist also revealed that she was feeling lonely and normally had trouble handling her feelings and behavior when she was attracted to women who were more forward in expressing their attractions. She admitted that she was having sexual fantasies about the patient but knew the patient was not an appropriate partner choice for her. The supervisor helped the therapist to see that she was caught up in her own feelings and interpreting the patient's behavior and feelings literally, thus losing sight of the clinical meaning of the patient's seductiveness and wishes to partner with the therapist. The supervisor helped the therapist to explore how to work with her countertransference in ways that would help her to stay in her therapeutic role with the patient and encouraged her to explore the possible meanings of the expression of the patient's attraction for the therapist.

Even when countertransference self-disclosure and confrontation and interpretation of enactments are carried out in a sensitive and tactful manner, the risk exists that many patients may experience these techniques as too blaming and assaultive, particularly at early points in treatment. Moreover, some followers of object relations theorists, such as Winnicott and Guntrip, would be focused on the degree to which patients are seeking new types of relational experiences and better responses to longstanding needs rather than always replaying their past pathological interactions. They would be more likely to rely on the containment function rather than to use confrontation and interpretation as techniques of first resort.

Despite their potential for disruptions of and impasses in the treatment relationship, therapists' problematic reactions may play a necessary and beneficial role in the treatment. When countertransference occurs or interferes with the therapeutic relationship, therapists' acknowledgment and processing of what is occurring, including mistakes and lack of empathy, can lead to productive and transforming experiences. Likewise, when therapists are pulled into repetitions of past traumatic relational experiences, they need, with the help of the patient, to stand back, observe, and reflect on what is taking place in the therapeutic interaction. This can lead to changes in the ways in which the patient views herself and others.

In clinical work with lesbians, heterosexual therapists who have a negative theoretical bias, heterosexist value system, or lack of personal experience and comfort in working with lesbians may react to them in ways that repeat the rejecting, disapproving, or unattuned experiences that the patients have experienced with significant others in their lives. For example, in working with a lesbian patient who expresses some regrets about her inability to have a sexual and romantic relationship with a man, a therapist, believing that it is preferable for the patient to achieve a heterosexual identity, might encourage her patient's fantasies about having sexual contact with men. This intervention might reflect her lack of understanding of the patient's need to mourn aspects of a heterosexual identity or her need to please the therapist. It also might constitute a reenactment of the patient's relationship with a mother who refused to accept her daughter's romantic interest in other women and insisted that she marry and have children. Moreover, in response to the patient's telling the therapist that she feels misunderstood, the therapist might interpret the patient's reaction as resistance rather than recognizing how her own values are influencing her work. Likewise, some therapists may not understand or may pathologize certain aspects of the lesbians' life experiences.

Other types of countertransference response occur when female therapists experience discomfort with a lesbian patient's growing attachment to them. They might inadvertently withdraw from the patient, fail to respond to the patient's need for more intimate and affectionate connection, or misread the patient's increased dependence and expressions of fondness for the therapist as signs of a beginning erotic transference. Moreover, in cases of a more intense transference that includes some sexual fantasies, the therapist might try to dilute this rather than recognize it as an important positive development in the transference.

Although heterosexual therapists need to bridge the differences in their sexual orientation, background, and lifestyle with those of their lesbian patients, lesbian and gay male therapists are not immune from having countertransference reactions that may be disruptive to the treatment. These can stem from their own identification with their lesbian patients or can be a result of personal and political values that they wish to impose on patients.

Summary

This chapter discussed eight major components of a treatment framework with lesbians:

1. Viewing the process of lesbian identity formation as a positive developmental achievement.
2. Demonstrating knowledge of lesbian life and culture.
3. Creating a collaborative treatment process.
4. Engaging in experience-near empathy.
5. Displaying realness, genuineness, and spontaneity.
6. Eliciting the personal meaning of lesbian identity.
7. Exploring lesbian narratives.
8. Reconceptualizing transference and focusing on counter-transference.

The following chapters discuss and illustrate these principles in more detail and show their application to work with lesbians across the life cycle.

Chapter 4

Lesbian Narratives and the Treatment Process

As discussed in chapter 3, enabling lesbian patients to relate their personal narratives about the discovery of their sexual identity and coming-out experiences is a crucial component of our psychotherapeutic approach. The timing and nature of this process differs from patient to patient because lesbians enter treatment for a variety of reasons that may or may not revolve around their sexual identity. They also differ in their self-acceptance of their lesbianism, trust of the therapist, and readiness to reflect on their life experiences.

In the beginning of treatment, it always is advisable for therapists to create a safe therapeutic environment in which the patient can talk freely. Providing a holding environment should take precedence over prematurely delving into the patient's deeper struggles related to her sexual identity. With patients who are dealing with coming out or other issues that are directly related to their lesbianism, it usually will be necessary for the therapist to engage early in the treatment in a nonthreatening exploration of the patient's feelings and experiences in regard to her sexual identity. For other patients, issues related to their lesbianism will emerge later in the work. For example, women who do not present with concerns related to their lesbianism and who show a relatively high degree of self-acceptance may be in treatment for some time before the exploration of the patient's sexual identity becomes significant. As is described in some of the case examples throughout this chapter, this discussion usually evolves when the treatment moves into a deeper exploration of the patient's personality, when the patient confronts new challenges in her life, or when current events trigger unresolved issues. In these instances, it may be beneficial for the therapist and patient to talk about the ways in which the patient has managed her self-identification and coming-out process.

The Narrative Process

Working with lesbian narratives is an ongoing process of discovery for both therapist and patient. The therapist must be open to the patient's experience of herself and must encourage the unfolding of her personal story, which may evolve and change over time. The therapist needs to be attuned to the themes of the patient's narrative and to its sometimes contradictory or changing nature. As the therapeutic relationship deepens, the patient and therapist may feel freer to explore more charged material. At various points, the patient may elaborate on her story or tell it differently. The therapist may help a patient to reformulate her understanding of the past and to recognize her own strengths and developmental achievements. During treatment, the patient may rework her narrative as she gains increasing levels of emotional understanding. The following case examples illustrate how therapists elicit and work with patients' narratives at different points in the treatment using the principles described in chapter 3.

A Crisis Around Delayed Coming Out

Ivana, a 25-year-old American-born child of Croatian immigrants, was a third-year medical student when she entered treatment. She requested that her insurance company recommend a therapist who was knowledgeable in the treatment of gays and lesbians. Ivana had just ended a brief intense relationship with a classmate, Jenny, to whom she was emotionally and sexually attracted. When she and Jenny began to have some physical contact, Ivana broke their connection because she became acutely anxious and guilty. Ivana did not know if she could exist without seeing Jenny, for whom she longed but was too frightened to seek her out. She was having trouble concentrating and doing her work.

The following dialogue occurred in the first session with the therapist.

P: This is the first time I've let myself get so close to someone. Deep down, I've known I was a lesbian for many years but I didn't want to believe it. I felt so ashamed and was afraid I would disgrace my parents. They expect me to marry and have children. I've never been interested in men but I don't want to give up the security of being in a straight marriage. No one knows how I feel. I'm finding it more and more difficult to lie to my parents when they pressure me to get married. I feel like I'm a fraud. I keep making excuses to get out of blind dates with men that my friends and family members arrange.

T: Living with a secret can be very stressful but you seem to feel that you have no choice.

P: My parents have tried to be modern but they could never accept my being with another woman. I can't accept it. I just don't think it's right. I haven't had a lesbian as a friend until now but I think lesbians are screwed up. I don't feel like hanging out in bars and having sex all the time. I feel bad talking like this. Can you understand how I feel? I don't know if you're straight or gay or if you have worked with anyone like me.

T: You are not so very different from other women with whom I've worked. I understand that you are troubled by your attraction to another woman when you and your parents have such negative feelings about lesbians. It is not unusual for people who are drawn to members of the same sex to take in the derogatory views of others, especially if they have not had positive role models.

P: So you don't think I'm strange?

T: No, I don't. You said that you didn't know whether I was straight or gay. Would you feel more comfortable if you knew whether or not I was a lesbian?

P: I'm not sure. If I knew what your sexual orientation is, I might feel pressured to be what I think you want me to be. Either way I'd be anxious.

T: It seems that feeling pressured to be what someone else wants you to be is an important issue for you. It may be hard to be yourself if you think it conflicts with what someone else wants.

P: I feel like Jenny and my mother are pressuring me but in opposite ways. I feel good when I'm with Jenny until she wants to get physical. I'd like that too but I get too anxious. Then I talk to my mother and she asks me if I'm dating. I want to scream. I don't know what to do.

T: I know you feel an urgency to resolve these issues but it is important to give yourself some time to sort out what you are feeling and what you want to do. You and I can do this together.

During the next several sessions, the therapist tried to quell Ivana's panic and sense of urgency and to gain her trust. After a month, Ivana reestablished contact with Jenny but tried to keep their relationship platonic.

P: I was with Jenny last night and we were watching the show *Ellen* on television. Ellen's parents were visiting her and her female lover for the first time. It was funny but I thought that I would never be able to introduce Jenny to my parents if we were together. We had a fight about this. She just doesn't understand what it has been like for me all of my life. Her parents seem okay about her being a lesbian. My parents live in the dark ages.

T: How do you think their cultural background influences their views?

P: They try to be modern but they are very traditional. They're not as open as people who are American-born. They have a lot of old-fashioned ideas about everything. I couldn't wear makeup until I went to college, and even then they hated it. They used to embarrass me with my friends. I know I shouldn't feel that way. They can't help it.

T: It's not unusual for children to feel pulled by the culture of their parents and the culture they have to deal with every day.

Later in the session, the therapist began to explore Ivana's beginning awareness of being attracted to other girls.

T: We haven't talked much about what it was like for you growing up and when you became aware of your attraction to other girls.

P: I think I've always gravitated to women more than to men.

T: What do you remember about that?

P: I can remember fantasizing about being physically close to other girls when I was about 13. I knew that I shouldn't be having such feelings but I couldn't stop. I used to try to force myself to think about being with boys sexually but the idea repulsed me.

T: What did you do?

P: I didn't tell anyone. I just knew that it was wrong.

T: How do you think you knew that?

P: I'm not sure. I didn't know what a lesbian was until later. Kids can be cruel when someone is different but my parents used to talk about my getting married and having children even when I was little. I knew what they expected of me. I'm an only child and they came to this country so that I could have a good life. They only want what is best for me and I want to make them happy.

T: You must have felt very bad.

P: I even used to make myself date guys but it didn't work for me. I just can't deal with them.

In the following session, Ivana returned to the subject of her parents.

P: I don't think they could imagine that being with a woman would ever make me happy. It's not part of their world. Sometimes I agree with them.

T: You are afraid you will never be happy as a lesbian?

P: But that *is* who I am.

T: But you are fearful that you will always be unhappy. It's not clear which upsets you more, disappointing your parents, feeling that they will reject you, or thinking you will not be happy with another woman.

P: Sometimes I feel confused. I don't always know where they leave off and I begin. They're very opinionated and they have always expected me to share their views about everything. I have always tried to live up to their expectations.

T: You care about them a lot but you seem to feel that they would not care enough about you eventually to accept you if you live your own life.

In a subsequent session, Ivana brought up a telephone conversation with her mother, who attacked her for isolating herself socially and not trying to meet eligible men.

T: It must have been very hard to listen to her, given what you are going through.

P: Maybe she's right and I should try to go straight.

T: Is that something you want me to help you with?

P: Maybe I'd be happier but I know that I can't be with men. I have these strong feelings for Jenny. They feel right to me but I feel bad about them at the same time.

T: You seem to equate being attracted to other women with being a bad person.

P: I've always felt this way. I knew I had to keep my feelings secret. I buried myself in my schoolwork. I often had stomachaches.

Later in the session, Ivana returned to the telephone call with her mother.

P: It's strange. I felt like I had a pit in my stomach when I got off the phone with my mother last night and when I talked to Jenny on the telephone. She told me that she couldn't understand why my attitudes about being gay are so negative. It's true I haven't really known many gay people who were out. I guess I've just accepted what everyone else thinks.

T: Are you connecting being sick to feeling pulled?

P: I hadn't thought of that. I guess it's possible.

T: You mentioned that you have taken on others' attitudes about gays. Where do you think your ideas came from?

P: I'm not sure. I just grew up in an environment where everyone had similar values and opinions about everything and no one dared to be different.

T: Do you remember anything specifically that was said about being homosexual?

P: Not exactly. [long pause]

T: What are you thinking?

P: My mother is not very affectionate. I know she loves me but I remember her telling me when I was a child that I was too big to hug her. It used to make me feel bad. Once I know that she pushed me away and called me a baby.

T: Do you think it's possible that this was because it was her issue and not because there was anything wrong with you? Children naturally want to enjoy physical affection with their mothers.

P: I just knew I felt ashamed of wanting to be close to her.

T: It's sad for you to feel ashamed of your natural feelings. Perhaps you came to connect your mother's negative reaction to your affectionate overtures toward her with your feelings that there is something wrong with you if you want to be close to other women?

In this early phase of treatment, the therapist and patient explored Ivana's negative feelings about lesbians, fears of her parents' disapproval and of bringing shame to them, and need for their validation. She also supported Ivana in creating a zone of privacy and independence in which she could pursue her own life without feeling that she had to report all her activities back to her parents. On one occasion after several months of treatment, the following interchange took place.

P: I want to ask you something. I think I'm ready to know whether or not you are a lesbian.

T: I will answer you, but I'm wondering what makes you bring this up today.

P: Well, I think you are but I find myself wishing that I knew someone I admired who also was a lesbian. I think it would make me feel more hopeful that I don't have to be a second-class citizen.

T: Well, you are correct that I am a lesbian. It's important that you could ask me. What's your reaction?

P: I feel good but I'm a little ashamed of all the bad things that I have said about lesbians. I hope you haven't taken what I've said personally.

T: It's important that you feel free to express your thoughts and feelings.

In the following sessions, Ivana began talking about how she could manage her parents while having a romantic relationship with Jenny. After six months, Ivana and Jenny became involved sexually and developed a more committed relationship while continuing to live apart. Although Ivana continued to be anxious about her parents' learning about her sexual identity, she was able to contain her feelings. She eventually began to consider that her parents would not disown her or fall apart were they to learn of her lesbianism. After being together for a year, Ivana gathered the courage to come out to her parents and to tell them about Jenny. She prepared herself for a turbulent and rejecting response, which she hoped would gradually abate. Her parents' reactions were predictable but they never broke off their relationship with her. They refused to acknowledge Jenny, however. Ivana frequently spoke about her mother and her feelings of estrangement from her. When she brought up her most recent struggle with her mother a year and a half into the treatment, though, her evolving self-acceptance and greater separation from her parents' negative attitudes about homosexuality were evident.

P: I am feeling very distant from my mother. We only speak about superficial things and safe topics. I miss the way we use to be involved in each other's lives. I know it's because she can't get over my being gay. Sometimes she can't help herself and she starts attacking me. Over and over I hear in my head that thick accent of hers saying, "You're too pretty a girl to be like a man with a woman. It's disgusting. Nobody in this house taught you such things."

T: It seems like your mother thinks that her attacks will make you change.

P: She thinks that being a lesbian is a choice. She doesn't understand what it's like for me.

T: Although her attacks are painful, you seem to be feeling much better about yourself and stronger in your ability to be your own person.

P: I do feel better. That's why I can't understand why I'm so reactive to her. I have been working hard in treatment and I feel myself getting stronger every day.

T: It's understandable that you would like to share what's important to you with her and have her acceptance.

P: I miss our old relationship sometimes but I realize that I don't need her in the same way. But the stronger I get the angrier I am with her.

T: Perhaps it's safer to feel angry with her now that you rely on her less?

Later in the session, Ivana had the following insight.

P: I feel like our roles have reversed. It's as if she is the rebellious child and I am the mother. I wish that she could find a way to be more modern or more adult in her thinking. I know she loves me and thinks she wants the best for me, but I guess I'm just very frustrated with her right now. I used to worry about disappointing her but she keeps disappointing me. I'd like to have a different kind of relationship with her.

T: You have taken an important step in your life in being able to accept your attraction to other women and to allow yourself to have an intimate relationship with someone you love. It's understandable that you want your parents to recognize and support your achievements. But sometimes parents have a coming-out process of their own. Given your mother's background, it may take her more time to accept that you are not going through a phase and to mourn the loss of what she wanted for you. Because you and your mother have a history of being close, in time, both of you may be able to arrive at a better resolution.

P: I hope so. I'm sick of this trapped feeling I have with her. Sometimes I feel as if she is pressuring me to be straight for her own sake. If I'm straight she can relieve herself of the guilt she feels in having created a lesbian. A few weeks ago she actually said to me, "What if two very attractive men wanted to go out with you and Jenny." She just can't get it through her head that Jenny is more desirable to me than a man, no matter how handsome he is. I was so angry with her I said, "What would you do if a beautiful woman came on to you?" She didn't get the point I was making.

T: I can see why you got so riled up. She does not see who you are and makes you feel like you don't exist.

P: She only thinks about her own feelings. It's always about her. I never thought that my mother was selfish and childish. I used to look up to her. I always thought she was so wise. When I was a little girl, she would tell me about how she and my father came to the United States knowing only a few words of English and without much money and family support. I admired her for overcoming such hardships and leaving her country.

T: You seem to have a lot of her strength.

P: Maybe I do but I am very disappointed in her. I naively thought her experience with being foreign and having to assimilate would help her to understand my lesbianism. Unfortunately it doesn't. She still refuses to meet Jenny and she had the audacity to ask me to go to my cousin's wedding with a male date.

T: It's hard to face that your mother would rather have you inhibit what feels natural in order not to offend or risk the disapproval of others.

P: After a year of trying to get them to meet Jenny, I'm tired. They still expect me to come by myself to spend Easter with them as always. I told my mother I was part of a couple. She started carrying on. I told her I wasn't coming home alone. I feel bad but I can't give in to her.

T: It's difficult to have to pay such a price in order to be your own person.

P: She sacrificed so much for me. She worked like a slave in a sewing factory to put me through college and to live what she thought was the American dream. In all ways but one I have realized her dream. I wish that she could feel good about that instead of feeling that I've ruined her dream. I don't want to feel responsible for her any longer. She had her chance. I deserve mine.

Discussion

When Ivana entered treatment, she was highly anxious and terrified of committing to a lesbian lifestyle that she demeaned and that put her in direct conflict with her parents. It is noteworthy that she did not specifically ask for a referral to a lesbian therapist but to one who was knowledgeable about the treatment of gays and lesbians. It is possible that this reflected both her anxiety about her lesbianism and her internalized homophobia. The therapist focused on Ivana's current conflict, didn't press her to discuss her past experiences, and allowed Ivana's narrative to unfold. She attempted to provide holding and to develop a therapeutic collaboration before delving more deeply into Ivana's background and feelings about her sexual identity. It is noteworthy that in their early work together, the therapist refrained from disclosing whether or not she was a lesbian because Ivana indicated that she would feel pressured by the answer. The therapist did disclose that she was a lesbian later in the treatment, when it seemed therapeutically beneficial to be responsive to the patient's questions. There are many instances in which patients seek out gay-identified therapists or in which gay therapists disclose their sexual identity to a gay patient as a matter of course.

Gradually, the therapist delved more deeply into Ivana's discovery of her same-sex attractions and past struggles with her lesbianism. She helped her to identify the themes that were reflected in her multiple narratives of herself as a daughter, a lover, and a friend. These themes centered on her internalized homophobia, lack of acceptance of her attraction to women, loss of a heterosexual lifestyle, fears of disappointing her parents, and difficulty separating from her overly responsible and enmeshed relationship with her parents. Until the therapy, Ivana had never discussed her feelings about her sexual identity with anyone. The process of talking with someone she trusted enabled her to get in touch with deeper layers of her early experiences and to feel a sense of validation.

As Ivana felt stronger, was able to take more risks, and separated more from her parents, she began to reconstruct and reinterpret her own experience with the help of the therapist and her view of her family shifted. She began to express disappointment and anger at the ways in which her mother, in particular, had reacted to her when Ivana was younger and to the mother's ongoing lack of understanding and acceptance of her lesbianism. She began to feel empowered to be her own person.

It is possible that a therapist who agreed with Ivana's parents' views about lesbians, or who shared her internalized homophobia, might have supported Ivana's initial decision to break off with Jenny and might have encouraged her to remain more open to exploring a heterosexual identity and lifestyle. It is important to note that in this case, Ivana had identified her own attraction to women from an early age but was fearful of acting on her feelings. She had also sought out a gay-friendly therapist. This woman, also a lesbian, was attuned to the characteristic anxieties associated with coming out, particularly in the context of Ivana's family background, and helped her to move forward in her life.

A Deep Sense of Insecurity and Lack of Safety

Jody, 47-year-old editor and talented writer, entered treatment after the death of her father. Feeling stuck, she wanted to make changes in her life.

She described herself as a street kid who happened to be really smart and who had to raise herself, as her mother was crazy and her father never grew up. She said she had always played it safe, staying in a low-paying position for years because she was afraid to take on more responsibility or to look for a better job in a new setting; never completing book manuscripts for which she had numerous contracts; remaining in a small, cramped, and dark apartment in which she felt trapped in a city that caused her extreme stress; and never having a satisfying relationship with another woman for more than a brief period. Until recently, she thought that being poor was a badge of honor and saw herself as a social critic and outsider. Although she was in a relationship at present, her lover lived in another state. They saw one another at regular but infrequent intervals.

Initially, Jody seemed matter-of-fact about her being a lesbian. She knew the therapist also was gay because of the nature of the referral. Her history revealed that although Jody had known she was a lesbian from childhood, she had her first sexual relationship with a woman when she was in college in the 1970s at a time when she and her friends were experimenting sexually and many came out. She later worked in an office in which a large number of her colleagues were gay and lesbian. She was politically active in gay organizations and well-versed in the trends in gay and lesbian culture.

After six months of treatment that was focused on helping Jody decide what to do about her work life, she made a job change that gave her a promotion and a higher salary. Subsequently, she somewhat impulsively moved out of her apartment into a small rental house in an attractive beachfront community in New Jersey.

P: I just love the house. It has great views, and I can't get over all the space that I have. I really made the right decision for now. I don't think I could have managed if I stayed in the city any longer. Living by the ocean has been my dream for a long time.

T: You sound happy. What's the town like?

P: Well, it's a funny place. I keep expecting to see Tony Soprano and his Mafia friends appear any minute. People are friendly superficially, but I don't know if they know what to do with me.

T: What do you mean?

P: I don't know if they can tell that I'm a lesbian but I'm not married, I don't have children, and I ride my bike all over. There are no gay-owned restaurants or gay community. Maybe there are a few people hiding out like me.

T: Are you hiding out?

P: In a way, I am. I don't mind being by myself. I have always liked to spend a lot of time alone but I am a little frightened about being physically attacked. I even put new locks on the door. I don't know who might get a strange idea about harassing me in some way. They may not realize I'm a lesbian now but wait until Amy comes for a visit. My next-door neighbors will realize that we're together. I didn't really think about how I might feel in this kind of town. I was so focused on getting out of the city. I'm not sorry. I just have to adjust.

T: Is this a new or familiar feeling?

P: I guess I feel more vulnerable because of the move and where I'm living but I've always been concerned about people who were strangers seeing me with gay friends on the street or in a straight restaurant. It's not that I'm uncomfortable with straight people if I know them and feel that they accept me. I just feel nervous around strangers. You probably think I'm paranoid.

T: Sometimes there are real dangers out there. There are people who attack gays but it's also true that we carry old fears into new situations. What do you think is going on for you?

P: Well, I have always been frightened since before I was born. My mother's mental illness didn't help any.

T: What were you thinking of in particular about that?

P: I never knew what to expect. She was so unpredictable.

T: What about your father?

P: He just tuned her out and did his own thing.

T: It sounds like he tuned you out as well.

P: He found a way of surviving.

T: You were quite unsafe and unprotected.

P: I used to go to school dirty. I think the teachers felt sorry for me.

T: They didn't try to do anything?

P: What could they do?

In a later session, when Jody spoke again about her mother, the therapist asked Jody about her mother's reaction to Jody's lesbianism.

T: We've never talked about how she reacted to your interest in other girls.

P: I was at college when I came out. It was never an issue. That's not really true. When I came home for the summer, my mother found me with another girl in my bedroom. We were playing around and she went ballistic and made my friend leave the house. She actually went after me.

T: That must have been frightening.

P: Not really. I was bigger than she was. I just laughed at her. It made her furious. I was careful after that. I didn't want to upset her.

T: What happened after that?

P: I don't remember it well. I know we never talked about anything important. I think she just pretended that I was straight and didn't ask questions. Then she died suddenly just before I graduated.

T: What about your dad's reaction?

P: He didn't care. He was always in his own world. He and my mom never communicated much. I don't know if he stayed with her out of loyalty or dependence. Whatever I did was okay so long as it did not disturb his poker games and visits to the track. My friends have always been my family.

T: You have come a long way without a lot of help.

P: Maybe that's true. It's not something that I think much about.

T: You also seem to minimize any struggles with being a lesbian.

P: I was lucky to have a lot of friends who were gay. They have been a family for me. As an adult I've always been in a gay-friendly environment.

T: Your fear about attracting the wrong kind of attention has to come from somewhere.

P: I have had some scary experiences. I remember visiting a friend of mine upstate. We were in a gay bar and some straight guys came in and started harassing us. It got ugly because they were drunk. The bartender was a woman and I thought they were going to rape her. We were able to get out and we ran.

T: That was a narrow escape. That kind of harassment used to happen a lot.

P: What choice did we have in those days? We had to hang out somewhere. It's not like today. The baby dykes have so many choices. Then, you never knew what to expect. That was why I never liked the bar scene. There were other reasons too.

T: What was it like for you?

P: I never liked to drink so I was always anxious. I wasn't very good at playing the game. I didn't like the cliques and the way women would give me the once-over when I walked in and then act as if I had the plague or something. I tried to go with friends so I wouldn't have to be there by myself. You'd think women would be nicer to one another. Do you think I'm exaggerating? I don't know if you ever experienced the bar scene.

T: I don't think you're exaggerating at all. The bar scene could be fun but also intimidating and scary. Women had to have tough skins.

P: I realize as we're talking that having gay friends and being in the city, as much as I've hated it lately, have made me feel safer than I do living at the shore.

T: In addition to your feeling that the town is far from gay-friendly, perhaps some of your earlier feelings about not being safe are coming into play. You may be feeling that you are more vulnerable and that there isn't anyone nearby who cares about your well-being and will protect you.

In subsequent sessions, the therapist returned repeatedly to Jody's early fearfulness and the ways in which she learned to fend for herself.

T: I wonder how much of your playing it safe personally and professionally has reflected your attempt to be invisible and not attract negative attention and even physical attack?

P: You mean I'm not just a loser?

Ironically, Jody arrived at her next session acting quite cheerful.

P: You will never guess what happened. I was standing in my back yard and a cat was loose. A butch-looking woman about my age came out. I noticed her a few weeks ago and thought she was the daughter of an elderly couple who live in the complex. I asked her if it was her cat and another woman came out and said, "It's our cat." I couldn't believe it. We got to talking. Obviously they had seen me before and were comfortable coming out to me. [laughs] I have two dykes living next to me.

T: [Laughs] That *is* funny. Truth is sometimes stranger than fiction, as they say. Do you think there are other gays around?

P: No. They assured me we are the only ones. But it felt like a miracle. I know you think this is strange but I slept better knowing they are there.

T: I'm glad you did but I also think we need to talk more about the longstanding fears you have had about drawing attention to yourself as a lesbian and how these anxieties still may be affecting you.

Discussion

Unlike Ivana, who entered treatment because of conflicts about coming out and who needed to discuss her feelings about her sexual identity rather quickly in therapy, Jody entered treatment for problems that seemed unrelated to her sexual identity. Her initial narrative about herself as a lesbian reflected that she was comfortable with her sexual identity and au courant with what was politically correct. The central themes in her narrative centered on her identification with being a poor, streetwise individual who lived outside the mainstream and who was afraid to take risks occupationally, personally, romantically, and socially. It was only after many months of treatment, when she moved to a small town in which she experienced the absence of a supportive gay and lesbian presence, that some of her longstanding worries about being openly lesbian became apparent to the therapist. The move stimulated acute feelings of being unsafe. The exploration of Jody's fears led her to revisit many of her early family experiences as well as those connected to her discovery of her lesbianism and coming out. Her different narratives revealed that her current anxieties were multidetermined and complex in their origins. In part, they stemmed from her relationship with her parents and difficult early life experiences with a mentally ill mother and absent father. It also became apparent, however, that Jody had many threatening experiences being a lesbian in a hostile and nonsupportive environment. She had sought out a safer gay environment. The therapist's recognition of the connection between Jody's feelings about the impact of her sexual identity on others and her difficulties in taking risks in her life generally opened up a new pathway for exploration in the treatment.

Confronting a New Threat

Sandy, a 47-year-old nursing administrator, was living with her woman partner of 11 years when she sought treatment for depression and interpersonal problems that were occurring at the hospital in which she worked. She became angry when her subordinates made minor mistakes, impatient with having to teach other nurses what to do, and upset when her supervisees did not live up to her expectations. She recognized that she was overreacting but couldn't modify her behavior. She wanted to get along better and have less stress at work.

In briefly discussing her background, Sandy indicated that she had identified as a lesbian from adolescence. She was open about her sexual identity with friends and family but was more closeted with others. She said her coming-out process had been difficult but she felt she had put these early events behind her. The therapist did not pursue this further until a major crisis developed three months into the treatment.

P: I have to tell you about what happened. I can't believe it. It's my worst nightmare. My sister, Rose, announced that her new husband wants me to stay away from my nieces. I knew he was homophobic but this is so extreme. He's not the girls' father. He's known them for only three years. Can you believe that my sister said that she couldn't do anything about it? She says that she has to appease him. I don't know what to do.

T: What an awful development! Did you try to talk with Rose?

P: I did but I was so horrified by her reaction that I was practically speechless. I just can't believe that she can go along with him after all this time. She's not a child.

T: She doesn't seem to realize how painful it will be for you and the children not to see one another.

P: I have been like a parent to my nieces since her first husband left. I feel like they are my children too. I speak to Darla and Suzy every day. Rose is a very simple person. She is not able to help them with their schoolwork. She never applied herself in school or took risks to better herself.

T: I can understand how hurt and angry you are feeling. What do you think is going on for her?

P: She's just a wimp. She has always been drawn to men that are abusive and controlling. Her first husband abused her. He took off about five years ago without warning and does not give her any money. Her new husband isn't much better. I wish she would stand up to him. She always gives in to his demands, whatever the cost. She's frightened of being alone.

T: This is pretty devastating. Have you discussed this with other members of your family? Can anyone else intervene on your behalf?

P: My fucking parents! I asked them if they would talk to Rose but they urged me not to interfere with her marriage. They think that my nieces need a father more then a lesbian aunt. I'm so upset. I can't believe this is happening. I feel totally betrayed by everyone.

T: This is very painful for you. You are going to need your strength. You have had to endure a lot in the past.

P: You are so right. I just thought that things were getting better. Now this! I don't know whom I'm angrier at. My parents have always disapproved of me. I didn't speak to them for two years after I came out. I had to cut off all contact with them because of how they acted toward me.

T: How was your relationship with your sister affected?

P: My sister and I somehow maintained contact during that time but she never stood up for me and she was afraid they would find out that we were seeing one another.

T: What finally happened?

P: When I felt more comfortable being out and felt better able to weather their disapproval, I contacted them and somehow all of us figured out a way of being civil.

T: That took a lot. Do you think that time may help your current situation?

P: Maybe. I don't know. I just can't bear the thought of not being able to see my nieces.

T: It's very sad for you and your nieces.

P: My family has never stood by me. When I told my parents that I was a lesbian, my mother started ranting and cursing at me. One day she came to my best friend's house and started pulling my hair and dragging me out the door. My friend and I were just talking.

T: Unfortunately, you have a lot of experience handling your family's rejecting behaviors. It's impressive that you have been able to make a life for yourself.

P: I'm not sure that I have the strength to deal with this situation. You know, before this crisis with my nieces, I was plagued by the thought that they will withdraw or disown me when they get old enough to understand about my lesbianism.

T: You have had to pay a big price for your family's rejection of you.

In subsequent sessions, Sandy continued to talk about her family. At times when she was feeling less angry, she described another side of her parents.

P: What is so hard about them is that I know that if I were sick or needed financial help they would help me. They treat me so badly sometimes but they are also the people who have taken care of me. In their own strange way, they love me.

T: It must have been very hard not to know whether you were going to bear the brunt of their criticism and abuse or receive their love.

P: I'm luckier than my sister is. I was able to get away from their control and find a loving partner but Rose is totally dominated by them and the men she chooses.

T: What helped you to get away?

P: I just knew I had to. I turned a deaf ear and I tried to rely on myself. I never wanted to be like them. My mother is just so difficult. I get upset when I catch myself thinking or acting like her.

T: Do you have any of the same characteristics?

P: I guess I can be controlling, insensitive, and stubborn sometimes.

T: It sounds like you had to be in order to survive.

In a later session, when Sandy was talking about a recent work problem, the therapist returned to the theme of how Sandy had survived her family.

T: A few weeks ago, you talked about how you sometimes acted like your mother even though you don't want to be like her. I wonder if your work environment sometimes brings out the traits that you dislike in yourself?

P: What do you mean?

T: Perhaps one reason that you have difficulties with your staff is that you are carrying over the example of how your parents treated you and your sister even though you suffered at their hands. It also may be that the very strengths that have helped you to come out and live as a lesbian in the face of your family's rejecting attitudes and behavior have hardened you and undermine your effectiveness at work when you feel that others are not listening to you or doing their job properly.

In the following session, Sandy began by saying that she had been thinking about the way she handles situations at work.

P: Sometimes I find myself thinking that I should be more supportive of my staff and let go of some of my expectations of them but I worry that if I'm nicer, they will take advantage of me and I will be in a weakened position. It's like I don't want to let down my guard.

T: That's an important realization.

Later in the session, the therapist picked up on this theme.

T: Do you think your expectations of others may be too high in other situations besides work?

P: What are you getting at?

T: It's not hard to understand your feeling let down by your sister, who has really let you down, and your wanting her to stand up for you. At the same time, you have told me about her serious limitations.

P: I know that her life is hard and that she feels trapped. You think that I shouldn't just withdraw and that there's a way I can support her so that she will eventually stand up to her husband?

T: I think it's worth reflecting on whether there's another way to get what you want.

Discussion

Like Jody, Sandy appeared to be self-accepting of her lesbianism when she entered treatment for work-related problems. When three months later a crisis developed that revolved around her brother-in-law's extreme homophobic reactions, the therapist empathized with both the reality-based threats that confronted Sandy and her rage over her family members' lack of support. Sandy's subsequent description of her earlier experiences with coming out to her family reflected the narrative theme of how hard she had to fight against the family in order to express her sexual identity. In retrospect, Sandy saw that the fact that she had been able to assert herself and put some distance between herself and her parents appeared to protect her from her parents' controlling and abusive behavior. She recognized that, in contrast, her sister, who was more passive and dependent, had not fared as well.

In working with the theme of Sandy's having to fight for herself, the therapist and patient were able to identify the positive and negative consequences of Sandy's feistiness and struggles to live her own life. This exploration led Sandy to observe that her effort to escape her parents' domination had resulted in her becoming like them, that is, controlling, demanding, and critical when her authority was challenged. Working on her internal conflict freed Sandy to see her work situation and her relationship with her sister, Rose, in a new light and to deal with her current life situations more effectively.

An Unrecognized Compensatory Pattern

Patricia, a 40-year-old stock analyst, was in a 10-year mutually supportive romantic partnership with another woman, with whom she lived, when she entered treatment for work-related problems. She complained of exhaustion and a sense of depletion. She wanted to leave her job but was reluctant to have to make a change. She had achieved considerable success in her career but felt overwhelmed of late by what was occurring at her firm. She felt pressured to meet increased demands but also received less recognition and approval because of a massive reorganization. In discussing her work life, Patricia indicated that she did not try to hide her lesbianism from her colleagues but did refrain from discussing her personal life with them because the work atmosphere was generally conservative and not particularly gay-friendly. She did not attend work events with her partner. They socialized with their respective families and a small network of good friends. Despite her reserve at work, Patricia did not attribute what was happening there to any discrimination against her.

In an early session, Patricia and the therapist had the following dialogue.

P: I'm very lucky to have a partner like Katherine. She has been so tolerant of my mood changes since the changes at work. One day I'm on a high and the next I'm irritable and devising strategies to win the approval of my new boss.

T: A boss's approval can be very important. What feels extreme about your concerns?

P: I don't just want his approval. I want him to see me as a cut above my peers. I'm too preoccupied with him and his opinion of me and I'm too reactive to everyone else in the office. I can't stand it if anyone does well. I know something is wrong.

T: Is this new for you?

P: Well, I have always thrived on being acknowledged for giving 110 percent to my work. This year, two trade-paper articles described me as a person who anticipates consequences, as "an analyst who is always ahead of her game." Seeing that in print made me feel powerful. I like that I'm known for succeeding at new challenges.

T: What is making you feel that you will not be successful with your new boss, given that you have been successful in other situations?

P: My boss questions everything I do and is always looking over my shoulder. I'm working harder than ever but getting less for it. [gives numerous examples of boss's behavior] It feels futile. Maybe it is time to move on.

T: No one likes to feel unappreciated and to feel under scrutiny when she has proved her worth, but you seem to feel that he has made up his mind.

P: Of the five different division heads I have worked under, not one of them ever questioned my expertise until now. All of them gave me the authority to manage my group in the ways I thought best.

If this new manager is too much of a jerk to appreciate me, maybe I should leave. I'm so depressed.

T: It may be that his behavior may have more to do with him and little to do with you personally. Is it possible that the fact that you are not getting the recognition you deserve is making you doubt yourself?

P: I have been worrying that maybe I'm not good enough to get another job. I know that's stupid with my record.

T: It seems possible that you, like other very successful people who drive themselves to take on responsibilities and win the approval of others, have underlying feelings of not being worthwhile. You appear to need a lot of reassurance about your abilities.

P: I think I know what you mean. [laughs anxiously] Since this all began, Katherine says to me every day, "Stop driving yourself crazy!" Then my brother said, "You always get too caught up in what others think. Don't you see how old this is? You always needed to be the special one."

T: What did he mean?

P: I think he was talking about the change in me when I went to junior high. I feel a little embarrassed or maybe more ashamed talking about it. It's a long story and I don't know how it relates to what I'm going through now.

T: It would help me to know.

P: In the seventh grade, I was admitted to a junior high for gifted students. I was always the kind of kid who did well with little effort. I never really applied myself. My parents were not invested in my getting As, and they didn't really care whether I went to a good school or not. So I was totally unprepared for how competitive all the girls were. I felt very alone. [pauses]

T: Go on. What happened?

P: I ended up getting involved with a group of girls who were a little older than me. I think they liked me because I looked very butch, and some of the kids were experimenting sexually or on the verge of coming out. I enjoyed being part of the group and playing around with them. I always knew that I wasn't like my straight friends, so this group of girls allowed me to find myself.

T: You mentioned that you felt embarrassed and ashamed talking about this. I'm not sure why.

P: I'm not sure either.

T: What did it mean to you to know you were drawn to other girls?

P: I felt fine about it but I was very frightened of what my family and the other girls would think because they were openly disparaging of queers and dykes. I think that's when I became obsessed with being the best.

T: It's good that you were able to trust your instincts, experiment, and self-identify as a lesbian at that age in spite of your fears.

P: I'm surprised that I'm even talking about all this old stuff. I haven't thought about it for a long time.

T: You started talking about this because of your brother's comment. He seemed to imply that this was a turning point for you.

P: He thinks that I have had a desperate need to excel in school and at work and gain others' approval to make up for my being a lesbian.

T: What thoughts do you have about that?

P: I did feel that way when I was younger. But I have accepted who I am for a very long time.

T: Sometimes we carry over certain ways of coping with difficult situations and our feelings about ourselves into our adult lives. Perhaps your boss's lack of approval and his challenging behavior are bringing up some old deep feelings.

In later sessions, Patricia alternated between talking about her most recent interactions with her boss and her past work experiences. She had clearly driven herself, often to the detriment of her personal well-being and relationships, to achieve her career success. She also had intermittent depressions when she had difficult tasks in front of her or when others received promotions or open acknowledgment.

T: Unless you feel that people view you as the best, you feel worthless and ashamed. This makes you very vulnerable.

P: I don't know how to be any other way.

T: I'm sure. As a teenager, working hard and proving yourself seemed to help you deal with your lesbianism. Now, you are still driving yourself even though you have considerable accomplishments behind you and your lifestyle does not get in the way of your success or personal life. You still feel threatened in some profound way but I think you deal with that by working even harder.

P: I can't seem to stop. I'm getting burned out.

T: I think it is important for us to revisit your experiences as a child and adolescent in order to understand why your self-esteem is so shaky.

Discussion

Like Jody and Sandy, Patricia had lived openly as a lesbian for many years by the time she entered treatment and her presenting difficulties were not related to her sexual identity. They revolved around her work situation, in which she felt devalued by a new boss who failed to appreciate her past achievements and strengths. The therapist went beyond the manifest description of Patricia's current situation and explored the evolution of her self-concept. The main theme in Patricia's narrative revolved around her need to see herself as a talented, powerful, highly competent, and responsible person whom others regarded as special. Thus, her boss's treatment of her threatened the mainstay of her self-esteem. Early in their work together, the therapist recognized that Patricia had developed a perfectionist character style in order to deal with her fears that others would devalue and criticize her if they knew she was a lesbian. She drove herself to be the best in order to combat others' homophobic attitudes. Patricia began to see how a major part of her self-concept was rooted in her compensatory strategy to cope with her coming out in an antihomosexual environment. This realization enabled Patricia to see that her current work situation was stimulating an earlier traumatic issue. Feeling that she was devalued and unappreciated at work stirred up her underlying vulnerability and made her drive herself more. When she was not able to obtain the desired recognition she craved, she became very depressed. At a deeper level, her longstanding pattern of behavior may have helped her to compensate for some deep-seated doubts about her own self-worth that were associated with her own internalized homophobia despite her seeming self-acceptance. As the treatment progressed, both the therapist and patient became aware of the importance of revisiting the patient's early experiences with respect to her self-identification and coming-out process. The therapist–patient collaboration helped Patricia to understand the burden of the adolescent developmental tasks that she had to negotiate in the absence of family and cultural supports. Patricia was able to feel less driven, gained a greater sense of her own accomplishments, and became more self-directed.

Feelings of Aloneness and Abandonment

Barbara was a 35-year-old public service attorney who came for treatment a year after her partner, Ann, died in an automobile accident. She felt that it was time to move on but felt lost and alone. In order to keep busy and to manage her continuing grief, she volunteered to do pro bono work with a health center that served gay, lesbian, and transgendered adolescents.

In an early session, Barbara began to talk about an upsetting experience that had occurred in her volunteer position.

P: I want to be a positive role model for young kids who are coming out. But instead of helping them, I feel like a big failure. I find myself fighting back tears every time kids talk about their coming-out experiences. One very feminine boy was afraid to go to school because he feared he would be teased or beaten by some of his classmates. Another 14-year-old girl was upset because she thought her orthodox parents would disown her if they found out that she was attracted to other girls.

T: Hearing their stories seem to get you very stirred up. You seem to be putting a lot of pressure on yourself. Most people would find it difficult to listen to and try to calm adolescents facing such hurtful experiences.

P: I feel so vulnerable. I get too caught up in my own feelings. I don't know what to say. I feel totally useless. When I came home last night, a cloud of depression came over me. I tried hard to think through what was going on for me but I couldn't find the words to explain what was happening for me. It was as if I had no energy. I curled up into a little ball and cried until I fell asleep. I wished Ann were there so that I could talk to her.

T: It sounds like you felt quite deserted last night. I know how much you miss being with Ann but you have also talked about how Ann helped you to feel less alone for the first time in your life. Being without her makes you feel very vulnerable and brings you back to an earlier time when you had no one to turn to. Your volunteer work also may be bringing you back to that time. When you listen to the sad stories, you may be emotionally remembering what it was like for you.

P: I know what I'm feeling seems very overwhelming. I get a lump in my throat whenever I'm around the kids at work.

T: What were your own early struggles like?

P: [Sighs] That was so long ago. I thought I had put those experiences behind me. I came out as a lesbian at college when I was 18 but I knew I was attracted to women many years earlier. Most of my friends think I'm a model of being a well-adjusted lesbian. I've been politically active for a long time. I met Ann when I was 28.

She was the first person who made me feel loved. I have felt so alone since her death.

T: Perhaps a lot of old feelings are coming up for you that you may not have experienced during your relationship with Ann. You and I have not talked much about your own coming-out experiences were like. Working with adolescents may be reminding you of your own adolescent years.

P: That period of my life always felt so vague. Thinking back, I know now that I felt attractions to some of my girl friends and didn't share their feelings about boys. I never had a crush on a boy or on a movie star or anything like that. I didn't dare say anything to anyone.

T: That must have felt very lonely. How did you explain what you were feeling to yourself?

P: I didn't know what to think. I just remember feeling both excited and ashamed. I remember sleeping over at my friend Mary's house with some other girls. It was cold and we all got under the blankets together. Mary and I were rubbing against each other. I felt very excited. Then a few days later, Mary and I were holding hands in a friendly way and some boys at school began teasing us and called us dykes. I had never heard the word but Mary seemed upset and told me what it meant. After that she became more distant. I felt I had done something wrong. I missed her and felt so hurt.

T: That must have been very sad for you to lose your friend and be punished for having pleasurable and loving feelings.

P: [Tearful] I feel very emotional, like crying. This is stupid. I'm 35. At this age, I should be over what happened.

T: I don't know whether your parents or anyone else helped you with your feelings when you were younger.

P: Are you serious? My parents? The perfect WASPs. They still think I'm going through a phase at 35.

T: What has that been like for you?

P: [Sighs] That's a whole other story.

T: I think it's important that we continue this discussion.

In subsequent sessions, Barbara revisited the sadness of her adolescence and her feelings of abandonment when her best friend, Mary, cut off their relationship when she became frightened about its consequences within their peer group. She also began to discuss her feelings of despair in having parents who were self-absorbed and uninterested in what Barbara might be feeling. Retrospectively, she began to realize how she had to compensate for her vulnerability by becoming very self-reliant because she did not feel that she could turn to her parents. The therapist helped Barbara to recognize her strength in navigating her early years and particularly in dealing with her self-identification as a lesbian.

Discussion

This case example illustrates how the collaborative therapeutic process helped Barbara to understand how earlier issues in her life were contributing to her current grief and depression. Narrative themes around abandonment and loss were prominent in her history. Although the death of Barbara's partner had understandably left her in a grieving state, it also reactivated earlier feelings of being lost and alone. She also felt vulnerable and raw. Listening to gay adolescents' struggles around their sexual identity and coming out revived earlier unresolved aspects of the trauma Barbara experienced when she had to rely on her own inner resources at a tender age to cope with feelings of difference. Her sad reactions to their stories led Barbara to become aware of and reexamine aspects of her lesbian self-concept.

The therapist's interpretation of Barbara's responses opened up an avenue for Barbara to explore how her sad feelings and depressed mood conflicted with her longstanding adult self-concept of herself as a "model of a well-adjusted lesbian." Together, the therapist and patient discovered that Barbara's efforts to navigate the developmental tasks of her adolescent coming out without parental and community support had had a larger impact on her emotional makeup than she had previously believed. The therapist was able to explore collaboratively the psychic meaning that the patient's self-identification as a lesbian had for her. Through the therapeutic couple's fluid interactive process, the patient was able to construct within the narrative useful meanings about her earlier coming-out process. This in turn offered the patient the possibility for a healthier resolution and integration of aspects of her lesbian identity.

Chapter 5

Working with Transference

Lesbians display the characteristic range of transference phenomena with which clinicians are familiar but they also may reflect emotional themes related to the patient's sexual identity. The focus of this chapter is to suggest ways for therapists to address and work with both the obvious and more subtle manifestations of such transference expressions.

The Process

Locating the lesbian patient's transference within the here-and-now aspects of the therapeutic relationship, which includes all aspects of their conscious and unconscious interactions, requires the therapist to engage in a particular style of listening and collaborating. In clinical work with lesbian patients, the clinician must be especially alert to their need for the therapist to function as a selfobject or new object and must be mindful of their fear of being misunderstood, labeled, or rejected. Thus, allowing and even encouraging certain transference developments to unfold at certain times may be preferable to interpreting them too quickly or at all. Likewise, the therapist must be prepared to respond selectively to patients' needs as they are expressed in the transference. When the therapist invites the patient to reflect on how she is making use of the therapist's presence and personality, it usually is crucial for the therapist to help the patient understand the societal and cultural as well as familial factors that contribute to the patient's reactions. That said, therapists always must be self-scrutinizing with respect to the ways in which they organize clinical data and make technical decisions. Moreover, they must consider how patients perceive their participation and whether their participation may be stimulating or contributing to the transference reactions.

Playfulness and Seduction in the
Transference–Countertransference Dynamics

Dominique, a 49-year-old bar owner, sought treatment when her seven-year live-in relationship with Terry deteriorated beyond repair. Terry had been married previously and had a daughter who was now an adult. Terry saw herself as bisexual and continued to have relationships with men and other women intermittently during her relationship with Dominique, who felt she couldn't take Terry's affairs any longer. Dominique's description of herself as feeling lost and frightened was at odds with her outgoing and dramatic style. She said she wanted to move out but was terrified of living alone, and feared she would never be able to find another partner, let alone have a satisfying relationship.

A somewhat handsome although not traditionally attractive woman who dressed in a tailored but colorful manner, Dominique viewed herself as always attracting people to her by being charming and seductive. Her ability to do this had been an asset in building her successful business but not in her personal life. She tended to seek out and attract exciting women who were emotionally unavailable and unreliable and to make them be there for her in the ways in which she craved. She sought their love and attention but wound up feeling disappointed, deprived, and hurt. Because of her dependency, she had trouble breaking away from unhappy relationships. She longed to have a relationship with a woman whom she admired who would make her feel strong instead of needy and weak.

In talking about her early years, Dominique said that her mother loved her but was a depressive and a drunk. Her father was a philanderer who made her feel uncomfortable. Although he did not sexually abuse her, she always felt that he would hug her too tightly, stare at her in what felt like a sexual way, and kiss her on the lips. Although she was not a pretty child, Dominique had a voluptuous figure from an early age. Nevertheless, she became a tomboy and refused to put on a dress. "With the body of Monroe and the mind and face of a mob boss, you can imagine how weird it was for me growing up. I hated the sexual attention I got from guys." She felt pride in being accepted by older boys and in recognizing her sexual attraction to women at the age of 12: "I thought I had invented lesbianism." She compared her love of women with her gift for singing, which had set her apart from others in her large family. She found other gays and lesbians when she was 18 and utilized them for support and validation. She embraced her outsiderness by developing a career inside the gay community.

Dominique presented herself initially in a seductive and flirtatious manner. Her language was colorful and spicy and she always seemed to want to unnerve the therapist and elicit a more personal interaction. She worked hard to entertain the therapist and tried to engage her in playful banter. She showed awareness of being provocative but nevertheless had difficulty getting serious about exploring her problems, often stating that she needed the therapist to go at her pace.

P: [Speaking in a dramatic manner] Lisa is managing the bar while I'm here. Did I tell you that she's a partial transsexual? [laughing] I love her even if she has a dick because I know that she's an honest person. She keeps an eye on the pickpockets on my staff. My money is safe when she's the boss. So here I am. I can lie back and relax with you. Lisa reminds me of you. Both of you are tough, feminine, and good in business. That's the way I like my women. [joking] You got good door movement. [smiling, moving her eyebrows up and down as she leans over and rests her elbow on her knee and her chin in her hand] Lots of patients come in and go out and you collect your money when it's due! That last therapist I tried was too straight. Imagine me sitting with Pat Nixon. She was stiff and I felt she tried to control me with her intellectual talk. I thought she looked down on me. But with you, I can be myself, the dyke that I am. When I look at your face, I see that you get me, it's easy for you to be with me. I like that, I feel free when I am with you.

T: You seem to be having lots of thoughts about me today — what I'm like, how you feel with me, my femininity, my toughness, how I run my practice. I wonder what's going on for you?

P: Ah, come on, you're going too deep.

T: Too deep? You think so? I just want to know what's going on for you.

P: Let's stay light today. I just like being with you. It feels good to me. You're cool. I feel when I am with you that something good is going to happen to me. I like that we can play and work. It's like my business. I mix work and fun.

T: Sometimes the atmosphere that gets created between us does feel like the two of us are sitting on bar stools. It is enjoyable but I also ask myself if I'm going along with you in ways that may not be so helpful. I'm concerned that your need to entertain me means you don't think I am really interested in who you are or that you are being provocative and pushing boundaries with me for some reason.

P: I know I'm a trip but what can be so wrong? I like bar stools. That last therapist couldn't get me. I spoke queer, she spoke straight. There's no waste of time explaining things to you. We speak the same language. Once I said to her, "You know, women are like babies—you can always find something cute in them." Now, to me that's true, but she threw me a look that said "get a straight-jacket." Why should I pay someone to be uncomfortable? People don't come to my bar to have a bad time. They want to have a good experience. That's what I want too. There will be time to work on myself later.

T: It seems important to you that that I am on your wavelength and have fun with you.

P: I'm proud of who I am. I'm sick of being messed with. I have enough of that in my own family. Last night Cynthia, Terry's daughter, and her husband, Jay, and their 13-year-old daughter, Michele, came for dinner. Personally, I think the kid is a dyke. Cynthia loves me but she won't let the kid go to my bar 'cause it's a gay bar. Can you imagine! I wasn't going to bring her at night but during the day when it's closed or slow. I'd like her to see me work. Her parents think being gay rubs off. So I told Cynthia if it rubs off—how come you're straight? [pause] What an idiot, I am good enough for her mother but not for her daughter. I like being me. If people don't like that, they can shove it.

T: It is disappointing to be close to people who seem to reject a major part of you that feels so natural. I can see why finding a safe place with me is so important, a place where the self that you cherish does not feel intruded on.

P: You are right. It is important for me to have you accept me the way I really am. But, I notice that you do set some limits.

T: What limits?

P: Outside of this setup [therapy], it would be natural for me to hug and kiss my acquaintances when we meet, but with you I know I have to obey the professional boundaries. [laughing] I know there are certain restrictions and that you will only go so far with my stuff. Like when I ran into you on Fire Island, I knew I overstepped a boundary when I kissed you on the cheek. I wanted to see what you'd do. I liked that you accepted the kiss without a fuss and didn't push me away or get flustered. You were cool, so I felt good.

T: What did you imagine I was thinking?

P: I could see that you were happy to see me. You didn't get uptight. And I liked that your lover was cool about it. I assumed she was your lover. I know I'm right.

T: It seems like something important is happening between us that makes you feel open and comfortable but at the same time you try to test boundaries with me.

P: I like to do that. I know it makes you uncomfortable.

T: Perhaps you do that with me to find out if you can trust me to be there for you. You couldn't count on either of your parents. You never knew when your mother was going to withdraw or become wasted and whether your father was going to intrude himself on you sexually. That must have been very difficult.

P: I don't want to talk about them but it's true that I've always been disappointed by women whom I thought I could trust. I thought Terry loved me and would take care of me but instead, I'm not enough for her. Hey, would someone like you consider having a relationship with me? Could someone like you find me desirable? Don't get uptight. I'm not coming on to you. I just want to know if someone like you, your type, together, strong, and pretty, could be interested in me as a lover?

T: I certainly like and appreciate you and can see why women are attracted to you. I think it's important to understand why you want me to move out of my professional role and respond to you woman to woman.

P: I don't really want you to want me that way. I want you be my therapist but there is something I feel I need. If someone like you could care about me it would make me feel like I can be really successful in my life. I like that you watch out for my feelings; even the way you answered me was nice. I see how careful you are with my feelings. I didn't have enough of that growing up. I'm thirsty for more of that.

T: It seems you feel protected by me when you push the boundaries and I respond in a way that feels very safe and comforting for you.

P: Maybe I need to be sure that you don't have an agenda. Sometimes, I wonder why, in hell, was I attracted to all that wild and crazy stuff that Terry and I got into? We made each other miserable. My 90-year-old mother even said to me, "Keep your hands clean, Dominique. Didn't you come from enough trouble? Why go back into that mess? . . . Don't live like your father and I did. Find a nice woman that treats you with respect." I think she's

right, I think I couldn't help myself from diving into all that shit
with Terry. I have to move out and begin a new life for myself. But
I'm scared.

Discussion

In the initial phase of treatment, the therapist encouraged Dominique
to communicate her thoughts and feelings in a way that was familiar
and comfortable. She allowed the transference to unfold for her and
believed that a reservoir of information would eventually emerge without intensive exploration. The therapist responded to rather than interpreted the patient's stated wish that the therapist behave differently
than did the previous therapist, who frustrated her by being aloof and
making rigorous interpretations and who prevented her enjoyment of
the therapist. The therapist also tried to strengthen the therapeutic bond
by participating in interactions that captured their shared lesbian identity. She thought that this would build a sense of likeness and comfort
that the patient seemed to crave. Although the therapist engaged in the
patient's playfulness, she tried to maintain the boundaries that she
thought were necessary to protect the treatment. Had she refused to
play, she would have removed herself from a natural mutual rhythm
developing in the interaction and cut off the development of a twinship
and idealizing selfobject transference.

The therapist did begin to gently explore the transference implications
of what was occurring in the therapeutic interaction in order to see if
Dominique was ready to work at another level. At first, the therapist did
this out of some discomfort that she might be too permissive and thus
collude with the patient in a nontherapeutic manner. She explored the
subjective elements of the patient's transference by questioning the
patient about what she thought was the significance of what was occurring in the relationship. She also invited the patient to talk about how
she experienced the analyst's personal presence and participation. Although the patient resisted the therapist's initial attempts to probe in this
fashion, it is noteworthy that the patient began to share some of her
concerns in a more serious way when the therapist backed off and related
to where the patient said she wanted to be. The patient spontaneously
returned to an exploration of the transference and allowed for a fuller
understanding of the relational dynamics to emerge. It seemed clear that
Dominique was seeking new object experiences while at the same time
repeating aspects of her early relational patterns.

The therapist was able to avoid making a common therapeutic error when Dominique asked her if she could be attracted to someone like the patient. She did not experience the patient as literally asking the therapist to become involved with her romantically and did not become threatened by the question. Instead of remaining silent, disavowing any potential feelings of attraction, or reminding the patient of appropriate professional boundaries, the therapist affirmed her positive connection to the patient and validated her attractiveness. Concurrently, she invited the patient to talk about what was behind the question. Had the therapist heard Dominique's question as just another attempt to be provocative or had she utilized more confrontational, interpretive, or limit-setting interventions, she might have derailed the relationship and missed the opportunity to learn more about what the patient was truly feeling. After this exchange, Dominique was able to begin to use the therapist's renewed efforts to link the patient's behavior in the transference to her past life experiences.

From the beginning of treatment, the therapist wanted to help the patient and felt empathic with her relationship struggles. She felt a strong identification with Dominique's history and the issues involved in the movement from lesbian child to lesbian woman, especially the search for recognition in a culture that has limited models. The therapist never felt threatened by the patient's provocative banter or pushing of the therapist's professional boundaries. She did not believe that the patient would go too far and felt clear about her own limits. Nevertheless, the therapist felt uncertain, at times, about whether merely to respond to the patient as she wished or whether to help the patient to reflect on their interaction. She wondered if she were engaging in a repetitive reenactment of earlier relationships in which the patient would charm others and later feel disappointed. She also felt cautious because of her enjoyment of the patient and the developing twinship and idealizing transference. She was aware that their interaction allowed the therapist to express aspects of her own gayness that she often inhibited in other relational contexts.

Working with Angry Accusations and Negative Expectations in the Transference

Fredericka, or Freddie, as she often called herself, was a 34-year-old investment banker who sought treatment after being admonished by her firm's president for her confrontational and disrespectful manner. She thought that some of her struggle with her boss was a result of a constellation of minority issues that she dealt with not only at work but that had plagued her all her life. At her firm she was the only woman as well as the only person of color (the daughter of a German mother and African American father), she was significantly younger than her peers, and she perceived herself to be the only gay or lesbian in the firm. She attempted to deal with these issues in a previous treatment but terminated because she felt that the therapist didn't understand her.

It had been important for Fredericka to be a high achiever since early childhood and she took pride in doing well. In her current position, however, she felt fearful that her superiors would think that she was inadequate and not as good as others. She thought that she was hired because she belonged to a minority and believed that her boss had reservations about whether she was capable of competently managing the job at hand. As a result, Fredericka felt she had to try harder than ever to be at the top of her game. The position meant a lot to her but she herself was riddled with feelings of insecurity. She developed defensive strategies of striving for perfection and simultaneously being critical of everyone and everything. Consequently, she was unable to derive satisfaction from her accomplishments, experienced constant anxiety, and wished to escape.

The following excerpt is from the second session.

P: [Spoken in an aggressive and irritable tone] Making tons of money isn't worth it if I feel tortured every day at work. I feel as if I'm drowning. I'm constantly flying to different time zones and I haven't had a day off in a month. I feel desperate. I have got to get out from under all this pressure. Being around straight middle-aged conservative businessmen is draining me of my creativity. I need to be around more sensitive creative and artistic people. I have been thinking of returning to school for an M.F.A. in writing. I'll just have to compromise and learn to live with less, like normal middle-class people do. Even if my parents and friends think I'm nuts, I've got to save my sanity. They ignore what I feel. They say, "How can you throw away what you've worked so hard to achieve? Just learn to cope." That's easy for them to say because they don't have to deal with the stress.

T: It must be very lonely to not have anyone who understands what you are going through.

P: [Impatiently] Why do you think I'm here? I am alone. I don't think anyone really understands the extent of my suffering. My family and my friends complain that I never call them. They think I am selfish. But how can I call them when my job doesn't allow for down time and when I have an hour here or there all I want to do is sleep.

T: Freddie, you are speaking in a tone that sounds like you are angry or irritated.

P: People tell me that all the time. They say they can't talk to me. I tell them that I am hanging by a thread. I am burned out and have no patience.

T: Have I done something to aggravate you?

P: Maybe I'm worried that you are going to be like my last therapist, Lorraine. I terminated the treatment last year because I felt that she was on the side of my parents and friends who were wildly caught up in my having a successful job. She didn't understand what was stressing me and what I wanted.

T: What gave you that feeling?

P: I felt that she tried to discourage me from leaving my job. She would point out all the difficulties I might face if I quit, as if I hadn't thought about them. When I would tell her that she didn't understand how hard it was for me, she would say something like, "Because you are not ready to make a decision about leaving your job, you put me on the side of your parents, who want you to stay." Her saying that made me angry.

T: Her explanation was not what you wanted to hear.

P: I wanted her to say, "You're right. I do want you to stay" or "No, I don't feel that way." I wanted her to be real and not give me her bullshit interpretations. I felt that she didn't really like me and didn't care about how I felt.

T: It still seems to make you angry when you talk about it. You must have felt very let down by her. You felt vulnerable and needed an anchor, someone to rely on.

P: Look, I still feel vulnerable, and I feel like I am going to snap. I'm sick and tired of projecting a powerful image and relying on myself for everything. I need you or someone to tell me what to do. Should I just quit my job, or should I just bite the bullet and stay? If you don't tell me, I think I'll feel too frustrated and will not be able to continue.

T: You seem to see me as someone who knows the answers about what is right for you but withholds them in order to frustrate you. Do you think I'm really doing that?

P: I guess I'm used to everyone doing that. They all judge me and frown on what I say I want to do but they don't offer any solutions. Maybe it's unfair of me to put this on you?

T: What am I doing that makes you feel that I'm judging you?

P: I don't really feel that you are judging me but you do ask a lot of questions. I wish you had more answers.

T: It is difficult to always feel that you are on your own.

P: You better believe it!

T: I do. I wish I knew the right answers about what is best for you but I don't. We need to figure this out together.

P: I guess I know that. I just get frustrated. I've always been like that. I know I'm impatient. It gets me into trouble sometimes. It's important that I give therapy a chance.

T: I'm glad that you are going to give us a chance to work together. It's good that you are able to tell me what is bothering you about me. It helps me to understand you better.

In the next session, Freddie spoke more about her work situation.

P: For the last six years I have been surrounded by a pack of alpha males in competition for the top-dog position. Last week, my boss, the top dog, got mad at me because I didn't feed him what he wanted. He wanted me to tell him that I could close an impossible deal. So I said to him that I thought it was a waste of my time and that I had other deals more promising and deserving. Well, this asshole got infuriated with me. His testosterone level went sky high and I thought he was going to jump across his desk and attack me. After the meeting my immediate supervisor said, "If you want to make things easier for yourself, give him what he wants, play the game, feed his ego, and do your own thing. He will forget about the other deal. He sees you as one of the top tier. You have nothing to worry about if you suck up to him."

T: [Tempted to comment on the patient's negative attitudes toward men] You seem to have a strong need to say what's on your mind even if it hurts you. It's hard to hide your true thoughts.

P: No one understands what it has been like for me when others ignore who I am.

T: I was also thinking as you spoke how lonely and exhausting it must be to face prejudice on so many fronts. You are the only woman, the only woman of color, the youngest of your peers, and the only lesbian. I imagine that is a heavy burden and that you have had to deal with assaults on a daily basis.

P: [Laughs sarcastically] A heavy burden. That's an understatement. For your information, the guys in the group don't consider me black because as I was born of a white mother and because I have a German nose. These jerks need to ignore my Afro American heritage because it gets them too anxious. They ignore my lesbi-anism too. It's not talked about. I'm the only person at work who doesn't have a life outside of work. Nobody asks me whom I am dating. What is even more frustrating is that because I am a woman and a lesbian, I will never get the access to potential business opportunities that are part of being in the boys club. So even if I decide to stay, I'll have to work twice as hard to bring in my own business.

T: That is a heavy hand to play. It takes a lot of energy to cope with so much discrimination. When you have to hide so much of what you feel, it is sometimes hard to know who is really on your side.

P: Yeah, I think this discrimination battle has made me paranoid. I have trouble trusting anyone. I know I have a chip on my shoulder.

T: It's understandable that you distrust others, given what you have had to contend with in your life. Perhaps even if someone seems friendly and wants to help you, it is hard to trust his or her motivation.

P: I can see that. I'm like that with my boss. He jokes with me and seems to be supportive sometimes, but I don't trust him. I give him a hard time and never let him know I appreciate him. I think that I couldn't get comfortable with my former therapist, Lorraine, for the same reason.

T: It would be understandable if you felt that I was going to be like everyone else. Maybe you get angry with me for that in advance. If I say something that seems stupid or don't have the right answer, it confirms your fears. If I do seem tuned in, you're sure the other shoe is going to drop any minute. It's a dilemma.

P: Bull's-eye!

As the treatment progressed, Freddie decided to remain at her firm until she had amassed enough money to pursue an M.F.A. in writing and maintain a standard of living with which she felt comfortable. She was able to use the therapeutic relationship as an emotional anchor. She no longer acted out her anger in the workplace and her depressive symp-toms lessened. As a result, the patient and therapist were able to explore aspects of the transference that were shaped by both early childhood factors and the current therapist–patient interaction.

The following session occurred 10 months later.

P: Whenever I talk to my mother about leaving the investment banking to get my M.F.A., I feel horribly guilty, then angry. She has this nonverbal way of communicating her unhappiness and dissatisfaction. It was the same when I came out to her. Both times she said something like, "Freddie, you have to follow what feels right for you." But what she is really saying is, "Freddie, how could you do this to me? I worked six days a week in a department store to give you all the opportunities that I didn't have. How can you ruin your life?"

T: Have you talked openly about this?

P: We haven't talked openly since my coming-out years. From the time I was 17 to 21 we had a turbulent relationship. After that, we both got tired and made a silent agreement to keep peace.

T: I think this is the first time you have mentioned this.

P: I've been thinking about a lot of things lately. When I came out to myself at 17, I told her. I think she knew I was gay before me but she secretly wished that I would grow out of it.

T: What was that like for you?

P: She didn't give me a hard time. She just ignored me. I was luckier than my other gay friends—I didn't have to fight with my mother about my lesbianism. I was always into girls. Boys never interested me. So coming out seemed like a natural outcome. My mother and I did fight about my going out to the bars. She thought older women would take advantage of me. She is a beautiful woman and has had a lot of attention for her looks and was afraid of what it would do to me at such a young age. She thought being good-looking was a disadvantage. I think that all the attention she got growing up was very confusing for her. Her intentions were good in many ways but she didn't know how to be sensitive to my feelings. She was afraid to let me out without a chaperone. As if lesbians are like men.

T: What stands out for me in your description of your mother is how hard it is for you to be angry with her. You seem very protective.

P: [Angrily] That sounds very theoretical, very Freudian. Can you talk to me like a person? You're acting just like my first shrink.

T: I'm sorry. I was not aware I was doing that.

P: There are times when I feel you put distance between us. You're like my mother. You mean well but you don't always hear me.

T: What do you imagine is going on for me?

P: I guess there are times when I feel that you are bored or that you are thinking to yourself that I am just a lesbian who feels her mother didn't love her and carries a grudge against the world.

T: Why would I think that?

P: Maybe you secretly think that lesbians are fucked up and an African American lesbian must really be a case.

T: What am I doing to give you that impression?

P: I told you. You give me therapist answers. I came to you because I knew you were an expert on lesbian issues and I wanted to feel open and comfortable talking about my life. I also came because I didn't want to repeat the experience I had with my last therapist, who was very distant. But I have been seeing you for almost a year and we've not talked much about my lesbianism and when I do talk about it you don't seem that interested.

T: I was not aware that that was happening. Tell me what you think I have been missing.

P: I think I expected that you would ask me more questions, you know, about how I feel as a lesbian. But to be fair, I know I have been depressed and have had a lot of other things on my plate. There probably has not been enough time to talk about other issues.

T: Perhaps I haven't probed enough but it's not because I was not interested. I wanted you to feel comfortable.

P: How can I open up if you don't seem interested?

T: I can see what you mean. I'm acting a little bit the way your mother did even if it's for different reasons.

P: It is hard for me to sort out all these feelings. I feel very confused. There may be something to what you are saying.

T: I can understand your sensitivity to what feels like my disinterest. In addition to your experiences with your mom, you have also had to deal with being ignored every day at work by your peers and superiors.

P: Their avoidance is very hurtful.

T: I see how important it is for me to stay connected to how you feel. But I also was thinking that when I don't say the right thing, you lose connection with the parts of our relationship that are working. You have felt so battered for such a long time that it may be hard for you to see my lack of awareness as a temporary break that can be easily remedied by our talking like we are now.

P: I'll have to think about that some more. [pause] I think when I feel hurt by you, I just want to lash out. But I do feel better when we can talk things out like this. I do think that we have a good working relationship, but I do want more from you.

T: Tell me what you are thinking.

P: I'm not really sure. It's more of a feeling. I think it's about needing to feel safe. I saw my friend Marlene and her two-year-old yesterday. The baby seemed really happy and content when Marlene anticipated his every need. I know it's silly, but I felt jealous of the baby. I think when she paid attention to him, he felt protected.

T: It's understandable that you want to feel safe with me and when I say the wrong thing, you feel unsafe.

Discussion

Early in treatment, the primary focus of the therapist was on getting acquainted with Freddie and creating conditions for her to speak comfortably about her problems, strengths, and personal history. In their second session, the therapist was puzzled about the meaning of the patient's anger. After commenting on Freddie's affect, the therapist learned that others often experienced Freddie as angry. Nevertheless, the therapist tried to explore whether the patient felt that the therapist was doing anything to cause her to be angry. She did this to learn whether she was having some type of inadvertent negative impact on Freddie, to enable her to get in touch with what might be bothering her, and to give her permission to verbalize her concerns. This exploration opened up a way of talking about Freddie's considerable anxiety about whether the therapist would understand her and brought forward her frustration when people, including the therapist, did not give her the answers. Although the therapist's questions did appear to play a part in the patient's anger, it also was apparent that Freddie brought the expectation, based on her past relationships, that her needs were going to be continually ignored in the treatment situation. It seemed likely that Freddie's life experiences with what can only be called oppression also were contributing to her difficulty trusting the therapist. The therapist's sensitivity to this issue seemed to help Freddie stay positively engaged with her.

As the treatment progressed, Freddie and the therapist began working with deeper transference manifestations that were conditioned by an amalgam of complex conscious and unconscious experiences influenced both by the patient's past relationships and cultural experiences and by the therapeutic couple's current interpersonal interactions. The therapist understood that Freddie's distrustful reactions were in part based in her long history of traumatic difficulties managing her multiple identities as daughter of an emotionally unavailable mother and the cultural prejudice she experienced as a multiracial lesbian woman. Nevertheless, the therapist chose mostly to stay focused in the here-and-now aspects of the transference by exploring Freddie's fantasies and subjective experience of the therapist's participation. The therapist did this because she felt that she had to stay closely connected to how the patient experienced her and viewed her role in stimulating the patient's distrustful transference. She also believed that the patient's transference reflected her need for a new type of object who would try to understand Freddie's inner experience.

Bridging Differences of Gender Identity and Sexual Identity in the Therapeutic Dyad

Ellen, a 38-year-old theatrical stage manager who lived alone, sought treatment for depression. She presented as an intelligent, articulate, moderately overweight, large-boned, androgynous-looking woman with a good sense of humor. The patient had two previous long-term relationships with women but had not seriously dated for four years, when she became tired of the bar scene and repeated rejections. She felt desperately lonely. When meeting new women, she felt anxious and very self-conscious about her appearance. She described herself as "ugly, fat, and sexually undesirable." These thoughts were at odds with her work persona, in which she appeared and actually felt secure, competent, disciplined, and in control. She recognized that she often experienced these two somewhat opposite ways of viewing herself.

As the youngest of four daughters, Ellen felt that her self-involved, fashion-conscious mother criticized her for being overweight and for looking and behaving like a tomboy. Her mother was a petite and attractive woman who repeatedly took Ellen to diet doctors and sent her to weight-reduction summer camps. Ellen said she felt tortured by what felt like her mother's repulsion of her appearance. Her father, a kind but passive man who also struggled with his weight, was unable to protect Ellen from his wife because he too was dominated and demeaned by her. Ellen moved away from home when she was 18 in order to escape. In retrospect, she felt that she had been able to survive her mother's devaluation because of her close relationships with two of her sisters, who attempted to protect Ellen from their mother's verbal assaults. Ellen felt that her mother saw Ellen and her father in the same negative way. She considered them "unattractive slobs" on one hand but at the same time expected that they succeed at their respective jobs. Ellen was a good student and received positive attention from her teachers for her academic performance. School was often a refuge for her, and she had responsible roles in school organizations. She had a few good friends but was never part of the popular group of girls.

In a session about six months after treatment began, the therapist noticed that the patient blushed and became very self-conscious when she spoke of her feelings about her appearance and her difficulties coping with the lesbian bar scene.

P: All the women are so feminine and physically fit. I don't have a chance with any of the ones that interest me. I think the only way I am going to find a girlfriend is if I lose 30 pounds and work out. I can't stand how fat and ugly I am.

T: Ellen, I don't know if you are aware that when you talk about your appearance, you begin to flush, your voice quivers, and you look away from me as if you expect me to say something hurtful to you. What do you think is going on for you?

P: I don't know if I can talk about it. I just have to deal with it myself.

T: I can see you feel upset. What do you think is making you feel that you have to keep it to yourself?

P: [Forcing levity] Maybe if you put a bag on your head or put a mask on, I'd have an easier time.

T: Tell me more.

P: It's not so much of what you are doing but it is who you are that makes me uncomfortable. You are so attractive and I feel so ugly. You can't possibly understand someone like me.

T: Go on.

P: I know it's absurd and not politically correct to have such views but you act so femme and straight. It makes me uneasy. It doesn't end there either. I have a host of other politically incorrect attitudes. You're married. You have kids. You sleep with a man. That's it in a nutshell.

T: That's some nutshell. It's important that you are sharing that with me. How long have you been holding that in?

P: I guess I've felt that from the beginning but I was so depressed during the first six months in therapy and you were kind and supportive. But lately, now that I'm trying to date again, a lot of old feelings are coming up for me and I'm having trouble talking about them with you. I don't want you to be repelled by me or criticize me.

T: You feel that because I am attractive, feminine, and straight that I will not understand or appreciate you.

P: Well, how could you? I'm not deaf, dumb, and blind. I can see what's important to you. You are always impeccably dressed and coiffed and you speak the Queen's English in a ladylike tone. I start feeling like a big ugly drag queen or a man. You are perfect and I'm a mess. We're just so different.

T: It is true that there are ways in which we are different but does that mean that I cannot see the world from your eyes and appreciate who you are?

P: I believe that you mean well but I don't know if you can overcome who *you* are. It's just like my not being able to understand how you can be with men. You'll never get all the gender stuff I have to cope with.

T: Have I said anything that gives you that feeling?

P: Not really. Not yet but it would hurt me to open up to you and see disapproval or disgust on your face.

T: That would be very painful, especially because that experience was so familiar to you with your mother.

P: I don't think I will ever get over it.

T: It's true that you don't really know whether or not I am like her. How can I help you to feel that I can understand where you are coming from? I would like to try.

P: When you say things like that, I feel that I want to trust you but I don't want you to be overwhelmed by me. I want to be able to talk to you.

T: Why don't you try?

P: It's just that sometimes I feel like a monster. I don't even understand my own feelings. I don't feel like a man or a woman. I mean I know I'm a woman but my body feels gigantic and all wrong somehow, more like a man. But I don't really feel like a guy either. I'm more emotional and sensitive and I don't really act like a guy. Sometimes, I feel like I'm from another planet.

T: I guess you don't think that I ever have any of the same feelings.

P: How could you?

T: Well, not about the same things but feeling like an outsider is not restricted to lesbians.

P: Well I guess that's true, but I can't imagine that you have ever felt odd or different.

T: I grew up in an orthodox Jewish community and from a very early age, I knew I could not live that kind of life. It felt too restrictive for a woman. I couldn't express who I really was.

P: Was it hard for you?

T: I had to leave the community in order to be my own person.

P: Maybe your life hasn't been as easy as I thought. I never really thought about that. Have you ever read the Ursula LeGuin novel, *The Left Hand of Darkness*?

T: Yes.

P: When I was a child, I thought that I was very much like the characters in the novel, whose sex changed by the lunar calendar. Some months their bodies were female and some months their bodies were male. But there were also times when their bodies didn't fully transform into the other sex. They got stuck in the middle and lived as she-men, equally made up of both male and female characteristics. From as early as I can remember that's how I felt. Emotionally I always felt closer to women but in terms of my body I never felt I fit anywhere. I always felt like an outsider.

T: When did you know that you were a lesbian?

P: It took me a long time to understand about my lesbianism. Even in kindergarten, I loved being surrounded by women. I loved when those cute elementary school teachers touched me. I can remember the crushes I had then. Teachers liked to hug me because I was an affectionate and appreciative child. Mom's behavior toward me was so different. She always said, "I should have named you Jody or Leslie, not Ellen. It's too feminine for you." She couldn't relate to my interest in sports and to the fact that I looked awkward in a dress. It wasn't only my gender. She also thought I looked fat in a bathing suit when I was 10 years old. When I look back at those pictures, I was a rail with a tiny protruding belly. She just couldn't identify with me. She actually told me that her favorite baby had turned into a monster and that she should have named me Dykenstein.

T: It must have been painful growing up with a mother who couldn't appreciate you and confusing to have to manage both your mother's attitudes and your own feelings at such an early age.

P: To her credit, my mother did encourage my interest in the theater and took me to plays. But always there was something queer about me that didn't fit in. [laughs]

T: Like how you felt in the bar?

P: Yes. I wished I had someone with me to share the experience. I have a friend, Josh, whom I've known for years. He turned out to be a fairy. We had gaydar [gay radar] for each other before we even knew we were gay.

T: Sometimes girls have a way of knowing about their sexual orientation before they fully understand what it means. It was good to have someone to share in the confusion about yourself.

P: It's funny when you think about it. We were the campiest elementary school couple. In the third grade, he dressed us both as

Carmen Miranda with floral bedsheets and plastic grapes from my mother's fake-fruit centerpiece. [laughing] We went to the playground in drag. That was great. But the following year my gay expression took a nosedive. My girlfriend Suzie was forbidden to play with me because of my "lesbian tendencies." Her mother walked in when we were playing 007. I played the James Bond role and she, the damsel in distress. It was a scream, kissing, both naked on the bed, me with her father's hat and she lying with her mother's gloves. Suzie's mother told my mom, who called me "a stupid fat dyke." I didn't know what that meant exactly, but I knew it was bad.

T: Your mother wanted you to be straight and was afraid of your being different and intolerant of your not being the feminine daughter she desired. She seemed to have a rigid ideal that most women, even the women you call very feminine, would have problems identifying with. Perhaps she saw you as an extension of herself and had to make you over in her image.

T: What is it about me that sometimes makes you feel that I am on your mother's side?

P: I'm not sure. When I meet new women, particularly if they're attractive, I feel like I'm back with my mother. For example, right now, with you, I feel very masculine. Sometimes at work or with women at the bars I feel like a big lug, like one of those big awkward country-bumpkin dudes you see in the old westerns, those men who stumble over their words when they're around city folk. It's as if your femininity overpowers the worldly, sophisticated, and intellectual parts of my personality.

T: We have to understand more about what that's about for you but perhaps as you come to feel more understood by and safer with me, you will come to feel more comfortable and accepting of who you are.

In subsequent sessions, Ellen spoke in depth for the first time in her life about her negative feelings about her body and discomfort with her degree of femininity and masculinity. Although she felt ashamed and pained by her disclosures and remained somewhat wary of the therapist's reactions, she nevertheless seemed to welcome the opportunity to share this part of herself and to derive some comfort from the sessions. It was apparent that Ellen felt not only that she could not be like her mother but also that she physically resembled her father, who, like Ellen, was large and overweight. Her mother used to tell her angrily that she was just like her father and expressed dismay at having a child who was so unlike herself. She never expressed pride in Ellen's appearance. In school, Ellen tended to be accepted by the boys more than the girls.

The following interchange occurred after about a year of treatment.

P: I had a dream last night that really upset me. It's so strange. I never remember my dreams. I'm a little embarrassed by it. Do you do dreams?

T: Sure. What is embarrassing you about the dream?

P: I think you were in it. I was sitting at a bar in a lesbian club and there were all these attractive women who were talking to me, not just to be friendly but really coming on to me. I was flirting back and felt really good about myself. A woman who looked like you walked past the bar and I thought she was nodding approvingly. Then she disappeared and so did all the other women. I went to look for everyone in the bathroom but no one was there. I went back to the bar and sat but I became very self-conscious and thought I was stupid for sitting there. I wanted another drink but I couldn't get the bartender's attention. I felt like a jerk. I tried to use my cell phone to call a friend but it wouldn't work. I tried to leave but couldn't find my way out. It was awful. Then I woke up.

T: It sounds very frightening.

P: Yes. I couldn't get back to sleep for a long time. It had felt so good when the women were paying attention to me and when you walked by. Then everything went against me.

T: You have never had the feeling that other women, including your mother, find you attractive. Perhaps you are getting in touch with how much you crave that kind of positive attention from women, including me. But some part of you feels you do not deserve it or that it is stupid to think you can get it. You fear that I will be like your mother and take away your good feelings about yourself.

P: [Wants to say something but is having difficulty] I had the thought when I was here last time that I wanted you to think I was attractive—not in a sexual way, but just that you would enjoy looking at me.

T: It's good that you can tell me that. Why do you think you did not say anything then?

P: I was afraid. I thought you would get scared or be angry or laugh.

T: I guess it's hard to believe that I do think you are attractive.

P: I know I don't always try to look my best. It's like I've accepted that I can't attract other women, so I don't even try.

T: It's not hard to understand that you would protect yourself from disappointment. But what if you are wrong about not being attractive to other women? How would you like to look?

P: I don't want to be a femme like you. I know that's not me, but I'd love to look kind of put-together and sporty — not flamboyant or anything like that, but smart-looking. I'm not sure how to do this.

T: I don't think it should be so hard to look the way you want. If you're not sure how to go about this, there are others who might help you. You could get some tips from friends or even a professional.

Soon after this session, Ellen started dieting and exercising, showed more interest in how she dressed, and started to try to meet someone to date again. She began to have some small successes, which made her take more risks. She often recounted with enthusiasm her adventures with other women to the therapist in sessions and seemed to look to her for approval and validation. On one occasion, she came to the session and uncharacteristically was silent.

T: You seem unusually quiet.

P: I didn't really feel like coming today.

T: Did something happen?

P: No.

T: You don't seem to want to talk to me today.

P: Maybe I don't.

T: How come? Maybe I've done something to upset you.

P: You're paranoid.

T: Well, something seems to have changed between us. What do you think it is?

P: I really don't want to talk to you. I've said too much and trusted you too much. I knew it couldn't last.

T: I must have really let you down in some way.

P: Don't you know? I thought you knew everything.

T: I need you to tell me what I've done to hurt you.

P: Don't flatter yourself. You haven't hurt me. I just feel very disappointed.

T: Tell me about it.

P: I don't know what the point is of that.

T: You can give me a try.

P: Last time, I was talking about my new flame, Joanne, and how she thinks I'm strong and good-looking and wants to have sex with me all the time. I could see I was turning you off. I always knew your being straight would be a problem. You probably think that I'm some kind of freak.

T: [Startled and disturbed] I'm sorry and baffled that you feel that way after all this time.

P: Don't get upset.

T: [Emphatically] Your saying that is so at odds with what I have been feeling. [pause] Maybe I am reacting too strongly. Let's go back. Why do you think you are turning me off?

P: I think that when I tell you about my girlfriends, you're okay until I starting getting into sexual stuff. I've noticed that before. You get fidgety and look like it's hard for you to pay attention to what I'm saying.

T: I wasn't aware of doing that.

P: Maybe you think that lesbian sex is disgusting. I know you are going to say that I'm confusing you with my mother and maybe I do that. I also know what I experienced when I was here. You didn't ask any questions. You just let me talk.

T: Perhaps I didn't know what to ask without seeming too intrusive. I want to be there for you. It is true that I'm not used to hearing about lesbian sex but I don't find it disgusting. But even if I were a little uncomfortable in some way, would that mean that there is something wrong with you?

P: My mother makes me feel that way. I thought you knew how important it is for me to know that you accept and appreciate who I am. I need that to feel strong in myself. I don't want anything to stand in the way of that.

T: I do understand that it must have felt very bad to think that I was viewing you negatively. I don't know how to assure you that I don't feel that way. I hope you will give me another chance.

P: I want to but I don't know why you seem uncomfortable sometimes when I am talking about my dating.

T: I have to think about that more but I know I do feel that I want to say the right thing and not disappoint you in the way that your mother did. It's possible that I am not spontaneous enough. I suppose I could be anxious about hearing the details of lesbian sex but I truly do not feel disgust or disapproval.

P: Maybe you would like it. All right, I won't ask you if you ever tried it. You're very honest and sincere. I like that. A lot of good things have happened since I have been coming to see you.

Discussion

In the first excerpt, Ellen's initial experience of the therapist seemed multidetermined. On one hand, her negative feelings about her body, confused feelings about her gender-role behavior, and past relationship with an attractive, highly critical, and controlling mother appeared to set the stage for her difficulty trusting that the therapist could understand and accept her. At the same time, the therapist's physical characteristics, manner, style of dress and speech, and heterosexual identity stimulated the patient's transference. The therapist did not become defensive in the face of Ellen's accusations. She was able to remain empathically attuned to Ellen's concerns and to verbalize her genuine wish to put herself in Ellen's shoes and see the world from her eyes. Believing that the patient also needed some concrete evidence of the therapist's ability to understand her, the therapist used a personal self-disclosure to build a bridge between her life experiences and those of the patient. These interventions seemed to help Ellen to share her deeper feelings about herself that she had never discussed with anyone else. They opened up the exploration of Ellen's self-identification process, permitted the therapist and patient to understand their relationship more fully, and fostered the development of a more collaborative partnership than previously.

The dream that Ellen reported showed both the idealizing and mirroring transferences that had developed and the patient's lingering fears and negative self-concept. The therapist's ability to accurately interpret Ellen's wishes and yearnings and her anxieties about being demeaned and rejected seemed to help the patient to use the therapist as a mirroring selfobject. The transference showed a serious but probably inevitable disruption when Ellen began to feel that the therapist thought she was a freak after she shared her sexual exploits and increasing feelings of power in her dating relationships. Initially, the therapist was somewhat upset by the patient's accusations because they felt at odds with her positive feelings about Ellen's greater self-confidence. Believing that Ellen was distorting the nature of her behavior in the treatment, the therapist became defensive. Sensing her own strong affect, however, the therapist quickly tried to take a step back, shifted her approach, and tried to understand, with the help of the patient, what was occurring in her relationship with the patient. The therapist was able to hear the patient's concerns and take some responsibility for her possible role in contributing to Ellen's reactions. Rather than attributing the transference only to Ellen's projections based on her past experiences, the therapist reflected on her own behavior in the treatment situation. She used

Ellen's observations of her to deepen her understanding of her own inner experience. Her openness with Ellen allowed her to repair the transference disruption.

Understanding the Relational Yearnings Expressed in a Sexualized Transference

Cindy, a 29-year-old struggling actress who supported herself by doing word processing, entered treatment at a gay and lesbian counseling center after the breakup of a lesbian romance a few months earlier. She was drinking heavily and was having trouble getting up in the morning, going to auditions, and staying focused at work. She felt tired of having short-lived relationships but felt hopeless about her ability to sustain a close relationship. The intake worker urged her to go to Alcoholics Anonymous (AA) as a prerequisite for being assigned a therapist and Cindy followed through. When she began seeing the therapist, she was drinking less but was very anxious. She had trouble spending any time alone but didn't want to go to bars to hang out. She didn't know what to do to stay busy. In desperation, she reluctantly started attending more AA meetings.

Cindy had grown up in the Midwest. Her parents divorced when she was a child, and she remained with her mother and younger sister in a small, deteriorating house that was always a mess. Her mother smoked a lot of marijuana and brought her unsavory male friends and sex partners to the house. One of these men sexually molested Cindy when she was 13. She told her mother, who didn't see the man again but who was not a source of comfort to Cindy. Her father visited every other week but he was preoccupied with his work and personal life. He dated frequently and eventually remarried a woman who had her own three children. Cindy never felt a part of his new family, although she lived with him for a while when she was in high school. During those years and later, when she was in college, Cindy was very active sexually. She frequently had sex with guys just to keep their attention, which she was unsuccessful in doing. She never enjoyed these sexual experiences and was often drinking when they occurred. She became sexually involved with a woman as part of a threesome on one occasion and discovered she liked the encounter. She began to go out with other women, whom she had no trouble attracting. She loved the softness of their bodies and felt freer to enjoy herself sexually. Nevertheless, she was fearful of closeness, tended to keep her distance emotionally, and often broke off relationships when she thought she was becoming dependent.

The woman therapist quickly learned that when Cindy was by herself and felt anxious, she felt that no one cared about her and that she was an unlovable person. She did not know how to soothe herself. Although she seemed to engage positively with the therapist in sessions, she lost this connection as soon as she left the office and did not think about what occurred in sessions. Cindy acknowledged feeling that she wanted the therapist's help but feared becoming dependent on her. When Cindy came late for sessions or missed appointments, the therapist would first explore whether she was inadvertently doing something to cause the patient to withdraw or whether the patient was testing her interest. When this did not seem to lead anywhere, the therapist would empathize with what appeared to be Cindy's need–fear dilemma. This seemed to help the patient stay engaged with her, at least temporarily. In working with Cindy to find a solution that could help her to feel less alone and to stay connected to the therapist between sessions, the therapist suggested that Cindy keep a journal and write down her thoughts and bring the journal to the sessions. Cindy liked this idea.

After nine months, Cindy seemed to be more comfortable in sessions. She had stopped drinking and was doing somewhat better in her every-day life. Before the therapist took a one-week spring vacation, she tried to explore what her impending absence would mean to Cindy, who brushed the subject aside. She did know she could call the clinic if need be and she planned to attend some additional AA meetings. Neverthe-less, Cindy failed to show up for her first session after the hiatus. She did agree to come in when the therapist called her to reschedule.

P: I know you want to know why I didn't show up. I'm sure you think it's because I'm angry with you for going away but that's not it. [pause] I did have a hard week. I thought about you all the time. I tried to imagine where you were and what you were doing and then . . .

T: And then what?

P: I even imagined having sex with you. It was exciting and I mas-turbated. I imagined that when you came back, I would try to have sex with you, right here in your office. I was afraid to come to session. I didn't want to lose control or have to talk about this. I don't want to drive you away.

T: This is a safe space where we can talk about whatever you are feeling. What makes you fear you will drive me away?

P: I know you're not interested in me that way — I mean, sexually. You're too ethical even if you were interested. You wouldn't tell me.

T: I'm not sure that your fantasies mean that you are really interested in me sexually. You have been feeling more connected to me. I think it's possible that in my absence, you felt very alone and that your thinking about me was a way of feeling less alone. It was good that you could do this. But your thoughts about me also may have made you feel dependent and vulnerable and you became frightened. I'm not sure if your sexual fantasies represented another way of being connected or a way of protecting yourself emotionally as you have done in other relationships. Sex has often made you feel more powerful and helped you to keep emotional distance between yourself and others.

P: I did feel like I had lost you. I didn't know what to do.

T: It is not hard to understand that being emotionally dependent on someone is very frightening to you, given your past experiences. You were beginning to trust me and my vacation made you feel uncared about.

P: I don't want you to go away again.

T: I wish I could promise you that but I can't.

P: I know but I don't know what I'll do.

T: What I can promise is that I will try to find a way to help you through it. You seem very frightened of the idea. Do you think there may be something else involved?

P: I don't know.

T: Both of your parents left you very unprotected and you were sexually molested. I don't know if my being away stirred this experience up for you. Perhaps it's time to go into this more if you feel ready to do so.

P: That's a hard subject.

Discussion

Cindy showed more deficits and difficulties functioning in her everyday life (e.g., the absence of object constancy, an incapacity to soothe herself in positive ways, and a tendency toward impulsive and addictive behavior) than the other patients described in this chapter. This required the therapist to help Cindy to find ways of helping herself to maintain her connection to the therapist between sessions and to decrease her overwhelming sense of aloneness on one hand and fear of closeness and dependency on the other.

Although the treatment progressed and the therapeutic relationship appeared to provide enough holding so that Cindy was able to contain her impulses and to become positively engaged with the therapist, a major disruption occurred as a result of the therapist's short vacation. Fortunately, the therapist did not become frightened or put off by Cindy's account of the upsurge in her sexual fantasies about the therapist, and she did not see these as indicative of an emerging erotic transference. Instead, the therapist speculated that Cindy's obsessive sexual fantasies had operated to help her quell her sense of panic, aloneness, and disintegration. They held her together. In conveying her understanding of the role of Cindy's sexual fantasies to her, the therapist not only showed her attunement to the patient's inner states but also opened up a number of important areas of exploration.

Chapter 6

Working with Countertransference

Therapists who work with lesbian patients display the characteristic range of countertransference phenomena with which clinicians are familiar but they also may show special reactions to their patients' sexual identity, background, and lifestyle, irrespective of the therapists' sexual identity. It is advisable for clinicians to monitor and understand the nature of their countertransference reactions, whatever is triggering them, throughout the treatment. It is especially important to do so, however, when there is a disruption in the transference that threatens the treatment. Sometimes the therapist's own supervision or treatment may be used to gain such understanding. The focus of this chapter is to illustrate the process by which clinicians attempt to understand and address their countertransference reactions with their patients.

The Process

Countertransference is always at work in therapy because the therapist's values, attitudes, personality, cultural background, and theoretical leanings influence the ways in which the therapist perceives and interacts with the patient. It often operates silently and goes undetected until there is a disruption or impasse in the treatment. Like other patients, lesbians may trigger countertransference reactions that stem from their expectations that the therapist act in certain ways. In working with this population, however, both straight and gay clinicians face certain challenges. Similarities as well as differences between patient and therapist can stimulate nontherapeutic enactments, disruptions, and other types of treatment impasses. Thus, clinicians must be self-scrutinizing with respect to their attitudes, feelings, and biases about lesbians, able to recognize and bridge differences in values, background, and life experiences, and aware of similarities that might influence their identification with their patients.

Because both the patient and therapist exert an impact on one another and the therapist cannot always know what his or her countertransference is without the patient's help, clinicians often must engage in a collaborative process with the patient that clarifies what is occurring in the relationship. In many instances, it may be useful for the therapist to elicit the patient's thoughts about how the therapist might be affecting the treatment relationship even in the absence of a derailment. This type of intervention can move the therapeutic process forward as it helps patient and therapist to understand one another better and to stay on track.

Using Therapist Self-Disclosure to Explore an Enactment Stimulated by Internalized Homophobia

Jayne, a 41-year-old university librarian in a long-term lesbian relationship, was referred to a lesbian therapist by a lesbian physician because antidepressant medication was not sufficiently helping her to cope with her insomnia and depressed moods. The first nine months of treatment went along smoothly. At this time, the patient mentioned offhandedly that she and her partner were planning to attend a benefit in the gay community. The therapist, who also intended to be at the event with her partner, realized that she and Jayne needed to discuss the implications of their both being present at the same affair. It also occurred to the therapist that she and Jayne had never acknowledged or discussed the therapist's lesbianism. She did not even know with certainty that Jayne knew she was a lesbian in spite of her requesting a lesbian therapist from the referral source. The therapist thought it was significant that both of them had avoided this topic and asked herself why this might have occurred. She could not immediately come up with a reasonable answer. In the next session, the following interchange occurred.

> T: I want to bring something up with you. You mentioned last time that you were planning to attend the Gay and Lesbian Center Garden Party. I realized that we have never discussed your feelings about either of our sexual orientations.
>
> P: I guess we haven't. I've always assumed you were straight even though I did ask Dr. Q, who referred you to me, if she knew a good lesbian therapist. When I saw you, I didn't think you were a lesbian but I trusted Dr. Q's judgment. I liked how you handled things

and felt we made a good connection. [laughs] I didn't hold what I imagined as your sexual orientation against you. I'm an equal opportunity employer; I try to be aware of my homosexist leanings. Why are you bringing this up now?

T: Usually, if I think I might run into a patient outside the office at a community event or conference I think it's important to talk about it beforehand.

P: You mean you are going to the benefit too? So you are a lesbian. That's nice.

T: Actually, I was rather surprised when I realized that neither of us had brought up the subject. I wondered why.

P: I just assumed you weren't gay because of your femme look. I must admit that I have had moments of suspicion. I felt gay vibes when you guided me into directions I thought only lesbians knew — my confusing experiences in early childhood and your familiarity with lesbian sex and relationships. But I told myself, she's a therapist, it's her job to have knowledge of gays to do the work.

T: I wonder if you had any concerns about raising it with me?

P: Now that you ask me, I probably was afraid to think you might be gay. Maybe I worried that you would perceive me as coming on to you — as one of those [humorously] predatory lesbians who inflict their disease on innocent and confused straight women.

T: It's hard to be yourself when you think that others will view you as defective and dangerous.

P: During my teens and 20s, I had some horrifying and painful experiences with straight women who flirted with me. When I flirted back, they backed off and acted as if I was initiating coming on to them. First I thought they were doing this deliberately but then I realized they didn't see what they were doing.

T: Many lesbians have had that experience. It's very disconcerting and confusing and sometimes leads to feelings of shame.

P: Looking back, I see that they were probably interested in me at some level but were afraid of their feelings and projected all their crap on me. At the time I felt like a leper. I guess the old hurts still linger.

T: Yes, it is very hard when a woman seems to come on to you and you respond only to get rebuffed. It can be humiliating and crushing.

P: You say that like you know what I mean. I think I felt very alone and depressed. I used to blame myself. I thought there was something wrong with me. It's less masochistic to see that my depression was in response to having to come out by myself.

T: You did have to find your way without any models. I'm sure it made you stronger but that didn't eliminate the pain of it all.

P: So, to answer your question about why I didn't ask you about whether you were a lesbian, I was probably protecting myself because I learned to do this over the years. I have always kept certain boundaries with women whom I thought were straight.

T: You mean that if you had followed your suspicions about my being a lesbian and found out that you were wrong, the threat of your turning me off would have been emotionally unbearable.

P: I couldn't have taken that with you. You certainly gave me some clues but I can be pretty rigid and defensive where my sexual orientation is concerned. I don't always show how vulnerable and frightened I feel. Underneath, I feel like a little cat whose back goes up when she feels threatened.

T: You have had to look for clues in order to feel safe — to feel sure of others before allowing yourself to interact in an open way. What could I have done to make it easier for you to share your fantasies or thoughts with me?

P: Maybe if you had invited me to talk about my fantasies about your private life, I would have talked more. But then again, I'm so used to dismissing issues around lesbianism, I may not have come forward. We've spoken about how part of my early dyke training was to cut off aspects of my gay experience to protect myself from being rejected. I wonder why you never brought it up either. Maybe you are like me in some ways. We're around the same age, not from the new generation of lesbians who ceaselessly proclaim their rights, have formal weddings, and come out to their grandparents. [laughing] I can't imagine coming out to my 95-year-old immigrant grandmother. I think you and I may be made from the same cloth in this arena.

T: We are close in age and have had a lot of the same experiences and training.

P: Our generation grew up fearful of public displays and had to compartmentalize who we were. Having a split identity was a survival tactic. When you're called a fucking dyke like I have been, you learn to protect yourself from humiliating situations.

T: I know.

P: Maybe your armor comes on automatically like mine. If you don't think about it there is no pain, no anxiety.

T: You may be right. Maybe I was protecting myself in some way too.

P: I like when you are honest and open about yourself. It makes me feel close to you.

T: The closeness does feel good.

P: That makes me happy. I am really glad you told that you're a lesbian. It would have been hard for me to ask you. It makes me sad to think I would still not know if you had not brought it up.

T: About the party, how do you think you will feel seeing me there along with my partner?

P: I must admit, I am very curious to see your partner.

T: Curious?

P: I have this fantasy that she is brunette, tall, and thin and probably wears dresses.

T: Except for the dress, the description is similar to your appearance.

P: [Laughing] Really! Well, that's transparent.

T: I guess it is.

P: Does your girlfriend look the way I described?

T: No, she is short, blonde, and somewhat plump.

P: [Laughing] I am glad you will be at the benefit. It will feel good to know you are there and that I can share that with you. I feel very free right now, like a tremendous weight has lifted.

Discussion

When the therapist realized that she and Jayne had not acknowledged the therapist's lesbian sexual identity in the nine months in which they had been working together, she recognized that their avoidance of the subject required investigation. The therapist thought that by raising the issue, she would enable the therapeutic couple to understand their interaction rather than unwittingly continue in their mutual enactment. Initially, the therapist focused on how Jayne was contributing to the transference–countertransference dynamics. This process opened up crucial material and the therapist began to learn about Jayne's painful past experiences with straight women, her anxieties about how such women would view her, and her ways of protecting herself. The therapist's self-disclosure about her lesbianism was important in this exploration not only because she did plan to attend the same event as did the patient but also because it revealed that she had participated in avoiding the topic of her sexual identity. As Jayne spoke about her life experiences and fears, it was easy for the therapist to understand and be empathic with her struggles. In fact, the therapist felt quite identified with aspects of Jayne's narrative. When the patient commented that the therapist might also be protecting herself, the therapist realized that the patient's comment might be true and was able to acknowledge this openly. The mutual enactment between the patient and the therapist reflected a concordance between Jayne's and the therapist's life experiences and defensive organizations. Each had tendencies to protect herself from anticipated disapproval and rejection. Both had self-defined at the end of adolescence during the same cultural time frame. The therapist's honesty in revealing her own contributions to the enactment enabled a greater closeness and sharing to occur between patient and therapist, and this ushered in a new, more intensive phase of treatment.

A lesbian therapist who wished to maintain her anonymity might have decided not to attend the benefit, thus continuing to avoid having the patient see her lesbianism. Or she might have explored the patient's thoughts about her sexual orientation without self-disclosing and concluded that the patient was distrustful in the transference, not recognizing her own contributions. Although justifiable interventions on theoretical grounds, both options would have perpetuated a nontherapeutic collusive interaction and prevented the deepening of the therapeutic relationship and process.

From a broader perspective, this case illustrates that although many potential benefits accrue when a patient and therapist share the same gender and sexual orientation, this is not a panacea. Lesbian therapists who treat lesbian patients are not immune from countertransference reactions that are related to their sexual identity and that affect their understanding of and interventions with their patients.

Recognizing the Presence of a Negative Countertransference Reaction

Betty, a 65-year-old proprietor of a dog-grooming business, was referred to a gay, lesbian, bisexual, and transgender psychoanalytic training institute by a social worker from a gay center that she attended. Having been diagnosed and treated for an early stage of breast cancer a year before and facing her upcoming retirement, Betty became preoccupied with a sense of foreboding. She worried she might fall apart in the process of giving up a 30-year career that had given her joy and made her feel proud. Anticipating this considerable loss and frightened by the physical toll from her recent cancer treatments, Betty had begun to feel depressed and defeated. She felt very troubled by the image she now saw when she looked in the mirror. Once a tall and strong butch-looking woman, she saw a "scrawny and feeble old lady" in the reflection and longed for the time when she felt that femme women found her desirable. Although not presently in a relationship, Betty considered many of her past lovers her immediate family. Six of them lived close by and were friends of varying closeness. Betty was also active at the Gay and Lesbian Center but attending meetings there often made her sad. Seeing older and more frail gay men reminded her of the way she felt during the height of the AIDS crisis, when she witnessed the decline of many of her male friends and peers.

In sessions with her 32-year-old lesbian therapist, Betty dressed in casual men's clothes. Her hair was cropped short, her voice was deep, and she had a tough-looking manner. She could be mistaken for a man if one did not look at her closely. Initially, the therapist was supportive when dealing with the impact of Betty's cancer and the prospect of her retirement. As the treatment progressed, Betty began to feel more hopeful. She warmly called the therapist "honey" and looked to the therapist to validate her and to help restore her previous sense of strength and confidence. Rather than mirroring Betty, the therapist tried to explore and interpret the emerging transference. The patient became more depressed and began to feel at odds with the therapist. The following excerpts are from two sessions after approximately three months of treatment.

> P: I wish I could look in the mirror and see the person I was. You should have known me years ago when I was a lady-killer. All those beautiful ladies would get turned on and want to buy me drinks. I had my pick. It's probably hard for you to imagine.
>
> T: I wonder why you are bringing this up today?
>
> P: I woke up feeling blue and I began thinking about my life and some of the good times. I'd like to get back to who I was.
>
> T: I wonder if you want me to appreciate you in the ways the women in the bars did?
>
> P: Of course I would, honey. I'd show you a good time.
>
> T: You know that I can't cross professional boundaries.
>
> P: [Depressed] I'm sorry if I made you feel uncomfortable. I was just trying to lighten up. This has been the hardest year of my life.
>
> T: I know it has been very hard for you.

In the second of these sessions:

> P: When I looked in the mirror this morning, I felt that I looked like my mother did before she died. She was so tired and feeble. I tried to stop thinking about her. Then I made breakfast and I

remembered my father's mistress, Elaine, and I started to feel better. It was such a good feeling to think about her. I haven't thought about Elaine for a long time.

T: Tell me more about her.

P: She came into my life during the early 50s, when I was a teenager. Elaine always made me feel so good about myself. She was the only adult woman whom I could turn too to talk about my lesbianism. She was kind and a lot of fun. She was a big, curvy Jewish lady who was really gorgeous and a little eccentric. When we talked she would let me sit at the edge of her bed and stroke her beautiful minks. I miss her. She was like a Jewish Mae West. She'd say to me, "Honey, I like my men strong and my coffee weak." She wanted me to learn from her disappointments in love and tried to teach me how to read women. She would say [laughing], "Honey, there are women who will get you all excited and take all your dough and women who are boring but happy to make you a good pot of chicken soup. Go for the boring one, my puppy. She'll be less trouble." Elaine was terrific. She would tell me how I was handsome like my father. She'd say, "Honey, you're going to be talented with women like your father was." [to the therapist] What's the matter, honey? You look like you ate something bad. Did I say something that upset you?

T: What is your fantasy about that?

P: What do you mean, my fantasy?

T: Are you having any thoughts about why I look upset?

P: I have no idea. I was talking about someone who meant a lot to me and you were frowning. Maybe you don't approve of what Elaine said to me.

T: You seem annoyed.

P: [Sighs] Sometimes, I don't think you get me. I think you see me as an old bull dyke. Maybe you're one of those younger gals who think that women like me are not normal. You don't understand why we want to act like men. You don't know what it was like coming out in the 50s. Everyone was either butch or femme. That was how it had to be. I liked to feel that I could have the power men had. It made me feel safe. You girls today have had it a lot easier. You don't have to be afraid to walk the streets or go into a gay club. When we used to dance, there was a signal if the police were about to raid the place. The red strobe lights would go crazy. The clubs had men and women on separate dance floors and as soon as we saw the lights, we would all try to find partners of the opposite sex. I was never arrested.

T: I'm not sure why you think I can't understand your experiences.

P: You are of a different generation. You're at least 30 years younger than I am. Elaine never saw me as freak. She appreciated me. She understood me on a deep level and made me feel important. I'm not saying that you haven't helped me but I think we have some things to work out.

T: [Defensively] I have to think about that. It does seem that something is off between us.

After these two sessions, the therapist reflected on her work with Betty and realized that she had felt more empathic with her in the initial phase of the treatment. A second year trainee, the therapist brought this case to her institute supervisor, who concurred that she had moved away from a more empathically attuned stance and was, instead, using more experience-distant interventions. The therapist and supervisor, who had an open and trusting relationship, were able to discover what the therapist might be bringing to the interaction. The therapist recognized that she had felt more empathic with Betty when she was depressed about her illness and retirement than when she was talking about her sexual prowess and pride in her male persona. It seemed likely that Betty's need for mirroring around her proud masculine-identified sexuality and gendered self was coming into conflict with the much younger therapist's values and homophobia. In her personal life, the therapist tended to value androgyny and looked down at lesbians, gay men, and transgendered persons who conformed to what she saw as negative stereotypes. Moreover, she avoided associating with masculine women because she was fearful that people would label her as a dyke who rejected femininity. In addition, the therapist, who was a petite and youthful-looking woman, felt uncomfortable and belittled by the patient's calling her honey. The supervisor suggested that the therapist acknowledge her lack of attunement to Betty, respond positively to the patient's desire to talk about herself as a strong and powerful woman, and support her ability to regain her former sense of self. The supervisor also discouraged the therapist from making two types of interventions because she thought that they might have the effect of making Betty feel criticized and rejected. Thus, she advised the therapist not to self-disclose about the exact nature of her countertransference reaction and to refrain from interpreting the patient's behavior as a repetitive relational pattern reenacted in the present therapeutic relationship.

In the following session, the therapist tried to repair the disruption in the transference.

T: I have been thinking about our last session and I realize that you were right in telling me that I have been off in some way and not fully understanding and supporting who you are. I made you feel not good about yourself when that was not my intention. I'd like to be more like Elaine.

P: [Surprised] I would like that too. [with humor] You don't look like her and I don't think you are Jewish. Seriously, you did seem like her in a way when I first came to see you. I think that's why I felt comfortable with you.

T: What do you think changed?

P: I just have had this feeling that your life experience and mine have been very different and that you have a hard time with who I am.

T: That can't feel very good especially since you were trusting me and feeling freer to express yourself here. My responses to you undermined you.

P: I don't think it was that bad, honey. I don't expect a relationship to go smoothly all the time. I've been around the block a few times. I do like the way you are talking to me. It makes me feel that you care and don't always have to be right.

T: It is true that we are of different generations and that I have not experienced how hard it was for lesbians who came out when you did. I can understand that you have taken a lot of pride in feelings of personal power in the past and need to reconnect with those good feelings about yourself. I know you can.

P: Well, I don't think I can be a lady-killer again. But I would like to feel stronger and more alive. I might even want to get my feet wet with another woman. I'm not ready to give up.

T: I don't think you need to give up. You have been through a great deal. That has taken a lot of strength and physical and emotional energy. Your illness was a blow. It takes a long time before a person regains her sense of self. I think it's important for us to talk about what you might to do help you feel strong and vital again. There are a lot of ladies still out there.

P: That sounds good to me.

Discussion

In this example, the therapist's misguided interventions and her negative countertransference to Betty's need for mirroring of the masculine and powerful parts of herself threatened the selfobject transference. A therapeutic stalemate or premature termination might have resulted if the therapist had not appreciated the reasons behind her unempathic stance or modified her verbal and nonverbal interactions with the patient. Fortunately, the supervisory process enabled the therapist to get in touch with what was driving her unattuned interventions and to arrive at rectifying the disruption in her relationship with the patient. When the therapist attempted to repair the selfobject transference, she acknowledged the validity of some of the patient's observations of the problem between them and her own role in causing the disruption in their relationship. As the supervisor advised, the therapist refrained from exploring the degree to which the relational dynamics within the therapeutic couple reflected a repetition or mutual enactment of past issues. Likewise, she did not confess the true nature of her countertransference feelings because of their likely hurtful and nontherapeutic impact. Instead, the therapist empathized with what it was like for the patient to have experienced her lack of understanding and encouragement, acknowledged their generational differences, and supported the patient's ability to regain her former sense of self. In this instance, the patient did not press the therapist further to explain her mistakes and seemed reassured by the therapist's modified and more attuned approach.

Recognizing the Therapist's Insensitivity and Contribution to an Enactment

Wendy, a 30-year-old Irish-American legal secretary who was in a 10-year live-in relationship with Angela, her 39-year-old woman partner, entered treatment at a local treatment facility because she did not know what to do about their relationship. She felt Angela was involved with another woman and was gaslighting Wendy by telling her she was imagining things and paranoid when Wendy raised her suspicions with Angela. In describing the events of the past several months, Wendy cited numerous instances in which Angela's behavior indicated that she was having an affair and brought in copies of e-mail messages that reflected intimate and sexually suggestive exchanges between Angela and her alleged friend, Nancy. Wendy did not want to leave Angela and could not imagine life without her. Nevertheless, she described having been unhappy for many years in the face of Angela's withdrawal into work, disinterest in Wendy sexually, verbal abuse, and alcohol dependence. The couple socialized infrequently and was not connected to the lesbian community.

In speaking about herself, Wendy said that she had been a somewhat insecure and fearful child who lacked ambition. Her mother was a housewife and her father worked in construction. He drank excessively and was volatile and verbally abusive. She could not understand why her mother stuck it out. Wendy loved her mother but felt that she could never please her. Her mother was isolated socially, demanding of her daughters, and often preoccupied. She catered to her husband and subordinated her needs to his. Money was scarce, as her father's work was seasonal, and he was periodically laid off from work if the building trade was in a decline. Wendy went to work after she graduated from high school. She knew she was attracted to other women but did not have her first lesbian sexual experience until she moved out of her house when she was 19. Soon after, she met Angela, who swept her off her feet. Angela was a coworker who seemed strong, dynamic, and savvy and made Wendy feel special. They had some good times together but conflict arose early in their relationship. Wendy liked to be at home cooking, watching television, or reading when she was not working and wanted Angela to spend time with her. The latter often felt bored at home and wanted to socialize with others. Angela would become frustrated with Wendy's lack of interests and her social withdrawal. She alternated between coming up with suggestions about what Wendy might do to get out of the apartment and accusing her of being a couch potato and brain-dead. Angela also complained that Wendy did not try to satisfy her sexually. Although Angela earned more income than did Wendy, she did not budget well and expected Wendy to give her money when she frequently overspent. Wendy did not feel comfortable in her family's presence because of her father's continued drinking and her feelings of difference because of her lesbianism. She had initially tried to hide her relationship with Angela from her parents and sisters. Although she thought that they knew about her lesbianism, she never discussed her sexual orientation with them and did not bring Angela with her to family events. Her sisters were married and had children and she wanted to get closer to them but did not pursue this.

The therapist at the counseling center was a 30-year-old self-identified lesbian who, in personality, was the opposite of Wendy. The therapist was an assertive, self-confident, ambitious woman who was brought up in a financially comfortable, close-knit family that valued independence and set high performance standards. She came out as a lesbian in high school and after a somewhat rocky period, her parents and siblings seemed to accept her sexual orientation. Both politically active and connected to the lesbian community, the therapist and her partner of five years had an egalitarian relationship. They spent a good deal of time together but were supportive of one another's independent pursuits.

In the first several months of treatment, Wendy presented herself as a passive, dependent, and unhappy individual who felt trapped in a life over which she felt she had no control. Initially, the therapist empathized with how Wendy felt and tried to support her taking some steps that would give her a sense of greater power. When Wendy seemed unable to use this type of help, the therapist attempted to explore some of the origins of Wendy's sense of helplessness. At this time, however, Wendy was not able to reflect on her behavior. Instead, she repeatedly returned to reporting the latest indignities that she was suffering at Angela's hands and the reasons for her continuing suspiciousness of her. In response to Wendy's requests for advice, the therapist soon found herself making suggestions about what Wendy might do to handle the situation. Although Wendy seemed to appreciate the recommendations, she was not able to implement any of them. She would come to sessions berating herself for not being able to follow through and then would continue to speak about her unhappiness and worry about Angela. The therapist renewed her efforts to mobilize Wendy, only to feel frustrated by Wendy's passivity and helplessness. The therapist began to feel hopeless about being able to help her. She wanted Wendy to make a life for herself, to be firm with Angela or to leave her. On one occasion, the following interaction occurred.

P: Angela didn't come home until midnight last night. She said she worked overtime and then went out for drinks with a group from the office. I waited up for her and when she saw me, she was angry and accused me of being paranoid and controlling. I just can't take her lies and her drinking anymore.

T: I don't know if you are aware that you have said that many times before. You feel desperate but are unable to take any action that might help the situation.

P: You don't understand. If I try to talk to Angela and tell her what I expect from her and try to set some limits on her behavior, she'll tell me that I am too controlling. I want her to go to therapy but she won't. She says that I have the problem. I know I should leave her but something stops me.

T: What about going to the 12-step meetings we discussed? This would give you some support and help you get out of the apartment. I know there are some meetings for gays and lesbians.

P: I just don't seem to be able to get to a meeting.

T: Do you have the schedule?

P: I must have misplaced it.

T: I see you suffering but you seem to feel powerless to do anything to help yourself.

P: I just don't know what do. I need you to give me direction.

T: Well, I have been trying to do that but it doesn't seem to work.

P: You sound like Angela. I guess I am frustrating you. I don't want you to get tired of me.

T: What makes you think that I will get tired of you? Are you used to people feeling that way?

P: I just can see that you are disappointed in me. Your voice sounds a little exasperated even though you are trying to hide it.

T: I am frustrated but not with you. I am feeling at a loss as to how to help you. I sense that you have had this kind of experience with others.

P: [Looks upset] You just don't understand my relationship with Angela. I know that deep down she cares about me and I still love her. I don't know what I would do without her. I know that I'm unhappy but she's all that I have. I keep hoping she will get over whatever is going on for her.

T: I think it is important for us to explore why the relationship is so important to you that you are willing to suffer rather than break it off.

P: I don't want to suffer. I just know I can't leave.

After this session, the therapist brought this case to her peer supervisory group. She was troubled by the fact that she was frustrated with Wendy and that her interventions seemed to be making things worse rather than better. Although a few of her peers empathized with the therapist's frustration at having a patient who seemed so stuck in a bad relationship, several members of the group offered fresh perspectives on the case. One commented that she thought the therapist was caught up in an enactment with the patient to which both were contributing. She suggested that Wendy's passivity, feelings of helplessness, and help-rejecting behavior in relation to an idealized and demanding object who eventually became frustrated and withdrawn were repeating a longstanding pattern that was evident in her family of origin and her relationship with Angela. The peer further suggested that the therapist might be contributing to the enactment because, like others in Wendy's life, the therapist reacted negatively to her lack of assertiveness, colluded with her stated need for advice and guidance, and felt frustrated when Wendy seemed to reject the help that was offered. She thought that the therapist should use the mutual enactment to help Wendy understand this pattern. Another peer thought that Wendy was very identified with her own mother's passivity and helplessness but also was angry and frustrated at her mother for not leaving her father. She speculated that Wendy was inducing the therapist to feel her own frustration and hopelessness as a child. She thought that the patient was not ready to examine this dynamic. Still another member of the group thought that the therapist's expectations of Wendy to assert herself, to take action, and to be independent were too great and that she was missing how ill-equipped Wendy was in major ways. She thought that the therapist was acting like a demanding mother and needed to acknowledge this to the patient and go at a slower pace. She felt strongly that the therapist should not think in terms of enactment. Instead, she urged her to consider how her own values, personality, and background, which were so obviously different from those of the patient, despite their similarity in age, were influencing her view of the patient. She suggested that the therapist slow down, identify and validate the patient's strengths, and explore the deleterious impact of the patient's background, her experiences and attitudes about lesbianism and lesbian relationships, her negative self-concept, and her lack of feelings of entitlement.

The therapist felt somewhat overwhelmed by her peers' suggestions. On reflection, she felt that although Wendy was repeating a longstanding pattern in the treatment that she eventually needed to understand and modify, the first and most important issue that needed to be addressed was how out of step she was with the patient. With the help of her own treatment, the therapist acknowledged to herself how judgmental she was of Wendy's passivity, helplessness, subordination of her needs to Angela, dependence on her, lack of a strong sense of self, and lack of openness about her lesbianism. Wendy represented everything that the therapist had tried not to be. She recognized that it was difficult for her to accept where the patient was because it aroused her anxiety. She saw that her own standards for how an adult lesbian should be had prevented her from appreciating and validating what the patient had done to make a life for herself. She admitted that her own ideas about a good lesbian relationship had gotten in the way of her grasping how important Wendy's relationship with Angela was in providing a home and security. She realized she needed to be more patient and supportive and to gradually explore the depriving and unpredictable conditions of her family life and her lack of nurturing and protection, the absence of role models for assertive and independent behavior, and the impact of being a lesbian.

In a session soon after she met with her peer group, the therapist attempted to use some of her insights into what was occurring in the treatment and to approach the patient in a sincere and open manner.

T: So how are you doing?

P: Everything is the same. I haven't done anything about going to Al-Anon.

T: I wonder how you are feeling about our work together.

P: Actually, I was a little afraid to come here today.

T: Afraid?

P: I don't want you to give up on me.

T: Why would I do that?

P: I know you feel frustrated that I am not doing more to help myself.

T: [Tempted to explore whether Wendy felt others had given up on her, but staying with their current relationship] I'm sorry that I have done something to make you feel that way. [Wendy looks surprised] I have been thinking a lot about our work together. I think you were right when you said that you felt I did not really understand you. Perhaps I have let some of my own personal choices and background influence me and I have not been completely there for you.

P: What do you mean?

T: What you sense as my frustration may stem from my wanting you to move at my pace rather than at your own. I may have pushed you too fast to go to Al-Anon or socialize more with friends or become more independent of Angela.

P: You have good ideas but I just can't get myself to move. I think I need to be pushed.

T: I'm not sure about that. My pushing you feels like a lot of pressure and then you feel bad about yourself when you don't meet what you feel are my expectations and fear that I will turn away from you.

P: It's true that I get down on myself but I usually think it's because you're right and I'm wrong.

T: That's not a good feeling.

P: Yes. It's not. What I do think you're wrong about is my relationship with Angela. Maybe it's my fault because I know that I complain about her all the time and she can be nasty and difficult.

T: What do you feel I am wrong about?

P: You think I would be better off without her. You don't see the good side of her and maybe you don't see that I'm not the easiest person to be with. I can be very frustrating. [laughs] Like I am with you.

T: [Tempted to explore this more, but restraining herself] It must not feel very good to think I want you to break off with Angela when she means so much to you. I must confess that I have focused on how she is dragging you down. Is that just me or has it been hard for you to talk about the good parts of your relationship?

P: I've never had anyone with whom I could share my good feelings about Angela. I've never talked to my family about her except as a good friend. I think they would be happy if we broke up.

T: We've never talked about what it was like for you to discover your attraction for other women and to come out.

P: I've never been very out. It always scared me. Sometimes I think that's why I keep to myself so much. I think I'm sexually inhibited too. Angela teases me about how I'm not really a lesbian. Sometimes she gets really angry. She's more out there. In the beginning, she thought I would get over it and become more comfortable.

T: I wasn't aware until now that this was such a big issue between the two of you. I guess there is a lot we have to talk about.

Discussion

The interaction between Wendy and her therapist can be seen in many ways. It does seem likely that Wendy was bringing to the treatment certain longstanding patterns and expectations that influenced the transference–countertransference dynamics. One could say that her im-mobilization, helplessness, and complaining behavior was setting the therapist up to be demanding and frustrated and to see Angela in a one-sided fashion. Yet this lesbian therapist, who was similar in age to the patient but different in most other respects, had significant blind spots that stemmed from her own values, personality, and background. These contributed to her negative countertransference to Wendy, to her failure in understanding the patient more fully, and to her difficulty in achieving a collaborative therapeutic relationship.

After the first described interaction, in which the therapist and patient were frustrating each other, the therapist recognized that she was caught up in a relational dynamic that she did not understand. Her colleagues had good ideas about what the patient was enacting but also drew attention to the therapist's possible contribution. The therapist's willing-ness to scrutinize her own attitudes and feelings about Wendy in her own therapy proved to be a crucial factor in her gaining more under-standing of her countertransference and in correcting her approach. It is noteworthy that when she decided to take responsibility for her em-pathic failure in the treatment and to disclose sincerely some of the reasons behind it, the patient spontaneously began to own up to how she might be triggering the therapist and how this resembled previous interactions with others. Moreover, the therapist's attempts to establish more of a therapeutic partnership with Wendy led to another surprise, namely, that the patient was communicating only one side of her relationship with Angela. Exploration of this dynamic opened up a new avenue of investigation related to how Wendy had coped with her lesbianism and the role her own homophobia was playing in her relationship problems. By the end of this session, not only were Wendy and the therapist in a more comfortable place than they were previously, but the therapist had a better and revised understanding of Wendy's difficulties.

Recognizing the Clash Between the Patient's and the Therapist's Selfobject Needs

Theresa, a 28-year-old divorced social worker, sought treatment with a lesbian therapist for help in coping more effectively with aspects of her coming-out process. Although she had begun to self-identify as a lesbian 10 years earlier, her coming out had been delayed for many years because of her parents' interventions. When Theresa was 18, her parents, who were caring people and devout Roman Catholics, found love letters from a female classmate in Theresa's bedroom. Although her parents did not become angry or critical, they spoke to their priest, who suggested strongly that Theresa enter religious counseling. The parents believed that she would eventually outgrow her innocent crushes. Theresa, who was afraid of disappointing her parents and confused about her sexual feelings for women, complied with her parents' wishes and the priest's advice. For two years, she attended the religious group meetings, which encouraged homosexual abstinence and heterosexual conversion. Although Theresa was not committed to the group's religious and philosophical orientations, she did experience considerable external pressure to put aside her attractions to women. In order to appease her parents, the group leader, and some other group members, she decided to date men openly but had secret lesbian affairs when convenient opportunities arose. Looking back on this time, Theresa thought that her compliant nature and strong desire to be valued by authority figures helped her to escape from the overt humiliation that a few more rebellious members of the religious group experienced. Inwardly, she did not feel conflicted about her lesbian interests as long as they remained hidden from her parents and the group. Theresa convinced herself that it was better for her to marry and live a heterosexual existence. At the age of 21 she married one of the members of the group, whom she liked but did not love.

Throughout Theresa's marriage, she participated in sexual relations with her husband but continued to fantasize about being with women. Her husband, who also was conflicted about his sexual orientation, was determined to remain in a heterosexual marriage despite his homosexual urges. Because he worked long hours as a junior attorney and was preoccupied with his career goals, Theresa spent most of her social time without him and saw his absence as an opportunity to explore her interests in women without his knowing.

During the four years of her marriage, Theresa learned about lesbian life and became more secure in her career. She eventually decided that she was ready to risk her parents' disapproval and ask her husband for a divorce. Theresa's parents responded to the news of her plans in a way that she had not anticipated. Although they didn't understand the lesbian lifestyle, they told her that she was free to make her own decisions and they would not interfere as they had done when she was a teenager. In addition, they also revealed that they had mixed feelings about having urged her to join the conversion-counseling group previously. They recounted that they had felt frightened at the time and were at a loss about how to help her. Moreover, they disclosed that although they had hoped that her marriage would last, they were aware of the struggles she was having with her husband. Subsequently, Theresa and her parents joined Parents and Friends of Lesbians and Gays (PFLAG) together to help them understand more about the issues that parents of gays and their gay children face.

The following excerpt occurred three months into the treatment, when Theresa was beginning to get more involved with the lesbian community and bar scene.

P: Last night, I saw this very striking woman when I was on the bathroom line at Kitty's [a women's bar]. I desperately wanted to get her attention and say hello or acknowledge her in some way but all of a sudden I became really anxious and lost my opportunity.

T: [Knowingly] Those bathroom lines can be very intimidating.

P: They are my worst nightmare. I have a hard time getting myself to approach a woman. Now I know how my ex-husband felt. He often complained that women had it easy because guys always had to make the first move. Since I came out, I feel just like one of those hesitant, wimpy men that I used to hate. I become hopelessly inept when I want to impress an attractive woman.

T: Approaching women in the bar stirs up a lot of feelings that you will be hurt or rejected.

P: For me it's more extreme than that. I don't think I could bear the humiliation if I were rejected. I know myself. I'd probably go home and start crying and I would make myself crazy thinking about how ugly I am. I wouldn't be able to sleep for days. I get very depressed when I feel rejected. I think that's why it took me so long to come out. I wasn't strong enough to tolerate the rejection. But now that I am a true, card-carrying lesbian, I think its time for me to stop playing the straight girl game of waiting for others to approach me. I want to act like a lesbian.

T: There's not one way to act. You seem to be putting a lot of pressure on yourself. Although you have known about your attraction to women for years, adjusting to living in a new community with different customs and roles for women takes time.

P: I know you are right. But I'm also excited and impatient to get into the lesbian scene and do what lesbians do.

T: What do lesbians do?

P: They go to the bars like men and pick up women. I want to feel secure enough to be able to speak to women I don't know and ask them out. I can tell that you have never lost sleep over these kinds of self-esteem issues. I desperately want to be secure and assertive like you. Often when I am at the bar, I try to imagine how you would handle going up to a woman.

T: What do you see me doing?

P: I think you would have looked straight into that woman's eyes and communicated your interest in her.

T: That's interesting. Do you have any other thoughts about me?

P: When I am in the bars I sometimes think about how you looked and acted when you were my age. I imagine that you went to the bars to hang out with your friends and check out who was available. I bet you were so confident and secure that you could walk in alone, lean on the bar with your drink in hand and eye the babes until you found one that interested you. Then you would simply hit on her. I wish I could be like you.

T: You seem to see me the way you would like to be. It doesn't occur to you that I might not be as confident as you think I am.

P: I don't think it's a question of how I think about you. I think you and a lot of other lesbians are more secure in the bar scene than I am.

T: You seem to feel that you are the only lesbian who finds it difficult to approach other women.

P: [Deflated] I know I'm not the only one who feels this way but I want to overcome how I am. I want you to help me.

T: I know you do but I also think you may idealize others, including me, at your own expense. I wonder how you would feel if I weren't as strong as you imagine?

P: [Looks depressed] I came to see you because I needed a role model to help me find my way with all these new experiences. When I was growing up, I looked to my parents to help my younger brothers and me, and my sisters looked to me to guide and protect them in the ways that they needed. That's the way we took care of one another. Have I done something wrong in thinking about you the way I have? Are you angry with me?

T: No. You haven't done anything wrong. It seems to have made you feel stronger to think of me as confident. It gave you some hope that I can help you get where you want to be. I guess my trying to get you to put less pressure on yourself felt like I was telling you to resign yourself to being a wimp. I didn't mean to make you feel bad.

P: You always say the right thing. I feel much better.

T: What were you feeling when I suggested that your expectations of yourself were too high?

P: I thought you were reprimanding me. It reminded me of the way my parents would speak to me when they felt I was not setting a good example for my younger brothers and sisters. Irish parents place a lot of responsibility on the oldest child. I think that although they never said anything bad about my being a lesbian, I knew they silently communicated how selfish they thought I was to expose my brothers and sisters to my sexual experimentation. They were afraid that I would influence the younger ones into a homosexual direction because the oldest child holds a special place in the family. Secretly, I know my parents expected me to be the perfect child, which meant I was to uphold their values within the family and outside in our community.

T: So you felt that I was telling you that you were not doing it right. Having to maintain such a high standard can be emotionally demanding. Up until now, it seems like the price you've had to pay for feeling valued by your parents was to put aside your need to find your own way to explore your lesbianism.

P: I think that is why I'm so impatient to get into the lesbian scene. I feel a pressure to make up for lost time. I probably am pushing myself into situations I may not be ready for.

T: That is an interesting thought.

Discussion

During the session, the therapist realized that she was feeling uncomfortable with the patient's idealization of her, which was at odds with the therapist's actual personal experience. Her own desire to be seen accurately by Theresa made her want to correct the patient's perception of her as strong and confident in the lesbian scene. She responded to the patient's fantasies about her by making insensitive comments that interfered with the patient's need for idealization. In the session, the therapist quickly recognized that she had made a mistake and was able to get the clinical work back on track by showing that she understood what the patient needed. She did not have time until later, however, to think about what had prompted her insensitivity.

In reflecting on the session, the therapist acknowledged that she had a wish for the patient to see her for who she was, while the patient needed the therapist to accept and therapeutically respond to her idealizing transference. She needed to feel protected by and merged with a secure and powerful selfobject who possessed the calm assurance that she lacked. The therapist came from a similar family background and felt very identified with the patient. The therapist herself had hurtful and depressing experiences in maintaining her self-esteem as a lesbian in a religious community and within the lesbian bar culture. She felt that the patient was ignoring her subjective experience as a lesbian. This lack of validation revived the therapist's sad and painful feelings associated with her own coming-out process and thwarted her desire for a twinship experience with the patient. She longed to share their common experiences in their need to be accepted, acknowledged, and validated during their coming-out struggles. In thinking about her interventions, the therapist was glad that she had exercised some restraint and had not disclosed the true nature of her life experiences to the patient at this time because doing so would not have been therapeutic.

In this example, the mild selfobject disruption and its repair opened up an opportunity for the patient to explore the emotional consequences of her parents' pressure on her to uphold the family values for her younger siblings. It occurred to the therapist that her countertransference might have been stimulated, in part, by the patient's recreation of her experience of being pushed into the role of the idealized daughter in the therapeutic relationship. In this repetition, the patient took the role of her parents as the ones who idealize and the therapist enacted the role of the patient by feeling overwhelmed by the idealization. The therapist concluded, however, that interpreting this level of the transference–countertransference dynamics was not indicated at this time.

Chapter 7

The Initial Stage of Lesbian Relationships
Clinical Considerations

During the course of treatment, many lesbians grapple with how to find romantic partners but they vary considerably in their knowledge and confidence about the process of meeting and making connections with other lesbians. It is important for clinicians who work with lesbians to be familiar with the common concerns and situations that arise in lesbian dating and beginning relationships.

Issues in Dating and Beginning Romantic Relationships

Different mores than those that govern heterosexual dating and beginning relationships guide lesbian dating. Although lesbians are more visible and open today than previously, the culture does not provide a clear roadmap of how to proceed in developing same-sex relationships. Both past and current generations of women have had to experiment and discover the customs and unwritten rules of lesbian dating and coupling on their own. Moreover, different age groups have evolved somewhat different practices. Although some easily learn to navigate this uncharted territory and others gain experience over time and have developed good coping strategies, still others find the relational environment unfamiliar and intimidating. Some lesbians may be entering same-sex relationships for the first time, whereas others may have been away from the dating scene for decades and are returning to it after having had a long-term relationship. Some of this latter group may not ever have felt comfortable dating or may never have mastered dating skills.

The Effects of Life Stage and Sociocultural Issues

Clinicians must be sensitive to the common issues that lesbians of different generations present, the specific life stage concerns that they face, and their geographical, familial, and cultural backgrounds. For example, the first sexual experiences of adolescent and college-age lesbians often evolve out of deep friendships. When these young lesbians are ready to explore their interests in other women further, they may not know other lesbians or they may not know how to make contact with their lesbian peers. Moreover, they may be living with their parents or may be financially dependent on them. Consequently, they may experience constraints on their ability to seek out other women openly and may resort to secrecy in order to escape parental disapproval and rejection. Older lesbians who become single after having been involved in a long-term live-in relationship or who lack extensive dating experience may feel different constraints. They may feel uncomfortable and timid in approaching other women for dates or in initiating sexual involvements. Having been part of a couple for many years, they may have lost contact with the single lesbian community and may lack familiarity with its particular pressures and characteristics. Moreover, lesbians of certain ethnic and cultural groups that stigmatize homosexuality may experience considerable conflict about coming out and remain closeted even after becoming involved in a committed lesbian relationship.

The Impact of Female Socialization

In treatment, many of the questions and concerns that lesbians raise about dating and initiating relationships are rooted in the ways in which lesbians, as women, are socialized in regard to sexuality and its expression. For example, despite valuing freedom of sexual expression and nonconformity in gender roles and behavior, many lesbians, particularly those of more recent generations, may have been raised more traditionally and have difficulty acting in consonance with their beliefs. Like their heterosexually identified counterparts, taking an assertive stance or revealing their sexual interests may cause discomfort. This can result in their having difficulty flirting, knowing how to move from friendship to a romantic relationship, approaching other women for dates, and initiating sexual involvements. They tend to wait for the other woman to take the first step.

A related issue is that, even today, it is common for some inexperienced lesbians to feel confused about whether getting together is a date or a meeting between friends. It may be difficult for them to decipher whether another woman is displaying sexual or romantic interest unless that individual is overtly expressive. A recent study actually found that midlife lesbians (ages 40–60), who had a more consolidated sense of self and greater life experience in contrast to younger lesbians (22–39), were more serious about dating, clearer about whom they are interested in and who is an appropriate partner, more skilled in signaling romantic and sexual attractions, more confident in initiating dates and physical intimacy, and faster in moving forward (Rose and Zand, 2000).

The Effects of Discrimination and Internalized Homophobia

Although lesbians experience greater acceptance and legal protection for lesbians than previously, they continue to be marginalized and discriminated against in many areas — for example, child custody, taxes and pension benefits, inheritance, and medical issues. The therapist also must consider how this type of discrimination and other forms of anti-homosexual bias influence dating and relationship building. Clinicians must be vigilant so that they do not mistake or misinterpret a patient's behavior as an intrapsychic or interpersonal problem only, rather than as an offshoot of reality concerns. For example, in working with a lesbian who goes to great lengths to avoid being seen entering or leaving a gay bar, the clinician must consider the reality basis of the patient's fear that her job will be jeopardized if any of her coworkers see her.

An offshoot of the longstanding and continuing marginalization of homosexuals in society is that lesbians, unlike their heterosexual counterparts, need to develop their own rituals to celebrate important events, such as anniversaries, the making of a commitment, and the like. Even the seemingly simple definition of what constitutes the anniversary of a relationship and the question of when it should be celebrated are not universally established within the lesbian or gay community. The anniversary date can signify different occasions — the day the couple first met, the day that they began a sexual relationship, or the day the couple made a commitment to each other as exclusive partners.

Internalized homophobia and lack of societal and familial sanction also may exert a significant impact on lesbian relationships. It is advisable for clinicians to consider the roles that fear of exposure, lack of knowledge about available resources, and lack of experience with the lesbian community are playing in a lesbian patient's discomfort with or lack of connection to coworkers and family members or in her social isolation. When lesbians are closeted or feel inhibited about sharing aspects of their personal lives at work, they may restrain themselves from talking about the vicissitudes of everyday life, important events, and matters affecting their partners in the workplace and may refrain from bringing their partners to work-related functions. Sometimes members of a couple are not at the same point, either in the stage of their coming-out process or in their degree of openness personally and professionally. This may result in different comfort levels about whether to attend certain family and social events and about how to behave in public. For example, one member of a new couple may choose to go to family gatherings without a partner rather than risk parental disapproval. Likewise, another lesbian might find herself to be very self-conscious about her partner's use of words such as honey or darling around family members or straight friends. Or she may warn her partner not to display any physical or verbal affection when dining in a restaurant, so as not to risk being seen as lesbians by others.

It is useful for clinicians to recognize that some of the existing resources and ways of meeting other lesbians are rooted in the past social and economic climate for lesbians but have continued despite changing times. For example, the bar scene and dances arose to provide affordable and safe opportunities for lesbians to meet one another. They still are mainstays of the lesbian singles' world even though other options have now emerged—for example, becoming a member of or volunteering in gay and lesbian social and professional organizations, visiting Internet sites, and attending gay and lesbian benefits, social events, and conferences.

Lesbian Friendships and Dating

Another significant issue for lesbians that the clinician should understand is that dating and romantic relationships may evolve out of existing close friendships. In one study, 78 percent of the lesbian respondents reported that their first love relationship grew out of a friendship and also that they were friends before they became lovers with their current partners (Vetere, 1982). Changing the nature of a lesbian friendship and negotiating the transition can be challenging tasks. Sometimes it is difficult for lesbians to know whether their feelings for one another reflect friendly, sexual, or romantic interest. For example, an unattached lesbian who was a close and longstanding confidant of another lesbian found herself thinking about beginning a romantic relationship with her friend after the friend's separation from her lover of many years. After revealing her romantic interest to her friend, who was feeling alone and needy, the two women impulsively had sex with each other. Soon after, they felt confused about what they meant to each other and whether they could be a couple.

A related issue is that lesbians tend to place a high value on remaining friends with their past lovers, although a period of time may elapse after a breakup before the friendship resumes (Weinstock, 2000). This can have both positive and negative consequences. On the positive side, these past lovers become extended family, provide confirmation of the lesbian lifestyle, and constitute a crucial support system over the years. On the negative side, one member of a couple may be more able to do this than the other. Or members of a new couple may have to deal with the presence of each other's former partners and with the complex emotional bond that exists between ex-lovers who have remained friends.

It should be noted that the very smallness of the lesbian community and the dating pool often results in a lack of privacy or in situations in which women in certain circles may have had sexual and romantic relationships with many of the same people. Likewise, women who have been romantically involved with one another may have the common experience of encountering their former partners at lesbian events. Because of the frequent opportunities for closeness among lesbian couples and their female friends, it is not unusual for a lesbian to develop a romantic interest or flirtation with the partner of a good friend. Although this situation also arises in heterosexual relationships, it may not be as prevalent. It is less likely that the members of two different heterosexual couples develop close friendships with the partners of the opposite gender. The consequences of the intensity of lesbian friendships may be detrimental to the couple, causing jealousy, rejection, and betrayal.

Lesbian romantic relationships do not always grow out of friendships. An important facet of lesbian life is the tendency for women who may not have known each other very long to become quickly committed to each other, sometimes after their initial sexual experience. There is a joke in the lesbian community that when two lesbians are attracted to each other, one is likely to bring a U-Haul instead of flowers on their first date. This phenomenon may be related to women's desire for connection and their equating sexual pleasure with intimacy. Such bonding can have positive outcomes but often members of a couple who become involved rapidly may soon realize that they do not really know each other very well or their fantasies about the perfect relationship may be crushed.

Although the early stage of many lesbian romantic relationships proceeds smoothly, lesbians themselves have coined the term dykedrama to humorously depict the passionate, intense, and turbulent nature of romantic entanglements. The drama often revolves around frustrated expectations, jealousy, needs for attention and being special, betrayal, and privacy. Sometimes friends provide an audience to or are drawn into the drama. For example, a lesbian who was in a new but committed relationship ran out of the bar when she saw her partner flirting openly with a mutual friend. The other friends who were present came to her aid and tried to comfort her. Her partner soon followed and was angry at the lack of trust displayed by her lover. The couple went home together and argued for several hours, frequently calling friends to talk over the details of the event and to get their opinions about what had happened. Eventually, they each felt sufficiently reassured of the other's love that they were willing to set the incident aside.

The Role and Expression of Lesbian Sexuality

The role and expression of sexuality in lesbian relationships varies considerably from couple to couple. Although some lesbians are highly sexual, some studies have suggested that after the initial romantic excitement diminishes, sex is less of a central focus in lesbian couples generally than it is in heterosexual relationships (Falco, 1991). Several factors may account for this supposed difference. It is likely that many older lesbians, in particular, have been raised with considerable sexual inhibitions. Moreover, many women tend to place a high value on intimacy and connection rather than on sexual expression per se. They may enjoy certain aspects of sexuality, such as cuddling, hugging, stroking, and touching as much, if not more, than sexual practices that lead to sexual release. It has been observed that the deepening of intimacy in ongoing lesbian relationships sometimes is associated with a loss of interest in sex. Whether this is because of tendencies toward merger and a reliving of early childhood relational bonds or represents a variation of women's normal sexual behavior is a controversial issue.

An important feature of lesbian sexuality in many women today is the freedom to transcend traditional gender roles. Lesbians engage in different methods of sexual arousal. Many lesbians prefer vaginal or anal stimulation by manual or oral means, whereas others use mechanical devices or dildos. Like heterosexual couples who place a high value on emotional compatibility and intimacy, lesbian couples who form a strong connection may later struggle with the satisfaction of their sexual needs.

Although being more egalitarian in gender role behavior is likely the more usual pattern among younger lesbians, some lesbians, especially those who came out before the feminist and gay-liberation movements, may adopt traditional gender roles in their sexual behavior. For example, they assume either butch and femme roles, with the butch being the more assertive partner in the sexual play and the femme taking a more traditionally passive role. This can take the form of the butch partner being the top in the sense that she makes love to the femme partner (the "bottom"), whereas the femme is not expected or allowed to make love to the butch. In times past, some of this gender role playing may have resulted from how lesbians thought they should behave and from modeling their sexual behavior on a heterosexual prototype.

A Lesbian Adolescent's Normative Struggle

Diane's example shows how she experienced many of the normative struggles of adolescent lesbians and how the therapist addressed these in the treatment from a nonpathological assessment and informed stance. It also shows the therapist's use of herself in the treatment relationship and describes a treatment process that had the goal of helping the patient continue on her developmental path.

Diane, an attractive, outgoing 16-year-old high school student, was having sex with her girlfriend in bed at home when her mother found her. Although upset, her mother was not surprised because Diane had always seemed to be attached to other girls in a way that seemed sexual. The parents located a therapist for Diane at a local mental health center and at the therapist's suggestion, they joined Parents and Friends of Lesbians and Gays (PFLAG). The mother told the therapist that Diane had a tendency to jump into new situations without examining the consequences and that she and her husband were afraid that their precocious and impulsive teenage daughter was making a mistake that would cause her to be hurt. The parents seemed confused about whether they wanted the therapist to "fix" Diane and help her to adopt a heterosexual orientation or to assist her in coming out as a lesbian in a positive way.

Diane, who appeared to be struggling to separate emotionally from her parents, did not view their concerns as a caring gesture. She told the therapist she had reluctantly agreed to see her in order "to get them off my back." She said she was counting the days to when she could go away to college and live her life away from her parents' watchful eyes. She felt herself to be quite adult and was comfortable and excited at the prospect of becoming more openly lesbian and dating other girls.

The therapist, who was not a lesbian, was knowledgeable about and accepting of gay and lesbian life. In their first session, she was able to empathize with Diane's feelings about being pushed into therapy and with her likely distrust of the therapist's intentions. She said that she had no agenda to "fix" Diane but thought that she could be of help to her in sorting through the issues she was facing at this transitional point in her life. She said she knew that it often took a lot to be one's own person and to navigate lesbian life. Diane acknowledged that although she sometimes hated her parents, she also cared about what they thought and didn't want to alienate them. In discussing her eagerness to pursue dating women, she acknowledged that she found herself intimidated at times by the girls she wanted to get closer to and felt insecure and anxious about how to proceed.

Early in the treatment, Diane ventilated her concerns about her family. With the therapist's help, she recognized that although she wanted to gain independence from her mother, she also drew her mother into her private business as a way of staying close to her. The therapist helped Diane to consider how she might achieve more independence while staying connected and at the same time not provoking her mother by flaunting her sexual behavior in the mother's face.

As Diane became more involved in treatment, she spoke to the therapist more freely about her anxieties about entering the lesbian dating scene. Initially, she expressed concern about how to decide which girls in her social network were friendly or flirting with her and open to dating. She described a number of incidents in which she approached girls at school who responded negatively to her flirtations. She wasn't sure if they were not gay or were just not interested in her. Because Diane's few prior sexual experiences had evolved out of close friendships with girls who cared about her feelings, these rejections were painful. Diane began doubting herself and her attractiveness. These feelings dampened her excitement about exploring her new sexual and emotional expression.

The therapist helped Diane, who was understandably naive in these matters, to realize that her experiences with her peers were likely unrelated to her as a person but to realistic difficulties in being able to know who was a lesbian in a mixed, mostly straight, environment. They discussed the problems of knowing whom to approach when it is not clear who is a lesbian, as well as the fact that sometimes women pretend to be indifferent even when they are interested in pursuing a romantic relationship. They also talked about gaydar, or being able to pick up or send clues about being a lesbian, and how Diane would develop this capacity in time. During this time, Diane began to look to the therapist as an older, wiser, and supportive mentor and the therapist took on this role in part.

When Diane decided it was time to move out of the protective milieu of her friends and into the lesbian community, she began to attend drug-free teen events sponsored by the local gay and lesbian center. Initially insecure and anxious, she began to feel more connected to members of the group. Nevertheless, she felt uncertain about which of the girls she could consider a friend and which she was interested in dating and became uncomfortable when she learned that many of the girls had slept together. They often talked about the their experiences in a negative light and discussed each other's bodies in a provocative sexual way. Diane did develop a friendship with Janice, one of the members, but felt too vulnerable to reveal her romantic interest in her. She was fearful that she would be rejected and that the other girls would talk behind her back. Another love interest was Sherry but Diane held back because Sherry had broken off a relationship with Janice. Diane was fearful that pursuing Sherry or telling Janice about Sherry would alienate Janice. It was difficult for Diane to enjoy her new friends because of her anxieties, which began to feel overwhelming.

The therapist empathized with Diane's confusion about how to pro-ceed and helped her to consider and weigh the emotional costs of asking Sherry out and alternative courses of action. This discussion provided a road map for Diane to handle this situation and others that arose in the future. Diane was able to become more reflective on her behavior with others. The therapist helped her to explore her tendency to idealize potential girlfriends and her need for immediate responses, even though the consequences of her actions might result in her getting hurt. Because Diane continued to be upset about the exposure of dating someone in her friendship network, the therapist encouraged her to venture out beyond her clique.

As Diane gradually became more involved with the gay and lesbian community and her social network expanded, she found more opportu-nities to date girls outside her friendship group. Likewise, as she became more familiar with the nuances of the lesbian dating culture, her confi-dence increased and she felt more confident maneuvering within a variety of social circles.

Once Diane felt firmly grounded in these settings she began dating regularly. She seemed more confident and looked to the therapist less for guidance. At first she slept with a number of teens she was not seriously interested in. After a year of treatment, Diane met Frances and they became romantically involved quite rapidly. Diane idealized Frances, who was an emotionally stable, independent, high-achieving, and popular teenager. They began talking about going away to college together and Diane became more studious and serious about her college applications. Although Diane's parents were apprehensive about Diane's intense attachment to Frances, they liked her and thought she was a good influence on Diane. They were happy that Diane was actively trying to get into a good school and that she seemed more grounded. Diane and Frances were affectionate to each other but were careful not to be sexually provocative around either of their sets of parents. At this point, Diane decided to leave treatment because she felt she had gotten over her crisis and wanted to see what she could do on her own. Although the therapist thought that Diane could benefit from further treatment, particularly with respect to her underlying feelings of insecurity and anxiety, she recognized that Diane was doing better and was on track developmentally.

Negotiating Self-Esteem in Lesbian Relationships and Dating

Randy's case reflects how the need to move on with her life after the breakup of a long-term relationship brought up the question of how to remain friends with an ex-lover and stimulated longstanding issues related to social insecurity and passivity. It shows how the therapist was able to understand and accept the patient's tie to her ex-lover while helping her to set limits. It also demonstrates how the therapist addressed the patient's gender training and passivity in initiating sexual and romantic relationships.

Randy, a 32-year-old Jewish college administrator, was traditionally feminine in appearance. She had long, wavy brown hair and dressed in a slightly provocative manner that displayed her curvy graceful body. She entered treatment one year after she and Virginia, her female partner of five years, broke up because the latter wanted to date others. Randy wanted to move on with her life. An insightful person, Randy had been in therapy previously when she first came out as a lesbian.

During the first session, Randy said that although she continued to experience deep sadness over their separation, she accepted that her romantic relationship with Virginia was over. Nevertheless, she confessed having considerable difficulty in transforming their relation-ship into a friendship because of Virginia's active dating life. Randy explained that she wanted to be Virginia's friend because she was the person in Randy's life to whom she had felt the closest. She found it difficult, however, to listen to Virginia's exploits, not because she was jealous of the other women but because she was envious of the ease with which Virginia was able to meet others. Randy felt inadequate by com-parison. She tried to put on a happy face so that others would not see how she felt. She thought her friends and Virginia saw her as the less attractive, weaker, and less evolved partner and feared that if they knew she was upset about Virginia's success in dating, they would interpret her response as her being the broken-hearted lover who longed for Virginia. What was making the situation worse at the moment was that Randy wanted to start trying to meet other women and was afraid that she would freak out if she saw Virginia and another woman together at the bars or events that they liked to attend. She didn't know how to discuss this with Virginia. She wasn't sure what she wanted to say but also admitted never having been good at confronting difficult issues or being able to stand her ground when she and Virginia were together.

In early sessions, it became apparent that Randy had longstanding feelings of insecurity and self-consciousness, which had been masked by her relationship with Virginia. Randy had become involved with Vir-ginia a few years after coming out. She had some, but not a great deal, of dating experience. She felt disheartened when she thought about having to develop a new network of single friends and enter into the dating scene. Before beginning treatment, she had started to meet women through an Internet dating service because she had felt awkward and embarrassed going out to the bars alone. When she went to a bar, she stood alone for hours without talking to anyone and imagined that the women she was attracted to saw her as damaged and pathetic. Through the Internet, she met a few women she would have liked to date again, but she couldn't tell if they were interested in her. All the dates felt very platonic and she wondered why these experiences felt so different from those when she first came out. In exploring this issue with the therapist, Randy revealed that she always needed the other woman to be the leader, which meant to take the first steps in dating and sex. She described herself as the more passive partner with Virginia and felt that this had been a problem in their relationship.

The early work had two foci. The therapist showed that she under-stood the importance of Randy's continuing friendship with Virginia but helped her to consider whether it might be possible for Randy to set limits on how much Virginia shared with her about the details of her dating experiences. Likewise, the therapist supported Randy in having more open discussion with Virginia about ways in which they could allow each other some separate space for their efforts to meet other women or, at least, some advance warning about the likelihood of their encountering each other. A second focus was on exploring some of the factors that contributed to Randy's longstanding passivity and helping her to experiment with becoming more assertive.

Randy felt strengthened by the therapist's exploration of whether it was both advisable and possible for her to set some limits on Virginia. It was not easy for her to do this, however, because she did not want Virginia to know what was making her uncomfortable and also feared Virginia's reaction. The therapist helped Randy decide how she might approach the subject without revealing her innermost feelings and without coming on too strong. When Randy did approach Virginia, she was surprised by her response. Instead of being angry, Virginia said that she thought Randy liked to hear about her adventures because she had never said anything and seemed happy. She said that she talked about her experiences because she didn't want Randy to feel left out but would stop. Empowered by this interaction, Randy broached the subject of how to manage their social lives. It was logistically more difficult to avoid being in the same places socially but Randy and Virginia were able to arrive at some ground rules and bringing the subject up made Randy feel more in control.

Although Randy's recent experiences in the dating scene made her recognize that she should practice being more assertive, it was difficult for her to do so because her tendency to passivity was so ingrained. She continued to try to use the Internet to meet other women. When she did begin to date Miriam, a woman she met through the Internet, some interesting issues arose. Both women appeared to wait for the other to pursue setting up further meetings and to show romantic interest. Although they saw each other frequently, they remained platonic because neither felt comfortable initiating sex. Although they eventually experimented sexually and enjoyed each other's company, Randy did not feel excited by the relationship and felt they were better at being friends than lovers. She complained about this in sessions but confessed that she had not said anything to Miriam about her feelings. The therapist explored Randy's silence with Miriam and suggested that she might be fearful of rocking the boat because it felt safe to stay with Miriam in an unsatisfying relationship rather than to invest the energy it would take to find a more romantic involvement. Randy reluctantly acknowledged that this was true and that it was her usual pattern.

Randy eventually shared her concerns with Miriam, who actually felt similarly. They agreed to remain friends and go out together to meet women. Because both had felt very inhibited in single social settings and were predisposed to passivity, having a friend to go out with relieved some of the anxiety that Randy had previously felt in the bars. She spent sessions talking about her struggles with the bar scene until she met Annette, a soft butch who was into role playing. Annette made dating easy for Randy because she could play the more traditionally passive feminine role. She didn't have to initiate any of their social or sexual contact. But Annette was also possessive and wanted Randy to make a commitment before Randy felt she knew her well enough. Randy began to feel smothered by Annette's attentions and demands and broke off the relationship.

Although the therapist supported Randy's having taken the action of breaking off with Annette, she also observed that Randy, in allowing the relationship to become more involved, had again revealed her tendency to want someone else to take the lead, even if that person was not right for her. Randy herself was able to see her pattern clearly and seemed motivated to explore the meaning of this characteristic more fully. In discussing her upbringing, she discovered how her identification with her mother's adoption of a traditional feminine role with her husband played a considerable part in Randy's difficulty maintaining equality in romantic relationships. She realized that although she considered herself a feminist, her early socialization led her to wish secretly for someone to take care of her the way her father cared for her mother. Her early heterosexual training influenced her expectations to have her dates take charge, show interest, initiate sexual contact, pay the bills, and be the primary wage earner. She also fantasized about leaving her substantial job and raising children. During these sessions, Randy became aware for the first time how her traditional Jewish religious and cultural training, along with her mother's and sister's romantic aspirations, influenced how she conducted herself in dating and relationships.

Soon after, Randy met Rachel, another Jewish college administrator, who came from a similar background. Initially, this new relationship had a lot of sexual excitement. Randy noticed how she felt very different with Rachel and she was able to practice taking more responsibility in the relationship. Who paid for what and who initiated dates and sex became more equitable, they collaborated and negotiated more around their lives together, and they developed a deeper involvement. Although she had lapses, Randy felt free from the former restrictive traditional female gender role she had engaged in previously. After a year and a half of dating the couple moved in together and began to speak about how they would approach having a family. Both partners desired to have their own biological child and they joined a parents' group at the gay, lesbian, bisexual, and transgender (GLBT) center to learn how others have handled these issues. Randy terminated treatment soon after.

The Many Layers of Problems in Maintaining Romantic Relationships

In the next case, the patient, Suzanne, presented longstanding problems in sustaining romantic relationships and a tendency to confuse sexual behavior and emotional intimacy. The example shows the therapist's recognition that these difficulties reflected a complex mix of early family-of-origin issues and an absence of positive lesbian role models to help her in evolving her lesbian identity and learning how to be emotionally intimate. It also shows how the therapist integrated an insight-oriented approach with the use of the therapeutic relationship to provide new opportunities for relating and intimacy.

Suzanne, a 39-year-old androgynous and athletic carpenter, entered treatment because she felt lonely and depressed. She was tired of coming up empty. She had had a series of monogamous relationships that lasted one to two years and wondered why it was so difficult for her to maintain a longstanding relationship. She knew she was doing something wrong but didn't know what it was or how to be different. Suzanne described that since her late teens, she had often become quickly involved in exciting lesbian sexual affairs that often led to early commitments and breakups. Suzanne felt very comfortable in the bar scene and unencumbered by proscribed gender roles. Her conflict centered on intimacy. Although she had many friends and remained in contact with her ex-lovers, she felt something was standing in the way of her finding happiness in a long-term relationship.

The therapist's thorough exploration of Suzanne's relationships helped her to understand her tendency to quickly act on her sexual attraction to other women and to confuse sexual involvement with intimacy. Over the course of treatment, the therapist observed Suzanne a number of times when she was in the throes of her idealization of her conquest and of love itself. There was an addictive quality to her being drawn into the high excitement she felt when she met a new woman. Often Suzanne would dive into a commitment before she actually knew much about the other woman. She could not tolerate being in a state of ambiguity or uncertainty about the nature of the relationship.

Suzanne grew up in a small town. Her mother died when she was a child and she barely remembered her. Although she did not think that she was sexually abused, her father was quite seductive and an alcoholic. He had frequent affairs with other women and often brought them home. Suzanne felt dependent on him but he was erratic and unavailable emotionally. Suzanne emulated her older macho brothers, whom she saw as strong and independent. She was physically active and preferred playing with the boys on the street to playing with girls. She felt uncomfortable in traditionally female activities. In high school, she was often lonely and depressed. She did make friends and developed crushes on her female teachers. She felt very drawn to another girl in her gym class and they experimented sexually. Their relationship was short-lived because they both were fearful. Suzanne didn't know what being a lesbian meant but after the experience with her friend, she became more aware of her attraction to other girls and women. She did not know anyone who was a lesbian until she moved to a nearby city. She thought that relationships between women lovers must resemble the numerous and highly sexual relationships she witnessed her brothers having. Her first lesbian friends were somewhat older than she and tended to be into playing butch and femme roles with one another. Suzanne worked as a carpenter and eventually developed her own business, which did reasonably well financially.

The therapist, a nonlesbian who was open to and reasonably knowledgeable about lesbian life, felt that Suzanne's problems were multidetermined and based on several complex issues. Her history revealed early experiences of abandonment, aloneness, and instability, the presence of a sexually stimulating environment, use of her older macho brothers as role models for her adaptation, and the absence of lesbian role models to help guide her lesbian identity. In the lengthy treatment process, three major interpretations of the patient's behavior took center stage. First, the addictive component of her sexual encounters, her need to be high on love, looked as though it functioned to alleviate her depressed moods. When she was in this state, she didn't have to think about her loneliness or unhappiness. Second, having had no example or model to rely on in terms of lesbian dating and relationships, Suzanne did not know how to date and allow a relationship of emotional intimacy and love to develop over time. Moreover, in the absence of such models, Suzanne took on her brothers' behavior toward women and later was influenced by lesbian friends who were role-bound. Finally,

Suzanne had an overstimulating father and suffered from maternal deprivation and neglect. She came to realize how much she feared rejection and abandonment and used sex as a defensive maneuver. It appeared that her fast sexual involvements and romantic fantasies of having found the perfect relationship enabled her to feel safe without having to risk a deeper involvement that might result in abandonment. Although the relationships ended, she protected herself from being hurt.

The treatment process helped Suzanne to gain insight into the roots of her difficulties, given her family background, and also into her lonely struggle with her lesbianism. The therapist and patient discussed not only her early feelings of abandonment and the role that sexuality played in her childhood and later life but also the impact of the absence of lesbian role models in her developing her lesbian identity and learning about lesbian relationships. At many points in the treatment, Suzanne displayed the same behavior in the therapeutic relationship that she did in other relationships. She became seductive and somewhat assertive in trying to entice the therapist into a sexual relationship in what appeared to be attempts to protect herself from emotionally relying on the therapist. Without rejecting Suzanne, the therapist was able to refrain from becoming embroiled in an enactment of Suzanne's relational patterns and her seeming need for a highly charged sexual experience. The therapist was able to help Suzanne reflect on this pattern and its multiple meanings and become more emotionally involved in the therapeutic relationship, which provided a new experience of mutual caring and a safe emotional intimacy. Although there were turbulent times when Suzanne expressed frustration at the boundaries of the therapeutic relationship and verbalized feelings of rejection, she and the therapist were able to weather these storms.

A Conflict Between Old and New Attachments

In the following example, a middle-aged lesbian entered treatment because of a conflict she was experiencing between her new romantic relationship and her longstanding attachment to an ex-lover, who functioned as a close family member. As in the case of Randy, the therapist recognized and accepted the importance of the patient's friendship with her former partner. In this case, however, it also seemed to the therapist that the patient was fearful of involving herself fully in her new relationship and was not aware of the confusing messages that she was giving her partner. The therapist was able to help the patient to identify her own anxieties, to be more attuned to and reassuring of her lover, and to maintain her relationship with her longtime friend in a way that was less intrusive on her new partnership.

Jackie, a 51-year-old social worker, was shopping for a therapist from a list of lesbian-friendly providers given to her by her insurance company. She wanted help with a major dilemma she was facing. Just prior to meeting with the therapist, she had consulted with another clinician. Initially, she liked her but then left after a few sessions because the woman gave her advice that showed she didn't understand Jackie or lesbian life.

In her first session with the new therapist, Jackie announced that she was a lesbian and proud of it but was having a hard time dealing with her new lover, Ann, whom she had known for three months. Jackie said that Ann was the first woman she had been with for a long time who she felt was her equal intellectually and with whom she wanted to spend the rest of her life. They shared many interests and wanted to live together and Jackie felt good when she contemplated the move, except for one major problem that was causing severe anxiety, worry, and loss of sleep.

> Here's the deal. I have an ex-lover, Angie, who is my family. I have no one else. I do have some other friends, but Angie and I have known each other for 25 years. We were lovers for five of those years and have continued to be friends through her lovers and mine. . . . We've gone through hoops to keep up our relationship, even when we have lived in different cities. We have traveled together and spent holidays together when we had other partners or were alone. It's been okay until now for everyone. . . . Sometimes, there's been a little tension with our partners but we have worked it out. Once, one of Angie's partners hated me but she put up with me. . . . Angie's been with someone for the past two years. The problem is that now I've met Ann, whom I love dearly. But Ann can't stand the idea of my talking to or seeing Angie. She feels that her needs should come first and that I love Angie more than I love her. She does not want me to as much as speak to Angie. She's being totally unreasonable. So far Angie has been understanding. I've explained the situation and I do talk to her and see her occasionally but I don't like lying to Ann. I also know that if she knew, it would freak her out. I don't know if she believes that I'm not communicating with Angie. I know that she doesn't trust me. I don't really know what to do. I can't keep lying. I also miss Angie. I hope you

are not going to tell me that I should break off my relationship with Angie, like the first shrink I saw did. She clearly does not understand lesbians.

If the therapist had any thoughts about suggesting that Jackie put an end to her relationship with Angie, she clearly would not have given voice to them at this point. But the therapist actually was not thinking that. She did initially find herself wondering, on one hand, what expectations of a relationship or what feelings of possessiveness or jealously Ann might have and, on the other hand, whether Jackie was allowing her attachment to Angie to interfere with her relationship with Ann more than Jackie realized.

When the therapist asked Jackie why she thought Ann felt as she did, Jackie explained this in terms of Ann's inexperience and insecurity. She said that Ann, who was also a social worker but 10 years younger than Jackie, had led a sheltered lesbian life. She had come out when she was 27 and had been in only one relationship with a woman, Beth, for 10 years until she died of breast cancer. They had a very close relationship and had been devoted to each other. Jackie thought they were too close in the sense that they had isolated from others except for Ann's family, with whom she was close. When Ann and Jackie met, three years after Beth died, Ann felt that a miracle had occurred. She felt happy for the first time in years. Jackie felt that Ann was not accustomed to having to share her partner with anyone, that Ann experienced Jackie's relationship with Angie as a betrayal, and that she didn't realize that lesbians keep their ex-lovers as friends. It didn't occur to her that Ann might fear losing Jackie and being abandoned once again.

In subsequent sessions, the therapist explored Jackie's recent history of unsatisfying relationships and heard more about the presence of Angie as the only stable feature of her life besides her job. The therapist thought to herself that Jackie might be understandably fearful of living with Ann, despite her wanting the relationship, and might be clinging more visibly to Angie as a result. If this were true, she might also be communicating this to Ann in subtle ways, thus intensifying Ann's distrust and fears.

The therapist also learned that when Jackie introduced Angie to Ann, Ann said that she felt like an outsider and that Jackie had seemed more interested in what Angie thought than in how Ann felt. Moreover, in trying to explain how important Angie was to her, Jackie had taken a rather emphatic stance, insisting on her right to be friends with whomever she wanted and lecturing her on the significance of lesbian friendships. When Ann went ballistic and gave Jackie an ultimatum about her deciding whom she wanted, Jackie became frightened and backed off. Thus, Jackie never sought to understand more about and empathize with what Ann might be feeling in the light of her recent loss. The therapist's pointing this out led to an exploration of whether Jackie might also be fearful of loss, not just of Angie, who was a stable person in her life, but also of Ann. This led to a very productive exploration of Jackie's early feelings of loss and abandonment in her family of origin and her many years of feeling alone as a lesbian when she did not have a mutually caring relationship. She also acknowledged her politically incorrect gut feeling that lesbian relationships don't last, even though she knew intellectually that this was not necessarily true and she knew many couples who had been together for years. She laughingly said, "I guess this is the remnants of internalize homophobia in me. Somewhere I think I'll wind up as a lonely alcoholic who commits suicide or ends up in a nursing home." Jackie also began to talk about her sense of losing her youth and her spark and her fears that Ann would begin to feel that Jackie was too old for her and would become tired of her. The therapist linked Jackie's fears to her inability to give Ann the reassurance and feeling of being special that she needed in order to feel valued and secure; to help her talk through her own fears of loss; and to create some boundaries with respect to her relationship with Angie, so that it did not take center stage.

As Jackie began to experience her own feelings more deeply, she spoke of how meeting Ann was a miracle for her. Although she had kept trying to meet others, at some level she had given up on being able to find a true companion. "Maybe I am holding on to Angie for dear life and making Ann feel like a second fiddle. Maybe she is being more stubborn about my relationship with Angie than she would if she felt surer about me." Although she wanted a quick resolution to the problem, Jackie realized that she had to try to repair her relationship with Ann before normalizing her relationship with Angie. After about eight weeks of treatment, with considerable trepidation Jackie did share with Ann what had been going on for her, including having lied to her about not talking to Angie, and also acknowledged her failure in having tried really to understand Ann's feelings. Much to her surprise, Ann did not become angry but also seemed relieved about their being able to talk more freely about their fears over a period of several weeks. Although Ann still had trouble emotionally understanding the strength of Jackie's attachment to Angie, she did understand intellectually Jackie's need for family. Feeling better about their relationship, Ann went along with Jackie's need to talk to and see Angie as an experiment but also indicated that she expected Jackie to put some limits on the frequency and nature of their contact.

A Longstanding Problem in Achieving Intimacy

In the final case example, the patient, a retired, financially secure lesbian, whose life was dotted with short-lived and unsuccessful romantic relationships, entered treatment because she feared that her new relationship would turn out as had all her others. Although this older patient's longstanding problems with intimacy appeared to be contributing to her past and current relationship difficulties, she also continued to show a lack of acceptance of herself as a lesbian. Moreover, she had never learned how to manage the give and take of a relationship and had difficulty differentiating between the realistic concerns of a woman her age and her apparently selfish needs and unrealistic fears. The treatment had a dual focus. The therapist took an active role in helping the patient with her current relationship difficulties. She also helped the patient to understand the basis of her low self-esteem and negative self-concept and their impact on her life and to rework major aspects of her lesbian identity.

Ruth, a 66-year-old retired editor, entered treatment feeling that her relationship with Sarah was going downhill quickly and that she had something to do with its decline. This distressed her greatly, because she viewed her relationship with Sarah as her last chance. She and Sarah had been seeing each other for a year but more recently had been fighting constantly or keeping emotionally distant. They rarely enjoyed each other any longer. Although they shared similar cultural interests and had been sexually attracted to each other initially, they also came from very different backgrounds and had vastly different attitudes about almost everything—money, food, furnishing, neatness, leisure activities, and politics. Although they wanted to live together, they could not agree on how to make this happen. Neither of their apartments was big enough for two people. They didn't want to give up their homes but couldn't find another place that they could afford. Moreover, Ruth felt that they should move slowly and Sarah interpreted this as rejection. Ruth felt unappreciated and put down by Sarah, who saw her as a spoiled princess who had to have her own way. Ruth said that Sarah accused her of being cold and withdrawn and not making her feel special. Sarah seemed to feel that Ruth was going to leave her at any moment and saw rejection in almost everything that Ruth did. Ruth acknowledged that she did withdraw and become withholding when she felt that Sarah criticized and ridiculed her. She felt that Sarah was overly suspicious, continually misinterpreted her intentions, and accused her of being uncaring, which made Ruth enraged. In order to keep herself from lashing out she withdrew further or sometimes told Sarah to leave her apartment.

Although Ruth felt she had been very successful professionally, she thought she had made a mess of her romantic relationships. "I just don't know if I've ever been cut out for this sort of thing. I don't know whether I just am attracted to the wrong women or I do something that pushes them away." In this and later sessions she recounted her early history of short-lived affairs with very attractive women who were emotionally immature and her unsuccessful attempts at any romantic relationship that lasted longer than a year or two, although she had remained casual friends with numerous ex-lovers. Ruth had been a workaholic as well as a heavy drinker. She spent long hours at her job and was promoted to a senior position. Although alcohol consumption did not seem to be a problem currently, all Ruth's past relationships were characterized by a lot of drinking. Ruth socialized in the bar scene and at private parties. Still closeted as a lesbian to her family and at work, she said, "You know, we didn't talk about our being lesbians in those days. You didn't dare do that if you wanted to be accepted. You couldn't be seen in a nice restaurant with another woman who looked like a dyke. Not like now. You went where you wouldn't be seen by anyone who was straight and where you felt comfortable." Ruth had two disastrous brief attempts at living with another woman that resulted in her losing her belongings and having to find another apartment when the relationships ended. Otherwise, she always lived alone both in a small apartment that she owned and in a summer house that she had reluctantly sold several years earlier, prior to her forced retirement. Although she shunned contacts with the lesbian community, she had built up a network of friends over the years.

Ruth's parents were both deceased, and she had two older male siblings. She described her mother as strict, emotionally distant, and critical and her father as loving but absent. When he was around, the parents fought a great deal. Ruth always feared her mother's disapproval and when Ruth discovered her attraction to women when she was an adolescent, she kept her feelings hidden. She did not have a sexual relationship with a woman until she was a senior in a college away from home, when an older professor befriended her and soon dropped her. She felt deeply ashamed of her lesbianism and remembers becoming both excited and depressed by reading *The Well of Loneliness* (Hall, 1928).

She buried herself in her schoolwork and, after college, in making her way professionally. She periodically socialized in lesbian and gay bars and women who were often affluent and attractive came on to her. If she felt attracted to them, she would become quickly involved sexually before she knew much about them. Sometimes they became friends later. She never felt fully comfortable with sex, however, and this has always puzzled her. When she did become involved in a relationship, she hid this from her family and up until the time of treatment, she had never brought a date or partner to a family event. When the therapist asked how she would have managed to live with a partner in a long-term relationship, given how she felt about keeping her lesbian identity hidden from her family and coworkers, Ruth responded that it would have been difficult. When the therapist asked if she felt that lesbians were damaged in some way, she replied, "Well, they are, aren't they? I know that's not politically correct, but it must be so." When the therapist suggested that it was possible that Ruth had never truly felt it was all right to be with another woman, given her negative feelings about her lesbianism, Ruth acknowledged that this might be true.

Although the therapist discussed with Ruth the possibility of inviting Sarah to a session so that she could better understand the problems they were having, Ruth did not think that Sarah, who also was in therapy, would agree to this. Based on the information that she had, the therapist thought that Ruth's contributions to the tensions in her relationship with Sarah were being caused by a complex interplay of factors. At the manifest level, Ruth had never learned how to communicate positively, to show affection, and to compromise. She wanted to have her own way, was easily frustrated and sensitive to criticism, and tended to suppress anger and withdraw. She did not seem sensitive to what appeared to be Sarah's need for overt displays of affection, reassurance, appreciation, and input into decisions. Needing to be admired and respected, she had trouble dealing with Sarah's tendency to become accusatory and critical. It seemed likely, however, that Ruth was fearful of the closeness in the relationship and that she distanced in order to protect herself. The prospect of living with Sarah brought up realistic concerns that reinforced her fear of intimacy. She was worried about her past relationship failures and about making a major change in her life at her age, especially if there was a risk that the change would not turn out well. At a deeper level, Ruth had always felt that her lesbianism reflected a character flaw, had hid her sexual orientation from her family, and continued to fear their disapproval. It seemed likely that her internalized homophobia was also playing a role in her relationship problems.

Ruth felt frustrated by Sarah and blamed her for many of the couple's problems but she also recognized that her own longstanding difficulties were contributing to the tension in the relationship. She was motivated to work on her own role. The treatment alternated between a focus on helping Ruth deal with current issues and conflicts in her relationship with Sarah and a focus on Ruth's family background, experiences as a lesbian, and relationship struggles.

In exploring Ruth's history, it came to light that her expectations of relationships were charged and unrealistic. She often began a relationship with a highly idealized view of romance and felt infatuated. She expected her partner to understand her every need without having to communicate but spent little time trying to develop the relationship. Disappointment soon set in, along with frustration, conflict, and loss of sexual interest.

As noted earlier, the treatment initially had a dual focus. The therapist interpreted some of the issues that Ruth was having in her relationship with Sarah as normal, given the fact that she had never been in or learned to negotiate a committed relationship, lacked positive relational models and experiences, and did not know how to deal with conflict effectively. She validated some of Ruth's concerns about moving too quickly. Alternatively, the therapist focused on Ruth's unrealistic expectations, fears and communication problems, and patterns of withdrawal. The therapist helped Ruth to develop greater ability to verbalize her own needs and express her frustrations, to empathize with Sarah's needs and feelings, and to modify her expectations about what constituted a good relationship.

Although Ruth was 66, she had never talked with anyone about her experiences growing up, particularly with respect to the emergence of her feelings of attraction to other women and the impact her lesbianism had on her life choices and behavior. The therapist, also a lesbian, was 10 years younger than Ruth and had come out later in her own life. She had heard about but had not shared the experiences that Ruth had in the period of her coming out. Listening to Ruth tell what it was like to be in bars and public places and what gays talked about was instructive for her. Ruth seemed to enjoy the therapist's interest in her life and the therapeutic bond strengthened. At the same, the therapist was able to help Ruth reflect on how her early experiences led her to internalize certain negative attitudes toward herself and how, in turn, they affected her tendency to isolate herself, work long hours, and become involved in unsatisfactory relationships with other women. The therapist questioned some of Ruth's basic assumptions about herself and lesbianism and helped her to reframe her own experiences. Ruth began to understand the roots of her difficulties in showing affection and verbalizing appreciation. She saw that these characteristics were not only related to her experiences and identification with a somewhat cold and nonexpressive mother but also to her having exercised restraint on any show of affection with women from the time she was an adolescent because of her fear of exposure. The therapeutic process also helped Ruth to understand how her guilt about becoming involved in a committed lesbian relationship, her need for admiration, and her fear of becoming the prisoner of a critical mother had influenced and were continuing to influence her.

Ruth was able to practice new behaviors with Sarah and the relationship improved considerably, although problems remained, particularly around the issue of living together. At this juncture, Sarah agreed to seek couple treatment with Ruth so that they could work on their issues jointly.

Chapter 8

Issues in Midlife and Later Life
Clinical Considerations

The events of midlife and later life present unique challenges and opportunities. Most of the literature on lesbians addresses their coming-out experiences and relationships in adolescence and young adulthood. Their life course in later decades is not well delineated. Moreover, many stereotypes still exist regarding what lesbians are like when they age, such as the view that the older lesbian is a lonely and isolated woman who looks to her cats and alcohol for comfort and companionship. Although midlife and later life often reflect themes from the past, significant changes in identity are also possible (Kertzner and Sved, 1996). The way a lesbian responds to challenges at different life stages depends on her personality dynamics, strengths and characteristic ways of coping, degree of comfort with her lesbian identity, nature of her interpersonal relationships, and degree of support from her family and immediate social environment, the society, and the culture. As society has evolved in its greater acceptance of gays and lesbians and as they are more visible and confident, there is reason to believe that their life course reflects greater options than was true of previous generations. At the same time, discriminatory policies and barriers to full participation and inclusion still remain and have important consequences. It is important for clinicians to understand the life experiences of lesbians in midlife and later life.

General Considerations

Midlife lesbians are a diverse group, but, according to Kimmel and Sang (1995), white middle-class lesbians generally describe this period as the best in their lives. This has a number of possible explanations. Usually having coped with becoming economically self-sufficient since early adulthood rather than with performing the role of housewife or parent, they do not necessarily experience the empty-nest syndrome or the need to reenter the world of work after a long absence as they enter their 40s and 50s. Thus, lesbians have greater continuity in their work identities than heterosexual women who follow more traditional paths. This situation may be changing, as more lesbians are raising children than previously and opting to give up their careers (a path chosen by many heterosexually identified women) and as more heterosexually identified women maintain their work roles. Because lesbians usually have had to deal with the pressures of the work world, many have developed a sense of mastery and self-confidence in this area of their lives. Some lesbians come out for the first time in midlife; but many of those who have been out for most of their adult lives feel that they have paid their dues, are more self-accepting, and feel less concerned about others' disapproval. They come to midlife with a greater sense of freedom and power than they had previously. They want to enjoy their lives. Many, although by no means all, are in committed, long-term relationships with other women, derive satisfactions from their friendship networks, and are involved in the community.

Kimmel and Sang (1995) also point out potential problem areas. For example, because of having to depend on themselves financially and being subject to discrimination with respect to wages and possibilities for career advancement compared to men, lesbians are not necessarily financially secure in midlife and later life, despite their many years of gainful employment. They may face having to work long past the usual retirement age or to find ways to cut expenses. Financial planning for retirement becomes a necessity. Moreover, although the majority of lesbians are in couple relationships, they are much more likely to be living alone than their heterosexual counterparts and to look to their friends rather than family for support and concrete assistance. Many lesbians remain closeted as they age. It also has been noted that, in addition to having to deal with the health issues that all women have to face in midlife and later life, lesbians appear to be at greater risk for certain diseases. At the same time, they often have to deal with insensitive health care providers who lack knowledge about their specific concerns. Finally, although many major cities in the United States offer some assistance to aged lesbians and gay men, overall services are lacking.

Pressures on Long-Term Relationships

Both internal and external stresses can create conflict and challenges for midlife lesbian couples. Some of the internal pressures arise when the partners have different and sometimes conflicting goals and ambitions or when one wishes to change the relational dynamics with respect to power, decision making, autonomy, intimacy, socializing, coming out to the outside world, or sexuality. Some of the external stresses arise because of a lack of outside supports and recognition of the relationship, limitations on coming out, conflict with families of origin, and the effects of legal, economic, institutional, and societal discrimination (Falco, 1991, pp. 109–113).

Lesbian relationships differ considerably with respect to whether couples share power and decision making equally or are skewed. As with heterosexual couples, sometimes one partner's needs appear to dominate the relationship, especially if that person is financially more successful. When a pattern of inequality has been established, one partner may wish to change it, even if the relational dynamics have seemed to work for the couple previously.

Many women value relatedness and connection rather than separateness and autonomy. Although they express their need for connection in different ways, lesbian couples often achieve considerable emotional intimacy while each partner is able to express her own self-needs. A potentially problematic pattern found in lesbian relationships, however, is the couple's tendency to spend most of their nonwork time together. Sometimes each partner lacks separate friends and does not pursue individual interests. Some couples tend to isolate themselves from others. Although the couple may enjoy their close connection, which is sometimes attributed to a tendency to merge, the impetus to change this pattern also may arise if one or both members become frightened of their mutual dependency or feel stifled and lacking in sufficient autonomy and separateness. In another relational pattern, which seems to be less usual among two women, members of the couple may be organized around maintaining their separateness. In this instance, one partner may begin to feel a greater need for connection and intimacy. In yet a third pattern, the couple alternates back and forth between intense closeness and distancing behavior.

When members of a midlife couple are committed to their relationship, affairs that occur need to be understood as not only or primarily based on the attractiveness of a third person's real qualities but as a means of coping with the stresses of the relationship. An affair may represent the attempt by one member of a couple to get needs met that are being frustrated in the relationship, to express sexuality outside the intimacy of the couple relationship, or to deal with the fears associated with closeness, stability, and dependency (Slater, 1994).

The external stresses that affect lesbian relationships arise from the frequent lack of the support and recognition of family members. They are not available to celebrate rituals such as anniversaries, may refuse to invite the couple to family gatherings, and may not recognize a partner's rights with respect to medical decisions, housing, or finances. Moreover, the continuing legal, economic, and social discrimination that exists can have a significant impact on the couple.

Becoming a Parent

Unlike previous generations of lesbian mothers who conceived their children predominantly within heterosexual marriages and often were beset by custody issues, many lesbians today are choosing to have children by means of a private sperm donor, sperm donor programs, or adoption. They do not equate being a lesbian with having to give up the parenting role, and they feel more confident about being able to parent their children, because of the greater acceptance of nontraditional forms of parenting and access to a wide variety of social and legal resources.

Despite this major change, the decision to have a child, the practices of insemination and adoption, the process of coparenting, and the raising of a child in the face of continuing homophobic attitudes are often challenging. Although lesbian parenting is receiving increasing attention, this activity has few role models and little in the way of guides. It is, therefore, important for clinicians to make themselves aware of the unique challenges that face lesbian couples interested in creating families.

Even if both members of a lesbian couple may feel ready or at least agree to have a child, some of the stressful issues that come up revolve around the fact that traditional notions of parenting are often not operative in these families. For example, the question of who the mother of the child will be does not automatically follow from biological considerations but tends to be a matter of emotional or practical preference. Other questions arise, such as: What will the nonbiological parent be called? Will the parenting be shared equally? If he is known, will the donor play a role in family life? Who are the grandparents? Are the parents of the donor included? Is it desirable, as well as possible, for the nonbiological mother to adopt her partner's child legally? Once the couple has the child, lesbians, like their heterosexual counterparts, are also subject to feelings of jealousy and competition.

In many instances, parents, siblings, and extended family members are happy that a lesbian or lesbian couple is planning to have a child.

Increasingly, certain churches, synagogues, and other religious or spiritual centers allow children of lesbian parents to participate in naming ceremonies and other rituals. In other situations, the family may be lukewarm, negative, discouraging, and nonsupportive, or the lesbian couple may be estranged from their families and excluded from participation in religious occasions.

Lesbian parents need to plan where they want to live and how to select a school for their child. It is preferable to be in a place that has more diversity, greater acceptance of difference, potential resources, and supports. It is difficult when no other lesbian parents are nearby or when a child of lesbian parents is ridiculed, excluded, or stigmatized.

As time goes on, the parents will need to explain the nature of lesbian relationships to their young and adolescent children and to answer their questions about why their family is different. It also may be necessary to deal with the effects of questions or comments by the child's peers or with the continuing insensitivity or outright discrimination of teachers, counselors, and health personnel. Perhaps more difficult for the parents is their ability to deal with their children's reactions to their lesbianism. Even children and adolescents who enjoy loving relationships with their lesbian parents may go through different phases in their ability to accept and feel pride in who their parents are.

Finally, like heterosexual parents, lesbian couples sometimes separate. Financial, custody, and visitation issues may become complicated and contentious, especially because of the lingering lack of legal protection for nonbiological parents and grandparents.

Impact of Physical Illness

Midlife lesbians need to deal with the effects of menopause, the use of hormone replacement therapy, and a variety of other health issues, not the least of which is the possibility that lesbians, particularly those who are not childbearing, may be at increased risk for developing breast and ovarian cancer. The main problems with respect to the health concerns of lesbians stem from the health care system's lack of knowledge of lesbian health issues and its treatment of lesbians as if they are invisible (Kertzner and Sved, 1996). Moreover, lesbians may experience a lack of access to health care. When lesbians do receive services, health care personnel who are insensitive to their needs and concerns and can create obstacles that limit their partners' ability to visit, to be involved in decision making, and to receive support when they become the primary caretakers.

Parental Caretaking

Being a caretaker for an elderly or aging parent can be fraught with difficulties for any daughter but it can also have its rewards. Knowing that one is giving back to a loving parent whom one loves can make one feel good. This situation becomes more problematic if relationships with the parents have been strained, conflicted, or estranged. Such is the case when the lesbian caretaker has experienced disapproval and rejection by her family. Although it is possible that some repair of past injuries and some positive resolution can occur under certain circumstances, this may not always be possible. The situation can be especially difficult if the lesbian must return to a locale in which others are not aware of or continue to stigmatize her lesbianism. Under these circumstances, not only are past wounds and conflicts reactivated, but the lesbian also must continue to be closeted. She may then be deprived of the normal support that she might receive from others as well as from a partner, if her significant other is not free to participate. An alternative scenario is that intense family conflict occurs over financial issues and that siblings or other family members may attempt to exclude the lesbian from receiving a fair share of her inheritance on the basis of her sexual identity and lack of children. Legal assistance may be necessary but this is no guarantee that justice will win.

Planning for Retirement and Being Dependent

Because many aging lesbians achieve emotional and financial self-reliance, enjoy long-term couple relationships or their single life, develop solid networks of support, and plan well for their retirement years, they are able to live out their lives in the manner that they have chosen. For some, this may mean relocating to an environment that is friendly to lesbians and gays and that has an active gay and lesbian community. Although making this type of change can create stress, conflict, losses, and dislocation, the results may far outweigh the temporary negative effects.

For other lesbians, growing older can usher in dependence. Having been estranged from their families and lacking family support, they are dependent on their partners and friendship networks. Those lesbians who experience the death or deterioration of their partners or whose friendship networks dwindle over the years may be quite alone. Some remain connected to organizations that provide services and sources of recreation. Others are more isolated. Lesbians who came out during more oppressive eras may have maintained a closeted existence that they adopted in their earlier life for protection. They may be reluctant to disclose their sexual orientation to social service agencies, because they fear that they will be treated poorly. If they become ill or disabled, they may have to depend on health care providers who are homophobic or who may just not have experience with gay people. Moreover, although gay-friendly and gay senior organizations and retirement homes are growing in number, some older lesbians may not live in a geographical location that has such services or may not have the financial resources to avail themselves of more appropriate resources.

Dissatisfaction with a Longstanding Relationship

Melinda's case shows the dissatisfaction that arose in one partner in a lesbian relationship and the therapist's efforts to help the patient identify her relational needs and her tendency to replicate old patterns and to cope more effectively with her life.

Melinda, a 45-year-old Puerto Rican interior designer, was in a 12-year relationship with a successful novelist when she entered treatment for depression and episodes of extreme anxiety and irritability. She attributed these states to her increasing dissatisfaction with her domestic life and her increasing thoughts of separating from her partner, Harriet. Although Melinda still loved Harriet, she felt that they had become more like siblings than romantic partners, a state of affairs that appeared to suit Harriet more than Melinda.

In early sessions, Melinda presented as an attractive, striking, insightful, and warm person who revealed her creativity and design talents in her stylish clothes and unusual application of makeup. The therapist thought the patient used her physical attributes and unique fashion sense to shore up her brittle sense of self, which was evident in the ethereal quality of her engagement in the therapeutic relationship. When the therapist probed about the discrepancy between her powerful presentation and the elusive manner in which she interacted with the therapist, Melinda revealed that her behavior was driven by her fear of being humiliated by the therapist's harsh judgments about her incompetence. Projecting her own disparaging thoughts onto the therapist, she did not feel safe in revealing her true feelings about herself and her situation.

Gradually, Melinda disclosed her deep sense of failure in managing her career and her intense envy of Harriet's professional success. She resented the ways in which Harriet used financial generosity to keep friends and new disciples attached to her. She described how Harriet often picked up expensive tabs and was the first to rescue friends in crisis. Melinda also depicted Harriet's friends as frequently complaining about her self-absorption and insensitivity. Harriet surrounded herself with an entourage of adoring fans, who were less accomplished but who provided her with admiration and attention. She had difficulty recognizing and appreciating others' individual uniqueness and, therefore, was unable to develop deep intimacies with them. Sometimes Harriet would invite large groups of people over to the house or out to dinner but would then withdraw, leaving Melinda to tend to her guests.

Melinda was frustrated by Harriet's denial of problems in their relationship and her refusal to discuss them. At the same time, Melinda thought that Harriet expressed her dissatisfaction by overtly flirting with other women in Melinda's presence at social events. Because Melinda was aware of Harriet's sexual inhibitions, she did not think that Harriet would have sex with another woman. Eventually, Melinda's anger and frustration drove her into a number of risky affairs with a few of their mutual friends and one of Harriet's close work associates.

Melinda was embarrassed by her financial dependence on Harriet and her fear of losing the lifestyle to which she was accustomed. Complicating matters, Harriet owned the apartment in which Melinda's ailing parents lived. Although Melinda believed that Harriet would continue to support her financially if they separated, Melinda dreaded being subjected to Harriet's control. She thought that Harriet would decide where she would live and dole out her monthly expenses based on her mood. Knowing Harriet's vanity, she imagined she would be obliged to maintain a passive-dependent and subservient demeanor with Harriet. Melinda expressed considerable anger when she thought about the financial and legal protections allowed to straight women who adopted traditional marital roles by managing the household and the social duties of their husbands' careers. Melinda also feared falling into a deep depression were she to leave Harriet.

The therapist learned that the first few years of Melinda and Harriet's relationship reflected the following dynamics. Melinda, who lacked self-confidence and felt ashamed of her family's poverty and humble origins, was attracted to Harriet's sense of power, intelligence, energy, and career and financial success. Standing in Harriet's shadow, Melinda idealized Harriet and basked in the illusion of her love and admiration. Harriet's attention and generous financial support felt nurturing and protective. Melinda fantasized that her talents and ambitions would in due course be transformed to the level of her lover's professional achievements. Although the couple had sex early in their relationship, their sexual relationship was never active. It soon became evident that Harriet had little interest in emotional or sexual intimacy and had only participated sexually to ensnare Melinda. As the years passed, Melinda's dream of Harriet's repairing her inadequacies failed to have the same self-esteem–restoring effects that it once had. Harriet's excessive need to be shown loyalty and deference began to feel like a burden.

The therapist thought longer-standing difficulties were contributing to Melinda's current problems. Seeing herself as a talented and creative person who lacked the emotional resources and confidence to succeed on her own had been a familiar experience in her family. Melinda closely identified with her mother, a simple woman from a poor family in Puerto Rico, who spent her life bolstering her father, a laborer who was often unemployed. Although her mother was dutiful as a parent, she was preoccupied and often depressed. Melinda recalled feeling that she would never be able to leave the deteriorated neighborhood in which the family lived. A pretty and cute light-skinned child, Melinda was well liked by her teachers, who encouraged her artistic abilities. Melinda and her two brothers developed a close bond from early childhood. They were much older than Melinda, assumed a paternal attitude toward her, and played an influential role in her life. She and her brothers all turned out to be gay and supported one another. Her brothers were hard-working and ambitious, and, with Melinda's help, they built a thriving interior design business. As a little girl and later as a business partner, Melinda idealized her brothers' intelligence, professional savvy, and accomplishments. A teenager during the inception of the business, Melinda was strongly encouraged to contribute to the creative aspects of the business, whereas her brothers handled the business relationships and financial aspects of the firm. Sadly, her brothers' health declined during similar time frames and they died within six months of each other in the late 1980s. Alone for the first time and devastated over their deaths, Melinda attempted to maintain the business but failed. The demise of the business haunted Melinda because she felt she had lost, owing to what she believed her own incompetence, the only tangible tie to her brothers.

In addition to helping Melinda to identify her expectations of Harriet and sources of her feelings of disappointment and frustration, the therapist focused on how Melinda had replicated an early relational configuration with her brothers in her relationship with Harriet. Beginning very early in life with her brothers, she tended, in all types of relationships, to seek out people whom she considered more capable and attractive than she felt herself to be. Her devoted and submissive stance in these relationships was driven by her need to be emotionally replenished by an idealized other who valued her, until some disappointing event or experience destroyed her fantasy, leaving her feeling depressed, unfulfilled, and without hope. The therapist also helped Melinda to develop more compassion for her own life struggles, particularly in the light of such emotionally overwhelming circumstances as the loss of both her brothers and the business. In addition, the therapist and patient together created plausible interpretations about how Melinda's family had encouraged a certain type of dependency that made it difficult for her to pursue her individual ambitions autonomously. The therapist also interpreted Melinda's taking on a role with Harriet that she played in her family, of the one who subjugates her own passion and ambitions for the advancement and achievement of others. With a new appreciation of her own life experiences, Melinda was able to develop more clarity about her relationship with Harriet and begin to get in touch with her own needs and goals.

The therapist believed that the patient had developed sufficient emotional resources for her old object ties to be challenged. The therapist confronted the acquiescent manner in which she accepted the therapist's interpretations and viewpoints even when Melinda herself had equally important or better interpretations of her experience. Melinda, strengthened by the therapeutic relationship, which was based on mutual respect and enjoyment, began to integrate into her social life broader and more complex relationships with friends and work associates. She began to refrain from acting out by not having trysts with close associates, and, over time, her depressed moods decreased. Sleeping with her close friends had helped her to appreciate the deeper emotional connection she was capable of. With these friends, she evolved more intense and supportive relationships, even after they stopped having sex together.

Melinda no longer relied on Harriet for emotional sustenance and had less conflict with her, and the couple got along better superficially. Nevertheless, Melinda continued to feel unfulfilled in the relationship and wished to leave it. Her career conflicts and poor financial circumstances prevented this because Melinda felt that she could not return to merely subsisting financially in the way she had done previously in her life. On one hand, she longed for the type of financial settlement that her divorced heterosexual friends had obtained, and she verbalized her anger at the poor ways in which lesbians were treated by society. Alternatively, she realized that she had to overcome her impediments to building her career and earning more money on her own. This became a major focus of the next phase of treatment.

Disruption of a Longstanding Relational Pattern

Like the case of Melinda, Monica's example also shows the consequences of one partner's wish to change the relational dynamics of a long-term couple. It shows how the therapist helped the patient to recognize the unverbalized needs that led to a precipitous action that unbalanced the relationship and to improve her ability to be a good partner.

Monica, age 50, sought treatment because she had taken an action that created problems in her relationship with her partner, Brenda. In addition to their romantic partnership of seven years, Monica had been Brenda's boss for 17 years. Without discussing her intentions with Brenda, Monica suddenly dissolved their professional tie by taking a prestigious position as an editor for a widely read local magazine. She said that she wanted to actualize her career ambitions and realized that time was passing. This decision to pursue her independent career interests made Brenda feel betrayed and rejected and sent her into an agitated emotional state that Monica did not know how to handle. In addition, Brenda felt insecure and panicky about having to pursue new work opportunities on her own. Feeling devastated by Monica's actions and insensitivity, Brenda bombarded Monica with a litany of complaints that had been brewing for a long time. The more emotionally tuned in and vocal of the two, Brenda accused Monica of using her and not appreciating her devotion and support. She told Monica that she had felt abandoned because of Monica's absorption in her career and their lack of emotional intimacy. Feeling devalued and rejected, she was in no mood for sex. She also objected to the financial support Monica provided for her ex-partner and she complained of Monica's tendency to invite, without her permission, other former partners to family and social events. Finally, she accused Monica of not being committed to her because Monica avoided confronting her parents' opposition to their making each other the primary beneficiary of their estates and protecting Brenda financially. Brenda believed that Monica's parents were homophobic. In addition, Brenda, who had been living in Monica's apartment during their relationship and paying half of the mortgage, wanted further protection by having her name put on the deed. Monica felt that this complaint was unfounded and that she had been hoping that Brenda would take an active role in doing the legwork for the wills and deed although she had never asked her to do so.

Although the therapist initially found Monica to be extremely engaging, she could see why others viewed her of being self-absorbed and insensitive. She seemed to have difficulty understanding others' feelings that differed or conflicted with her own needs. Additionally, Monica often humorously rejected and devalued the therapist's interpretations and comments by calling them too emotionally elaborate and long-winded. The therapist decided not to confront these aspects of the transference until a firmer working relationship was established and the patient would be able to consider her interpretations seriously.

The therapist speculated that Monica, in addition to acting on her own career ambitions without regard to Brenda's feelings, was not in touch with her desire to rework the symbiotic nature of the couple's attachment that was evident both in their romantic relationship and work lives. It seemed that, for many years, each partner had functioned emotionally to stabilize the other's deep sense of inadequacy. For Monica, Brenda voiced emotional experiences that Monica had trouble grasping. She relied on Brenda's substantial intelligence and emotionally expressive and sensitive nature to guide her in arenas she felt ill-equipped to negotiate. Monica relied on Brenda to help her to manage her staff and to attend to many of the administrative aspects of her position that were not part of Brenda's job responsibilities. For Brenda, the couple's relationship seemed to be an extension of the symbiotic bond she had had with her alcoholic mother. In both relationships, she had difficulty separating her own needs and substantial accomplishments from those of others with whom she was intimately involved.

During the early phase of treatment, Monica presented herself as a victim of Brenda's relentless complaints, did not comprehend Brenda's subjective experience, and would not focus on her own contribution to the couple's problems. She lacked awareness of how her actions and her boasting about being at the top of her game unsettled Brenda. She argued that Brenda's insecurity was unfounded because she had achieved considerable respect in her field and was now thriving in a new position. Monica also rebuffed Brenda's complaints about how her inclusion of her ex-lovers in their social lives played a role in their unsatisfying romantic intimacy.

The therapist's persistent inquiry into Monica's feelings and experience revealed how abandoned she felt by Brenda's complaints and withdrawal of support. Deeper exploration traced these experiences to an earlier sense of abandonment in Monica's life. Her father, an extremely volatile and domineering man, although enormously bitter about his own failed business ventures, instilled in Monica an unwavering sense of herself as a person who could achieve unlimited success in her chosen career. During her childhood, Monica's father would become euphoric when she did well in school and won academic achievement awards. This attention from her father, although thrilling and confidence-building in her educational endeavors, did not help her to cope with the mean-spirited remarks she received from schoolmates about her being overweight and "dykey." Her parents turned a blind eye to her emotional struggles around her weight and her sexual orientation. The treatment revived memories of her seeking emotional support from parents who responded by saying things like, "If you think you are fat, lose weight," and, "If you're a lesbian, your life isn't going to be easy." Monica felt devastated by her parents' withdrawal in these emotional arenas.

As the therapeutic bond became stronger, Monica became less reject-ing of the therapist's drawing parallels between the dynamics of her relationship with Brenda and her parents. She began to recognize that, like her parents, she tended to withdraw emotionally when Brenda expressed her vulnerability. Over time, she also saw how she had internalized the traumatic aspects of her parents' insensitivity and lack of attunement by berating herself for being fat, in spite of her many honest attempts to control her weight.

Gradually, the therapist's genuineness, understanding, and empathic acceptance of Monica's profound vulnerability enabled more trust to evolve. This permitted the patient and therapist to become immersed in a more intensive exploration of the transference–countertransference dynamics, permitting a deepening of the therapeutic work. Since the therapist believed that Monica could now tolerate disruptions in their relationship, she chose to self-disclose her experience of the patient when her behavior was aggressive and domineering. Although the therapist's confrontation was uncomfortable for Monica, it enabled her to remember experiences she had as a child with her father, in which she felt suffocated by his overbearing nature. During such episodes she would withdraw to her bedroom and cry about her father's nasty and insensitive treatment of her. This memory and the therapist's self-disclosure enabled Monica to understand how her own behavior affected Brenda. Like her father, Monica had trouble being compassionate when someone close expressed vulnerability.

At one point in the treatment, it became apparent that Monica had developed and maintained a large circle of significant others, many of whom were former partners, in order to feel validated in her lesbianism. Their having fought family and cultural oppression together encouraged the establishment of powerful emotional bonds that outlived their ro-mantic attachments. This family of choice continued to provide ego-building supports and was a great source of comfort for them all.

Through a discussion of the significance of these friendships, the therapist helped Monica to appreciate that she was making Brenda feel like a second-class citizen and not showing her that she was special. Monica began to show some empathy for her partner's experience. Without losing touch with her own need to maintain strong ties with her friends, Monica decided to see her friends separately or to consult with Brenda before inviting them over.

In regard to her longest and deepest past relationship with the woman whom she continued to support financially, Monica and the therapist evolved a new understanding of the relational dynamics of that attachment. Dawn, who was 13 years older than Monica, embodied many of the same contradictory personality characteristics as Monica's father. In this relationship, however, she reenacted the regressive tie to her father by being the more fragile party. On one hand, Dawn expressed great admiration for Monica's intellectual abilities; on the other hand, she belittled her when she emotionally exposed herself. Although Monica continued to support Dawn once she had insight into these dynamics, she no longer felt the deep urgency to placate her when her Dawn engaged in such behavior.

The treatment process also enabled Monica to understand how her parents' negativity about her lesbianism had made her feel alienated and estranged from them in spite of their continued contact. Monica was able to confront her parents about their lack of recognition of her lesbian relationship as equal to that of a heterosexual marriage and their insistence that "family money" not be willed to Brenda. Likewise, Monica and Brenda made a date with a lawyer to set in motion the changing of the deed to their apartment. Most striking, however, was the couple's ability to move from a symbiotic attachment to one in which each partner was able to consider and value the other's needs.

Impact of a Lesbian Partner's Decision to Become Pregnant

A lesbian patient in a committed same-sex relationship, Maureen sought treatment for issues centered on her unsuccessful efforts to become pregnant. The treatment helped her to deal not only with the self-doubts that she had about her decision to become a parent but also with ongoing issues in her relationship with her partner even after the baby was born.

Maureen, an Irish Catholic 38-year-old television producer for a news magazine show, sought treatment with a lesbian therapist because of two failed attempts at artificial insemination, which were causing her to doubt her decision to become pregnant. She was having trouble deciding whether to proceed further with the insemination process but was reluctant to discuss this with Eva, her partner. She was worried about how her difficulty conceiving and her mood swings during and after the insemination cycles were affecting Eva, who was eager for the couple to have a baby. She was fearful that Eva would become profoundly disappointed and lose interest in her if Maureen was not able to conceive. Maureen reported that the couple found themselves easily irritated with each other and were less sexually intimate than usual. Maureen began to feel that their five-year relationship was shaky.

Maureen described Eva, who was five years younger than she and a freelance producer, as having higher aspirations for her career and more confidence than Maureen. She also described Eva as being emotionally immature and drinking too much at times to cope with the boredom and frustration she experienced when spells of unemployment thwarted her substantial professional ambition.

Early in the treatment, it became evident that Maureen's parents' uneasiness about children born out of artificial insemination was contributing to her questioning her decision to continue with this process. Although they had reconciled themselves to her lesbianism, her parents considered conception outside heterosexual marriage unnatural. Devout Catholics who were active in their local religious community, they preferred the couple to adopt. Although Maureen did not feel conflicted about her choice, she worried that her parents would not treat her biological child in the same manner as their other grandchildren and that her child would feel rejected. Maureen desperately wanted her child to have the experience of the connections that she had while growing up. Moreover, she was concerned that she would not be able to rely on her parents to provide the support that a child of lesbian parents might need in order to find a buffer against potential negative attitudes and stigmatization. Maureen and Eva had enjoyed close friendships with their friends, who did not have children themselves, but recently had felt some distancing from them. Although Eva's family was more encouraging, she did not have the close ties that Maureen had with her family.

The therapist thought that several factors were contributing to Maureen's dilemma. As with most couples who undergo artificial insemination, the stress of the procedures and her difficulty conceiving undoubtedly were bringing about self-doubt and couple conflict. The lack of family support and the subtle withdrawal of friends also seemed to be exacerbating the couple's feelings of aloneness. Additionally, Maureen was not able to share her burdensome feelings with Eva. Maureen also showed, however, longstanding issues around self-esteem and feelings of abandonment that seemed to be influencing her current reactions. In exploring her background, the therapist was struck by Maureen's incapacity to sustain a positive sense of self in the face of any conflict. This appeared to be a derivative of her strong identification with her mother. Although her mother had graduated from college in an age when this was unusual for women, like other women of her generation, she forfeited her dream of a law career to cultural and family pressures to marry and start a family. Nevertheless, she devalued her own accomplishments as a mother, wife, and active community volunteer and seemed to derive vicarious satisfaction and emotional sustenance from her husband's career ambitions and attention to her. Maureen believed that, at times in the marriage, her mother doubted her husband's commitment to her because of his refusal to listen to her concerns about their relationship and his unwillingness to discuss or work on the problematic aspects of the marriage.

After a period of empathizing with the multiple sources of stress that Maureen was experiencing and helping her to put this in a normal context, the therapist began to identify Maureen's reenactment of past relational configurations in her relationship with Eva. She focused on Maureen's identification with her mother as an insecure partner who devalued her own accomplishments, needed constant reassurance of her lover's interest, and was unable to communicate her feelings or to cause conflict. Additionally, she learned how she maintained a regressive tie to her parents by not confronting them about their ambivalence about her lesbianism and wish to have a child.

The therapist worked with Maureen on taking more risks in communicating her feelings to Eva and on sustaining her ability to discuss areas of concern and conflict. Maureen was able to talk to Eva about her fears of being abandoned and her distress over Eva's drinking. The couple reaffirmed their commitment to have a biological child, and they both decided to attend a prospective parents group at the local gay, lesbian, bisexual, and transgender (GLBT) center to meet other couples who were trying to have children. With the therapist's and Eva's encouragement, Maureen became more assertive with her family. She engaged her parents in a discussion about their homophobic attitudes toward the insemination process. Although her parents were defensive and reiterated their concerns initially, Maureen's mother called her soon after their discussion and told her that she and her husband just wanted Maureen to be happy and that they would try to accept her decision.

Maureen's fourth try at insemination succeeded and the pregnancy and birth of a daughter went smoothly. Before the birth, each partner chose a role in the parenting process that seemed comfortable. Maureen was to become the primary caretaker and Eva would share in the responsibilities. Because the couple needed money and Eva's income was higher, they decided that Eva would continue working and Maureen would take a year's leave from work and then try to get an early shift when she returned full time. Soon after the baby's birth, however, Eva, who initially had no interest in being a birth mother, began to become envious and excluded from the biological mother–baby relationship. Although Maureen tried to attend to Eva's needs and encouraged her to have her own biological child when the couple were emotionally and financially capable of supporting a larger family, she secretly believed that her partner was not emotionally suited to be a primary parent. Eva's larger-than-life personality and penchant to engage in impulsive whims, which were part of what made her attractive to Maureen, caused her anxiety when she entertained sharing her thoughts with her partner.

The therapist spent a considerable amount of time exploring with Maureen her anxiety about challenging Eva's general tendency toward competitiveness, which was having a disturbing effect on their domestic lives. Like her mother, she had chosen a partner who embodied a charisma and strength of personality that she coveted. Facing Eva's weaknesses was particularly jarring. In so doing, she had to confront on a deeper level her own loss in having a relationship with a partner who had some major flaws. Moving into the more adult competent role with her partner enabled Maureen to relate to Eva more realistically and nonjudgmentally. In turn, Eva became more supportive of Maureen's pursuit of her own personal and professional needs. Eva did not pursue having her own biological child and the couple made strides in managing their coparenting roles in a harmonious manner.

Impact of a Lesbian's Serious Health Problem

Connie had the double trouble of having to deal with her partner's illnesses and her parents' deterioration and difficulty taking care of themselves. Both situations drained her and brought up difficult emotional issues, which the treatment helped her to work through.

Connie was 48 when she entered treatment at the strong urging of her office manager at a New York City law firm, where she was employed as a legal assistant. Her supervisor had received numerous complaints about Connie's irritability and shortness with coworkers and the attorneys for whom she worked, her increasing careless errors, and her uncharacteristic absences. Her supervisor knew that Connie was dealing with many personal stresses and had cut her some slack but felt compelled to be firm with Connie about the need to improve her work performance.

In her initial session, Connie told the therapist that she had contemplated coming to therapy before but had put it off because she did not know how she would fit it into her already overburdened life. As she related her recent difficulties, Connie began to cry and commented, "I guess I do need to talk to someone. I feel like I'm losing it." The therapist soon learned that Connie was dealing with several major life events that had occurred in close proximity to one another. Two years earlier, Alice, her female partner of 10 years, had been diagnosed with breast cancer. She underwent a lumpectomy and a course of radiation therapy. A year and a half later, Alice was diagnosed with ovarian cancer and underwent extensive surgery and a short course of chemotherapy. Because both cancers were caught in an early stage, she had an excellent prognosis but the two separate diseases and treatments had taken a physical and emotional toll on the couple. They had some close friends but had not felt like socializing. They had few family supports and were both closeted at work.

Connie expressed some anger when she described her experiences with the health care system. She said that during Alice's first bout of cancer, Connie had a very hard time getting Alice's doctors to give her information. They seemed not to acknowledge her relationship with Alice and continued to ignore her when she forced the issue. The couple fared better during the second episode when they sought out a surgeon and an oncologist who were recommended to them by a friend. On at least one occasion, however, Connie had to ask the surgeon to intercede on her behalf with the nursing staff at the hospital where Alice underwent surgery, because they would not give Connie permission to stay overnight in Alice's room right after her operation.

In addition to dealing with Alice's illnesses and treatments, six months before Connie entered treatment and at the same time that Alice was diagnosed for the second time, Connie's 79-year-old father, who lived in a suburb of Boston with Connie's mother, had an incapacitating stroke. He was sent to a nursing home because his 78-year-old wife was not up to taking care of him at home. Prior to the stroke, he had carried the brunt of household responsibility. Connie's two older brothers and their wives looked in on the mother but resented Connie's lack of involvement, despite the fact that her relationship with the family had been strained for many years because of their disapproval of her lesbianism. Although her siblings and parents knew that she was living in a committed relationship with another woman who was undergoing cancer treatment, they nevertheless told her that she should come back to

Massachusetts and take care of her mother. They minimized her concerns and were unable to understand the fact that Alice needed her and that Connie did not want to be separated from Alice at this time. Accusing Connie of being selfish and irresponsible, her brothers also told her that they would make sure she never inherited a dime from the small estate her parents would leave when they died. Connie told the therapist that their threats did not bother her because she never had any interest in her parents' money. What upset her was that they succeeded in making her feel guilty even though she knew that she was doing the right thing by staying with Alice. Connie decided that she would try to visit her mother and her father every other weekend, which did not satisfy her mother or her siblings. Her mother was demanding and critical and her siblings and their wives barely spoke to her and did not invite her to their homes. She barely knew her nieces and nephews. These trips were exhausting and nonrewarding and brought up old issues for Connie. She said that she could live without her mother and siblings' approval, as she had had to deal with their rejection of her sexual orientation and lifestyle much earlier in her life. What upset and angered her were her brothers' continuing to treat her like a pariah and making her feel that she was not a part of her family of origin. At a time when she worried about something happening to Alice, Connie felt very alone. To make matters worse, Connie felt that she could not talk to Alice about her fears because Alice was depressed and worried about her prospects for living cancer-free. Moreover, Alice felt angry and abandoned when Connie left her to visit her mother. The couple began to have the first acrimonious verbal fights of their long relationship. Connie felt burdened and did not know where to turn. Although work had helped her to cope with Alice's first bout of cancer, it was draining her currently. In the absence of any family leave policy that she, as a lesbian, was eligible to use to take care of Alice, it had never occurred to her to ask officially for time off related to her parents' physical problems.

The therapist, a middle-aged lesbian, whose partner was a breast cancer survivor of seven years, felt very empathic with Connie's story. She felt removed enough from her own painful experiences so that she felt she could work with Connie. In fact, she thought that her own life events might facilitate the treatment. Sensing that Connie was emotionally and physically exhausted, she explored the possibility of Connie taking some time off from work in order to help her to recoup some of her energy while she sorted out the emotional issues she was facing. This proved to be a workable solution, because Alice had returned to her position in advertising and finances were less of a problem.

The treatment had several foci. First, it seemed apparent to the therapist that Connie had not been able to deal with her depression and anxieties about Alice's health problems and their implications for the future. Having busied herself with being a support for Alice, not wanting to burden her, and not having anyone to whom she could really talk, Connie had acted in a very stoical manner and kept her feelings to herself. In the initial phase of treatment, the therapist helped Connie to discuss the events of the past two years, her feelings about them, and her fears. A major issue that emerged in the sessions was Connie's realization that, on one hand, she and Alice needed to work on reestablishing their closeness rather than pushing each other away, but also, on the other hand, they needed to work on expanding their separate friendship networks and interests. Connie thought that her dependence on Alice, although gratifying, was also frightening. She saw that she had looked to Alice to provide her with the love, constancy, and security that she had not experienced with her family of origin and that the thought of losing Alice terrified her.

A second focus of the treatment was on helping Connie to stop protecting Alice from her concerns and to open up communication between the two of them. One of the factors that enabled this was the fact that Alice had completed her chemotherapy, had recovered from her surgery, and was feeling better physically. She also was attending a support group for women with cancer that was given by a private organization that she learned about from other patients. The therapist agreed to have some couple sessions to help in this process. These meetings worked out very well in that Connie and Alice were able to talk about things that they had been keeping to themselves and this relieved them.

Yet a third crucial treatment focus addressed Connie's guilt and anger about her role in the family and her feelings of rejection and aloneness. With the therapist's help, Connie recognized that one impetus for her biweekly visits to her mother was her fear that Alice would abandon her, thus intensifying her wish to become closer to her family. In sessions, she revisited her traditional Irish Catholic family background, the events that led to her coming out, her move to New York, her remaining closeted to family, her eventual disclosure of her lesbianism to them, and their rejecting reactions. She came to a different appreciation of her own struggles and strengths and recognized that her family members not only were stuck in their biased ways of thinking but had also not been very loving to and supportive of one another. Connie saw that she could not change her family but that she could assert herself to a greater degree in arriving at a solution for how the siblings would address her mother's caretaking needs in a way that would be better for Connie. By this time, Connie had returned to work. With Alice's support, Connie continued to visit but less often. More important, with the help of the nursing home social worker, she called a conference of her brothers and sisters-in-law to discuss what each member could and could not do. She remained firm in her position despite some attempts at provocation by her brothers. The nursing home physicians indicated that Connie's father, who was improving somewhat, would be able to manage in an assisted living facility, and they all decided to encourage the mother to join him in this living arrangement. Although it took some doing to accomplish this, their efforts were eventually successful. Although Connie's relationship with her family remained strained, Connie felt stronger and she and Alice were doing better together. They began to believe the doctors' favorable prognosis for Alice's surviving her cancer and went about moving on with their lives with a renewed sense of closeness and purpose.

A Senior's Struggle with a Homophobic Institutional Environment

In the final case example, Martha, an elderly lesbian who had a history of political and social activism, found herself in a nursing home in which she had to cope with the homophobic attitudes of the staff and other residents. The treatment not only helped the patient in her struggles but also helped the therapist, who coincidentally turned out also to be a lesbian who found the nursing home's environment oppressive.

Martha, age 82, had been in failing health for some time and with the help of friends entered a nursing home. Martha had founded a lesbian organization five decades earlier and 20 years before the Stonewall riot ushered in the gay and lesbian liberation movement. This very vibrant woman, who had been known for her strong commitment to gay and lesbian causes and who was considered by many to possess limitless energy, intelligence, and humor, was having trouble adjusting to the restrictions of her failing health and declining mobility. In addition, she felt depressed over the loss of her work as an activist. Because her mind was still as sharp as it always had been, it was particularly painful for Martha and her friends to have to place her in a nursing home. To make matters worse, in order to have good relations with her caretakers and the other residents and to receive the same attention given to others, Martha felt that she had to monitor aspects of her lesbian identity for the first time since her early adulthood. In addition to being dependent on others, having to cope with the home's homophobia, after years of her fighting for the right to live openly as a lesbian, caused her to become withdrawn and depressed. Her friends were saddened by Martha's decline and depression and contacted the nursing home's social worker, who was a clinician with a part-time private practice. Coincidentally, she also was a lesbian who was open selectively about her sexual identity in her personal life but who was closeted in her position at the nursing home. Like the patient, she felt that the staff would not welcome her disclosure of her sexual orientation. Although she thought some of the staff suspected that she was a lesbian, the professional atmosphere engendered a "Don't ask, don't tell" policy. She remained in her position because she needed the income and enjoyed her work with the patients.

After meeting with Martha's friends and learning about her life and concerns, the social worker consulted with her private practice supervisor to explore different ways of approaching her work with Martha. The story about Martha touched her greatly. Before meeting Martha, the therapist was concerned about her identification with the patient in regard to their feelings about the homophobic tone of the institution. She found herself having powerful fantasies of protecting Martha from the staff that she experienced as insensitive. With her supervisor, she decided that if Martha was amenable to working with her, she would disclose her sexual orientation and validate Martha's difficulties adjusting to an unfriendly environment. Although the social worker thought that such an engagement with the patient might expose her professionally, she felt prepared for the consequences. She acknowledged to her supervisor that the prospect of working with Martha had actually helped her to get more in touch with her own anger at the administration's negative attitudes toward gays and lesbians and her own collusion with its homophobia by staying closeted.

During their first meeting, the social worker saw that Martha felt profoundly lost in the unfamiliar and personally constricting environment. Because Martha knew that the social worker had been contacted by her friends and informed about her unhappiness, the therapist was able to draw her out rather quickly about her feelings about being a lesbian in a hostile setting. The therapist shared her similar experiences in an atmosphere that discouraged her own coming out.

Although Martha was initially responsive to the social worker's overtures and spoke of her own life and struggles readily, in time she began to question the worker about her life and wondered why she subjected herself to such an emotional compromise in her work. Martha's inquiry into the social worker's predicament had an interesting effect on her. Although she first was taken aback by the questions, she quickly realized that the patient seemed more lively than she had been previously in their meetings. She wondered if she had stumbled on an important way to help Martha. Rather than discouraging Martha and redirecting her, she permitted Martha to show the activist side of her personality. She acquiesced to the patient's endless battery of questions. Her openness to Martha's need to find a new cause revitalized them both. The features of Martha's personality obscured by her depression were coming back and the social worker enjoyed being Martha's new project. With the worker's encouragement, Martha became involved in her old gay and lesbian projects by phone and through her political contacts encouraged the nursing home to conduct diversity training for the staff.

Chapter 9

Experiences of the Lesbian Therapist

Being a lesbian therapist whose patient load includes lesbians in treatment can be a rewarding experience as well as one that has special trials and tribulations. In this final chapter, we would like to share some of our thoughts and impressions about the issues that lesbian therapists encounter.

Impact of Homophobia in the Professional Community

It is easier today for gay and lesbian trainees and clinicians to come out in professional circles and in their publications and presentations than it has been previously. Nevertheless, lesbian therapists continue to describe professional situations in which they encounter homophobic and antihomosexual attitudes and practices. A clinical supervisor at an analytic institute recently asked a candidate if she thought her lesbianism would interfere with her ability to understand and treat a heterosexual male patient who suffered anxiety in his relationships with women that inhibited his sexual performance. The supervisee replied, "It surprises me that you do not think that my being a lesbian might help me relate to his experiences with women." Because the institute advocated non-discriminatory policies on gay, lesbian, bisexual, and transgender (GLBT) issues, the trainee took the risk of challenging her supervisor's prejudicial assumptions. The burden, however, of confronting his homophobia was on the trainee. Not everyone is able to do this. It is not unusual for individuals to become anxious, defensive, or remain silent. A therapist who recently graduated from an analytic institute told her noninstitute therapist that she was deeply pained by her decision to remain closeted during her training in the face of the blatant homophobia of peers and instructors in her classes:

I just sat there. I held in everything that I wanted to say and was frightened that everyone would see what I was feeling. But I just sat there. . . . I'm angry with myself about that. I have always thought it was important to help patients feel self-accepting and open and there I was—frightened to say a word. . . . I just felt that I had worked too hard to get where I was to jeopardize my career. I think it was wrong but I'm not sure if I would have the courage to act differently if I faced that same situation today. Things have changed but not all that much. Sometimes I think that the changes are about political correctness—not about how people really feel.

Another continuing situation that lesbian trainees or therapists often experience in training institutes and mental health clinics is receiving only gay or lesbian referrals. This practice usually is rationalized as being good for patients to be assigned a therapist who shares a similar sexual identity with the patient. Unfortunately, it usually also reflects the bias that a lesbian therapist will not be able to be as helpful to a nongay patient. For example, a candidate, who was out as a lesbian in her predominately heterosexual psychoanalytic institute, complained about being pigeonholed as the lesbian analyst by the majority of heterosexual clinicians in the setting. She hoped that the reason behind her being assigned only gay and lesbian patients was her colleagues' erroneous assumption that it was her wish to specialize in treating homosexuals exclusively. When she questioned some of her associates about this, they admitted that they felt conflicted about the treatment implications of a lesbian analyst treating heterosexual patients, although many of them readily treated homosexual patients. They had difficulty explaining their double standard. Over time, the therapist's confrontation of her peers had a positive outcome. Nevertheless, she found the whole experience extremely distressing. Having to educate colleagues, with whom she had worked closely for several years, about their theoretical and personal biases made the therapist feel resentful and vulnerable. The same therapist also had the frequent experience of having her peers and instructors ask her for information about gay and lesbian life when a homosexual patient was discussed in her classes. She had a mixed reaction to this. On one hand, she was glad to be able to share her knowledge and experience. On the other hand, she felt singled out because of her sexual identity and distressed that her colleagues and instructors were so limited in their own understanding of gays and lesbians. To help her shoulder some of the responsibility of addressing the prejudices and discriminatory practices of homophobic training analysts, supervisors, and instructors at her institute, the therapist contacted the GLBT division of her professional association to intervene on behalf of patients and trainees.

As discussed in chapter 2, the foundation and evolution of psychoanalytic theory and practice gave rise to discrimination against gays and lesbians with respect to their becoming psychoanalysts. Although in some of his writings Freud supported social tolerance for homosexuals, believed that they should not be excluded from the psychoanalytic profession, and wrote that changing sexual orientation was not an appropriate treatment goal, he also contradicted these views in other writings. Because oedipal theory was built on the axiom that healthy psychosexual maturity culminated with one's gender identification, developing a heterosexual object choice, and being able to have genital sexual intercourse, it created a theoretical rationale for seeing homosexuals as immature and pathological. This view lingered and perpetuated heterosexual bias in the psychoanalytic community. It was compounded when ego psychological and object relations formulations redefined homosexuality as a form of developmental arrest. For many years, the psychiatric establishment embraced the view that homosexuality was pathological and psychoanalytic institutes in the United States selectively and openly rejected gay and lesbian applicants.

One therapist described the trauma she experienced during her interview to become a psychoanalytic candidate in the mid-1980s, a decade after both the American Psychiatric Association and the American Psychological Association changed the diagnostic category of homosexual from a mental disorder to a normal variant of human sexuality. The interview committee was composed largely of traditional male analysts, who extensively questioned her about her sexual orientation. Although the candidate was proud of the positive strides she had made to cope with her sexual identity in an nonsupportive environment, she was devastated when one of the analysts told her, in a belittling manner, that she was obviously depressed and had probably been her entire life. The second interviewer asked her how she could possibly manage her countertransference with male patients when she obviously did not like men. The third interviewer told the candidate that psychoanalysis could help her and suggested that she undergo a thorough in-depth analysis with him before reapplying for training. The candidate received a rejection letter from the institute, stating that a future application might be considered. The applicant spoke to colleagues about what had transpired and found an institute that was more friendly to gays and lesbians. Nevertheless, because of these unsettling experiences, she retreated into the closet for the duration of her training.

Adding insult to injury, the candidate's analyst, whom she found to be very accepting, caring, and usually helpful, commented on her having revealed her sexual orientation during her interview, by saying, "You really got yourself into a very sticky situation. I wonder why you needed to come out as a lesbian in the interview?" Vulnerable to her analyst's interpretation and to others like it, it took the candidate many years to recognize that her analyst's attitudes reflected her own biases. She was unable to support the patient's courage in coming out. Nor did she express anger or dismay that the patient had to be exposed to such aggressive antihomosexual behavior or be put in the position of remaining closeted in order to gain acceptance in the institute. This example also exemplifies the different cultural sensibilities that often arise between the gay and heterosexual communities. Her analyst had little awareness of the negative emotional consequences that gay and lesbian therapists experience when they feel compelled or choose to hide their sexual orientation in order to feel safe.

Another example that reflects a surprising degree of ignorance about gays and lesbians is an incident that occurred when a student at a mental health clinic of a major New York City university tried to recruit a social worker for a GLBT clinic. The director of the clinic asked a former lesbian employee to recommend someone for the job. Although the woman she suggested had been in a lesbian relationship for seven years earlier in her life, she was currently married to a man. She considered herself to be bisexual with strong lesbian leanings and had many lesbian friends. When she told the director of the clinic about her background in their interview, he thought she was lying about her lesbianism in order to appear qualified for the position. A heterosexual man, the director had little knowledge about the variety of ways in which nonheterosexuals define themselves across a sexual continuum, despite the fact that he was trying to hire a GLBT worker. In his mind, people were either gay or straight. Needless to say, the applicant did not get the job. Another staff member told the former employee who referred the woman that the director had shared his pride in having detected a fraudulent applicant.

In stark contrast to the above examples, many psychoanalytic institutes and mental health institutions are aware of their past discriminatory practices and policies and are trying to correct them. Not only are they teaching theories that are more affirmative of GLBT experience, but they also are hiring experts to reach out to the GLBT community and are openly discussing the impact of homophobia in the field of mental health. For example, homophobia was the topic of a recent American Psychological Association yearly conference. The financial strength of

GLBT organizations has been a factor in making these changes possible. They have supported legal issues that protect GLBT mental health professionals and have supported theoretical revisions of traditional mental health approaches. In fact, one heterosexual clinician and teacher related an interesting experience she had at a GLBT-aware institute when teaching a course on Freudian theory. The class became very angry and argumentative when she began to teach Freud's *Three Essays on the Theory of Sexuality*. Unaware of the contradictory aspects of his writings, the students objected to the homophobic content of Freud's theories and the necessity of learning his work at all. The students were also not aware that the teacher had written a paper revising oedipal theories to include homosexuality as an achievement equal to heterosexuality. The instructor found the students' lack of motivation to learn traditional theory disappointing. She believed that in order to discard traditional theory, the students needed to have a foundation in the historical evolution of psychoanalytic theory. This incident reflects an instance in which some students do not want to study or consider theories that are not politically correct.

Being Out in Publications and Presentations

Whenever clinicians share their ideas and work in their writings or professional presentations, they risk possible criticism. The nature of the exposure is different, however, when a lesbian clinician publishes or presents material in which she reveals her sexual orientation or discusses ideas and cases in ways that challenge prevailing heterosexist views. She is exposing not only her ideas but also her identity; thus, if criticism follows, she may have to defend not only her views but also herself. Even a confident person must be prepared to be stirred up by having to reexperience the questioning and disapproval of lesbianism in her professional life that she likely faced in her personal life. This requires taking certain risks as well as developing a thick skin. This type of public self-disclosure is different from the self-disclosure in one's personal life, which tends to be more discreet. One has no control over how far information that is shared in a public forum travels and how it gets used.

Although positive benefits can accrue from being out as a lesbian in professional circles, it also can have negative repercussions about which one may not even be aware. One therapist who published and spoke professionally on a frequent basis on subjects that were unrelated to sexual identity was asked to write a chapter on the treatment of lesbians

by a colleague who knew through his personal contacts that she was a
lesbian. When she was in the midst of her writing, one of her longstanding friends, a heterosexual woman therapist, asked her if she was worried about people who weren't gay reading the chapter and if she was
going to include the publication in her curriculum vitae for everyone to
see. When the author asked her what difference it might make, her friend
replied, "Well, it's different if I know you're gay or if everyone knows
you are. Aren't you afraid that some people will label you a lesbian
therapist and they may not invite you to speak on other subjects or refer
nongay patients to you?" The author responded that she actually had
thought of that and had in fact avoided being more open publicly about
her lesbianism until then. "I just feel like it is time for me to give back. I
guess I won't know if I'm not invited to do things professionally or if
I'm not referred patients because of my lesbianism. What will be will be."
In retrospect, she also realized that this good friend had her own anxiety
about being known to be close to an out lesbian. She became more aware
of this dynamic when she did become more visible as a lesbian in the
professional community. She observed that some of her heterosexual
colleagues and friends appeared nervous when hearing about her more
public lesbian-related writing and activities and seemed to avoid the
topic rather than show their interest.

A Clinician's Lack of Personal Privacy

A major issue that lesbian therapists who choose to work with lesbian
patients continue to encounter is managing the boundary between their
personal and professional identities. Lesbian therapists may wish to
socialize with other lesbians and have the same need for connection and
validation that their patients have. The smallness of the lesbian community generates situations in which therapists and patients run into one
another at community and social events and in settings commonly
frequented by lesbians. This small town atmosphere can cause the
lesbian therapist to experience a lack of privacy that may have an impact
not only on the clinician but on the patient's treatment as well. One
therapist related that she couldn't go to a popular beach or a local
supermarket in a summer resort community in which she has a home
without encountering a present or former patient. She learned to manage
these chance encounters in a friendly and matter-of-fact manner for the
most part. Nevertheless, she could not nor did she want always to
monitor whom she was with, what she was wearing, and how she was
behaving. Although some of her patients accepted and even felt good

about the accidental meetings, it always aroused curiosity about the therapist's personal life and relationships. One borderline patient threatened to track down the therapist's house, and although she firmly cautioned the patient against doing so, for a time the therapist was anxious that she would carry out her threat. Another therapist, who was trying to reconnect to lesbian social activities after the death of her partner, learned that one of her lesbian patients planned to attend a meeting of a classical music lovers' group that she had joined. Because this group was important to her, the therapist wanted to continue to attend meetings, but she also did not feel that it would be good for the therapy for both her and the patient to be at the group at the same time. Yet she did not feel that it was right for her to prohibit the patient from ever attending the meetings. When the therapist brought the issue up with the patient and tried to work with her to find the best way to handle the situation, the patient admitted that her wanting to attend the group was not a coincidence. She had learned from a friend that the therapist had been at a meeting and this fact motivated her to want to join. She said she fantasized about just showing up and surprising the therapist. This discussion was fruitful in terms of revealing transference issues but made the therapist quite anxious, which the patient seemed to enjoy. "I'm playing with you. I'm not really interested in coming to the group. I just wondered how you would react to my being there." Needless to say, the therapist was relieved. At the same time, the therapist realized that the patient had "spies" at the group meetings, if she wanted them to report on the therapist's behavior.

When treatment begins, it is not uncommon for lesbian therapists and their patients to be unaware that they have crossed paths with significant people in one another's lives. In the course of treatment, the patient sometimes inadvertently becomes friendly with people who know the therapist. For example, during a session, a therapist who had been treating a patient for three years realized that she was dating a woman who had sex repeatedly with the therapist's partner and continued to have contact with her. It did not seem that the patient knew about this connection as yet. The therapist did not know whether and how to address the issue. Initially, she thought that she would wait for the patient to find out the information on her own and work with the transference implications as they arose. She turned to her peer supervision group for advice. The group members questioned the therapist's plan, because it seemed too traditional a stance. They believed that the patient might experience the therapist's technical strategy as deceitful and uncaring when she inevitably learned of the relationship between her girlfriend and the therapist's partner. Furthermore, they questioned

whether the therapeutic couple might become entrenched in an enactment in which they avoided discomfort by sidestepping the extra-
analytic material. The therapist acknowledged to the group that the idea
of talking with the patient about their partners' relationship aroused
anxiety. She realized that she feared that the patient would de-idealize
her and see her as less able to help her. The fear of the patient's entering
into a full-blown devaluation of her—a fear rooted in the therapist's
personal life experience—presented a formidable challenge that the
therapist felt ill-equipped to handle. One peer group member wondered
if the patient might not feel closer to the therapist if she knew about the
connection. The therapist became even more anxious when she realized
that the patient might indeed have access to considerable personal
information about the therapist. The therapist came to the realization
that her anxiety about her being de-idealized and exposed, although
understandable, were really her own issues. After considering the many
facets of her dilemma, the therapist decided she had to raise the subject
with the patient, discuss the meaning that it had for them, and to work
together on how best to protect their work together if it continued.

Lesbian therapists confront an array of professional and personal
concerns when they are out simply socializing with friends or looking
for new relationships. Although the selection of venues for meeting
women is now wider, bars have historically played a key role in developing contacts with other lesbians. More recently, the Internet and GLBT
organizations have become popular resources for lesbians to make new
connections. Using any of these venues can feel daunting to lesbian
therapists because they may encounter past, current, or future patients
who see them interacting in social situations. Consequently, lesbian
therapists often approach these social opportunities with considerable
caution, may develop a tendency to avoid being out in public, or may
become anxious about exposure.

In the following example, a complicated transference–countertransference dynamic was triggered by a therapist's chance social meeting
with her patient. The therapist had a few drinks at a downtown lesbian
bar and was obviously a bit tipsy when a patient walked in. They greeted
each other and then tried to ignore each other's presence until the
therapist soon left. When the patient came to her session the following
day, she bombarded the therapist with a battery of personal questions
about her partner status and her alcohol use. Although the therapist felt
comfortable dealing with the transference implications of their meeting,
she became conflicted when the patient said she wanted to terminate
their treatment relationship so that they could date. Because she had not
had an intimate relationship for a long time and felt very lonely, she felt

vulnerable to the patient's demand. For many months prior to the accidental meeting, the therapist had been discussing her attraction to this patient in her own analysis. The patient's physical style embodied the type of woman to whom the therapist felt most attracted, even though she was quite certain that the patient was not emotionally suited to her. For a few weeks after their chance meeting in the bar, the therapist engaged in an enormous struggle to anchor herself emotionally during the patient's incessant flirting and demands to transform their relationship from a professional one to a romantic one. Despite her feelings for the patient, she had no intention of acting on her feelings. She was cautious about doing anything that might intensify the patient's sexual longing. Although she recognized her role in the patient's transference, she believed that disclosing her countertransference would be too sexually stimulating for the patient. She responded to the patient's request for validation by acknowledging how important it was for them to discover the meaning of this new desire to obtain a deeper intimacy with her. Theoretically, the therapist believed that an honest self-disclosure would be too traumatizing for the patient, because with this patient it would have reenacted her boundary difficulties with her parents. What the therapist did choose to disclose was how their accidental meeting had had a strong effect on both of them, and she emphasized that they needed more time to understand its meaning. In addition, the therapist addressed aspects of their concordant identification as single lesbian women and opened up a conversation about the specific issues that arise for women during the dating process.

Another lesbian therapist who had trouble finding a way to manage the personal constraints and transference complications that arise in the types of situations described above decided not to treat lesbian patients. She felt that this would enable her to have the freedom to socialize in the lesbian community without tension and anxiety.

Impact of Homophobia in Work with
Heterosexual Patients

When gay or straight patients see a therapist, they often automatically assume that the therapist is heterosexual unless they have prior knowledge of the therapist's sexual orientation. Consequently, heterosexual clinicians usually do not have to deal with the issue of self-disclosure. Nor is it necessary for them to be concerned about the ramifications of revealing a stigmatized sexual orientation if a patient expresses curiosity about the therapist's relationship status. The heterosexual therapist does not ordinarily have to worry about the patient's negative judgments of his or her sexual orientation or of the financial and professional consequences of becoming known as a heterosexual.

The main issue that sometimes arises when a lesbian or gay patient enters treatment with a heterosexual therapist is whether the therapist will be accepting and knowledgeable about the patient's sexual orientation.

When a heterosexual patient sees a lesbian therapist, at some point in the treatment the patient may become curious or have fantasies about the therapist's personal life. In order to manage discomfort with having to reveal one's lesbian sexual identity, the therapist may practice more traditionally and refrain from disclosing any personal information. Although this stance may protect the therapist, in many instances it can hamper development of a deeper and more vital therapeutic intimacy. Therapists may adopt such a stance to avoid having to deal with a patient's negative judgments, not wanting to lose referrals if the word about her lesbianism gets out, and not wanting to have one patient share personal information about the therapist with another patient. This strategy does not always prevent the patient from sensing or knowing about the therapist's sexual identity. One therapist was not fully prepared for her patient's confrontation of her with respect to her lesbianism. The patient, a 40-year-old divorced religious Jewish woman who wished to remarry but tended to be hypercritical of the men she met, overheard a conversation that one of her straight married friends had on the telephone. The friend was a colleague of the therapist and had referred the patient to the therapist originally. The friend indicated that the therapist had recently lost her female partner of many years. Although the fact that the therapist was a lesbian was not a complete surprise to the patient, she had a strong reaction to learning this might be true. In probing about the meaning that learning about the therapist had for her, the patient said, "I'm not homophobic at all. What you are is your own business, but it worries me that you won't be able to help me deal with my issues about men." She explained that the therapist might tend to take her side against the men she met. After exploring this issue further in numerous sessions, the therapist and patient continued to work together. Nevertheless, the patient, who was pessimistic about her chances to remarry, decided that she wanted to find another therapist. She thought that it might help her to have a therapist whom she felt had achieved what she wanted for herself. The therapist recognized that for this patient, being able to idealize a therapist might be an important part of her treatment and the therapist was not sufficiently idealizable.

Nevertheless, the therapist felt upset about what had transpired and wondered what she might have done differently.

Lesbian therapists who are willing to self-disclose often find themselves considering numerous factors in deciding what to do when a heterosexual patient becomes curious about her personal life. Deciding when it is appropriate to disclose her sexual orientation to a particular heterosexual patient can become a challenging technical issue that has different ramifications for different therapeutic couples. For example, an attractive married heterosexual woman sought treatment because of depression, anxiety, and low self-esteem that affected her ability to get close to woman friends and to pursue her professional goals. She was a perfectionist and could be quite judgmental and critical of those, including her children and friends, who did not live up to her standards. Her brother was gay and the patient often talked disparagingly about his lifestyle, even though she liked his partner. The therapist's office was in her apartment and the patient saw her early in the morning. About a year into the treatment, the patient was talking about her sister from whom she was estranged, when she fell silent. When the therapist probed about what she was thinking, the patient commented that she thought the therapist lived alone until she saw the same woman leave the apartment twice while the patient was waiting for her session to begin. She thought the woman looked somewhat like the therapist and must be a relative. She decided the woman was the therapist's sister and that made her feel good. She said that she liked the idea that the therapist was not alone and was close to a sibling. She went on to talk more about her sadness at not having a good relationship with her own sister. The therapist did not think this was the right time to disclose anything about her personal life, because the patient was deeply involved in her own transference fantasies. As the therapeutic bond deepened, the patient became somewhat embarrassed about her dreams that revealed her growing attachment to the therapist. At the same time she felt good about her increasing comfort in the relationship. When she finally began to express her curiosity about the therapist's personal life after two years of treatment, she acknowledged that it had occurred to her that the therapist was a lesbian. The therapist asked her what it would mean to her if it were true. The patient responded, "I don't know. I think I'd be okay with that. I wouldn't have said that a year ago. But you have really helped me and I admire you. I'd just be embarrassed about everything I've said about my brother. I've been looking at him a little differently. He's happy. I'm not." Curiously, the patient still did not ask the therapist directly if she were a lesbian until a month later. She began a session with a dream that revealed her increasing curiosity about the therapist. "Okay, I think I'm ready to know. I've been thinking that you can't be living with your sister. What New York City therapist lives with her sister? Are you gay? You don't have to answer that. I know the answer." The therapist responded, "I guess you do. So what do you think?" The patient responded, "I've been realizing lately that there are a lot of really great women out there who just happen to be gay. I'm learning."

To Disclose or Not to Disclose with Lesbian Patients

A lesbian patient often knows a lesbian therapist's sexual identity at the beginning of treatment because the patient seeks out a therapist of the same sexual orientation. Although lesbian therapists do not always self-disclose as a rule, if at all, sometimes lesbian clinicians reveal their sexual orientation early in the treatment out of a conviction that it is colluding with homophobia to withhold this information. They also believe that the lack of positive cultural role models necessitates their acting as a role model, mentor, and educator for the lesbian patient. Moreover, at times transference developments seem to require self-disclosures and refraining from revelations of this type can obstruct or derail the treatment.

A potential hazard of lesbian therapists' working with lesbian patients stems from their often close identification with many aspects of their patients' lives or their wish to gain approval, recognition, and admiration from the patient that they may not have received from significant others. The treatment situation may become a place in which the therapist feels comfortable in revealing or verbalizing certain aspects of sexual identity and lifestyle that she may ordinarily be unable to talk about. Sometimes, therapists may be too casual with the patient or experience a false intimacy. They may feel a strong countertransference impulse to share personal information, even when this may be contraindicated. For example, with a patient whose transference dynamics are driven by ties to early object experiences with narcissistic and intrusive objects, self-disclosures may be experienced as burdensome, self-aggrandizing, or meddling. Likewise, it may be crucial for the therapist to refrain from impinging too much on patients who need to feel that they are mastering certain types of experiences on their own. One therapist shared an upsetting experience with a patient that had just occurred. She told her peer group that she felt she had made a serious clinical error. With the help of other members, she recognized that she had been blinded by her own countertransference fantasy that her patient would benefit from her sharing her own struggles as a lesbian and appreciate the therapist's life experience. Consequently, she failed to anticipate correctly and interpret the transference implications of her self-disclosures to her 26-year-old lesbian patient. The patient became angry and accused the therapist of being like her self-involved, self-aggrandizing, and devaluing mother when the therapist revealed some of her own knowledge of the lesbian bar scene and dating process learned from her personal experiences. These comments were in response to the patient's concerns about her lack of dating experience and her problems maintaining relationships with women who were suited to her. From the history gathered over the course of treatment, the therapist knew that the patient's mother had difficulty relating to her daughter as a separate individual with needs of her own. The patient interpreted the therapist's revelations as self-serving and insensitive to her as a person. It made her feel that the therapist didn't really know who she was and had not been listening during all the time she was in treatment. In response to these accusations, the therapist initially felt rebuffed and unappreciated by the patient. Then she realized she had made a mistake. Because of their positive working relationship, the therapist was able to work this through with the patient in the weeks following the incident.

The Lesbian Therapist's Rewards

Clinical work generally has rewards that keep therapists going despite the challenges and stresses that they face on a daily basis. Significant benefits occur for lesbian therapists who choose to work with lesbian patients. Lesbian therapists who have been able to achieve some sense of personal and professional satisfaction despite their stigmatized identity and past struggles often feel that they want to make it possible for others to reap the same benefits. It is heartening to see patients grow who have battled with internalized homophobia, family and peer disapproval and rejection, and job discrimination and other forms of prejudice. The therapeutic process also helps the therapist to express and validate her own identity. Although sometimes revisiting one's own early traumatic experiences can be painful, it also is empowering and reparative. Some patients' means of coping with their identity struggles can be a source of learning and even inspiration. Lesbian therapists who come into professional contact with one another can have the experience of collegiality rather than the isolation that they may have felt previously. Finally, they can feel that they are contributing to social change.

References

American Psychological Association (1991), Bias in psychotherapy with lesbian and gay men [final report]. Washington, DC: American Psychological Association.

Appleby, G. A. & Anastas, J. W. (1998), *Not Just a Passing Phase: Social Work with Gay, Lesbian, and Bisexual People*. New York: Columbia University Press.

Aron, L. (1991), The patient's experience of the analyst's subjectivity. *Psychoanal. Dial.*, 1:29–51.

_____ (1996), *A Meeting of Minds: Mutuality in Psychoanalysis*. Hillsdale, NJ: The Analytic Press.

Baptiste, D. A., Jr. (1987), Psychotherapy with gay/lesbian couples and their children in "stepfamilies": A challenge for marriage and family therapists. *J. Homosexual.*, 14:223–239.

Bayer, R. (1981), *Homosexuality and American Psychiatry: The Politics of Diagnosis*. New York: Basic Books.

Benjamin, J. (1988), *The Bonds of Love: Psychoanalysis, Feminism, and the Problem of Domination*. New York: Pantheon Books.

_____ (1994), Commentary on papers by Tansey, Davies, and Hirsch. *Psychoanal. Dial.*, 4:193–201.

_____ (1995), *Like Subjects, Love Objects: Essays on Recognition and Sexual Difference*. New Haven, CT: Yale University Press.

Berger, R. M. (1992), Research on older gay men: What we know, what we need to know. In: *Gay and Lesbian Lifestyles: A Guide for Counseling and Education*, ed. N. J. Woodman. New York: Irvington Press, pp. 217–232.

_____ & Kelly, J. J. (1986), Working with homosexuals of the older population. *Soc. Casework: J. Contemp. Soc. Work*, 67:203–210.

Bergmann, M. S. (1973), *The Anatomy of Loving*. New York: Columbia University Press.

Bernard, D. (1992), Developing a positive self-image in a homophobic environment. In: *Gay and Lesbian Lifestyles: A Guide for Counseling and Education,* ed. N. J. Woodman. New York: Irvington Press, pp. 23–32.

Bion, W. (1962), *Learning from Experience.* New York: Aronson.

Blanck, G. & Blanck, R. (1974), *Ego Psychology in Theory and Practice.* New York: Columbia University Press.

———— & ———— (1979), *Ego Psychology II: Psychoanalytic Developmental Psychology.* New York: Columbia University Press.

Buloff, B. & Osterman, M. (1995), Queer reflections: Mirroring and the lesbian experience of the self. In: *Lesbians and Psychoanalysis: Revolutions in Theory and Practice,* ed. J. M. Glassgold & S. Iasenza. New York: Free Press, pp. 93–106.

Burch, B. (1993), *On Intimate Terms: The Psychology of Difference in Lesbian Relationships.* Urbana: University of Illinois Press.

———— (1997), *Lesbian/Bisexual Experience and Other Women: Psychoanalytic Views of Women.* New York: Columbia University Press.

Butler, J. (1990), *Gender Trouble: Feminism and the Subversion of Identity.* New York: Routledge.

Cass, V. C. (1979), Homosexual identity formation: A theoretical model. *J. Homosexual.,* 4:219–235.

Chevalier, J. (1893), *Inversion Sexuelle.* Paris: Masson.

The Children's Hour (1961), Motion picture. Screenplay by John Michael Hayes from an adaptation by Lillian Hellman. Directed by William Wyler. MGM Home Entertainment.

Chodorow, N. (1978), *The Reproduction of Mothering: Psychoanalysis and the Sociology of Gender.* Berkeley: University of California Press.

———— (1989), *Feminism and Psychoanalytic Theory.* New Haven, CT: Yale University Press.

Coleman, E. (1982), Developmental stages of the coming out process. In: *Homosexuality and Psychotherapy,* ed. J. C. Gonsiorek. New York: Haworth Press, pp. 31–43.

DeCrescenzo, T. A. (1984), Homophobia: A study of the attitudes of mental health professionals toward homosexuality. *J. Soc. Work & Human Sexual.,* 2:115–135.

DeLaCour, E. (1996), The Interpersonal School and its influence on current relational theories. In: *Inside Out and Outside In,* ed. J. Berzoff, L. M. Flanagan & P. Hertz. Northvale, NJ: Aronson, pp. 199–220.

DeLauretis, T. (1994), *The Practice of Love: Lesbian Sexuality and Perverse Desire.* Bloomington: Indiana University Press.

Deutsch, H. (1932), On female homosexuality. In: *The Psychoanalytic Reader,* ed. R. Fleiss. New York: International Universities Press, 1948, pp. 208–230.

_____ (1944), *The Psychology of Women*. New York: Grune & Stratton.

Drescher, J. (1998), *Psychoanalytic Therapy and the Gay Man*. Hillsdale, NJ: The Analytic Press.

Ehrenberg, D. B. (1995), Self-disclosure: Therapeutic tool or indulgence? *Contemp. Psychoanal.*, 31:213–228.

Eisenbud, R. J. (1982), Early and later determinants of lesbian choice. *Psychoanal. Rev.*, 69:85–109.

Ellis, H. (1897), *Studies in the Psychology of Sex*. New York: Random House.

Falco, K. L. (1991), *Psychotherapy with Lesbian Clients: Theory into Practice*. New York: Brunner/Mazel.

Forstein, M. (1988), Homophobia: An overview. *Psychiat. Ann.*, 18:33–36.

Fosshage, J. L. (1991), Beyond the basic rule. In: *The Evolution of Self Psychology: Progress in Self Psychology, Vol. 7*, ed. A. Goldberg. Hillsdale, NJ: The Analytic Press, pp. 64–74.

Freud, S. (1905), Three essays on the theory of sexuality. *Standard Edition*, 7:125–243. London: Hogarth Press, 1953.

_____ (1920), Psychogenesis of a case of female homosexuality. *Standard Edition*, 18:145–172. London: Hogarth Press, 1955.

_____ (1931), Female sexuality. *Standard Edition*, 21:221–243. London: Hogarth Press, 1966.

_____ (1933), Femininity. *Standard Edition*, 22:112–135. London: Hogarth Press, 1966.

_____ (1935), Anonymous (Letter to an American mother). In: *The Letters of Sigmund Freud*, ed. A. Freud. New York: Basic Books, 1960, pp. 423–424.

Friedman, R. (1988), *Male Homosexuality: A Contemporary Psychoanalytic Perspective*. New Haven, CT: Yale University Press.

Frommer, M. S. (1994), Homosexuality and psychoanalysis: Technical considerations revisited. *Psychoanal. Dial.*, 4:215–233.

Fuss, D. (1995), *Identification Papers*. New York: Routledge.

Gair, S. R. (1995), The false self, shame, and the challenge of self-cohesion. In: *Lesbians and Psychoanalysis: Revolutions in Theory and Practice*, ed. J. M. Glassgold & S. Iasenza. New York: Free Press, pp. 107–123.

Gerson, S. (1996), Neutrality, resistance, and self-disclosure in an inter-subjective psychoanalysis. *Psychoanal. Dial.*, 6:623–645.

Gilligan, C. (1982), *In a Different Voice: Psychological Theory and Women's Development*. Cambridge, MA: Harvard University Press.

Glassgold, J. M. & Iasenza, S., eds. (1995), *Lesbians and Psychoanalysis: Revolutions in Theory and Practice*. New York: Free Press.

Goldner, V. (1991), Toward a critical relational theory of gender. *Psychoanal. Dial.*, 1:249–272.

Goldstein, E. G. (1994), Self-disclosure in treatment: What therapists do and don't talk about. *Clin. Soc. Work J.,* 22:417–433.

———— (1997), To tell or not to tell: Self-disclosure of events in the therapist's life to the patient. *Clin. Soc. Work J.,* 25:41–58.

———— (2001), *Object Relations Theory and Self Psychology in Social Work Practice.* New York: Free Press.

Gonsiorek, J. C., ed. (1982a), *Homosexuality and Psychotherapy: A Practitioner's Handbook of Affirmative Models.* New York: Haworth Press.

———— (1982b), Introduction: Present and future directions in gay/lesbian mental health. In: *Homosexuality and Psychotherapy: A Practitioner's Handbook of Affirmative Models,* ed. J. C. Gonsiorek. New York: Haworth Press, pp. 5–7.

———— & Weinrich, J. D. (1991), The definition and scope of sexual orientation. In: *Homosexuality: Research for Public Policy,* ed. J. C. Gonsiorek & J. D. Weinrich. Thousand Oaks, CA: Sage, pp. 1–12.

Gorkin, M. (1987), *The Uses of Countertransference.* Northvale, NJ: Aronson.

Gould, D. (1995), A critical examination of the notion of pathology in psychoanalysis. In: *Lesbians and Psychoanalysis: Revolutions in Theory and Practice,* ed. J. M. Glassgold & S. Iasenza. New York: Free Press, pp. 3–17.

Greenberg, D. F. (1988), *The Construction of Homosexuality.* Chicago: University of Chicago Press.

Greenberg, J. & Mitchell, S. (1983), *Object Relations in Psychoanalytic Theory.* Cambridge, MA: Harvard University Press.

Greenson, R. (1967), *The Technique and Practice of Psychoanalysis, Vol. 1.* New York: International Universities Press.

Guntrip, H. (1973), *Psychoanalytic Theory, Therapy, and the Self.* New York: Basic Books.

Hall, R. (1928), *The Well of Loneliness.* New York: Avon Books, 1981.

Hanna, E. A. (1993a), The implications of shifting perspectives in countertransference on the therapeutic action of clinical social work. Part I: The classical and early totalist position. *J. Anal. Soc. Work,* 1:25–32.

———— (1993b), The implications of shifting perspectives in countertransference on the therapeutic action of clinical social work. Part II: The recent totalist and intersubjective position. *J. Anal. Soc. Work,* 1:53–80.

Harris, A. (1991), Gender as contradiction. *Psychoanal. Dial.,* 1:197–224.

Herek, G. M. (1984), Beyond "homophobia": A social psychological perspective on attitudes toward lesbians and gay men. *J. Homosexual.,* 10:1–21.

_____ (1995), Psychological heterosexism in the United States. In: *Lesbian, Gay, and Bisexual Identities over the Life Span*, ed. A. R. D'Augelli & C. Patterson. New York: Oxford University Press, pp. 321–346.

Hetrick, E. S. & Martin, A. D. (1988), Developmental issues and their resolution for gay and lesbian adolescents. In: *Psychotherapy with Homosexual Men and Women: Integrated Identity Approaches for Clinical Practice*, ed. E. Coleman. New York: Haworth Press, pp. 25–43.

Hoffman, I. Z. (1983), The patient as interpreter of the analyst's experience. *Contemp. Psychoanal.*, 19:389–422.

_____ (1991), Discussion: Toward a social-constructivist view of the psychoanalytic situation. *Psychoanal. Dial.*, 1:74–105.

Horney, K. (1924), On the genesis of the castration complex in women. In: *Feminine Psychology*, ed. H. Kelman. New York: Norton, 1973.

_____ (1926), The flight from womanhood. *Internat. J. Psycho-Anal.*, 7:324–339.

_____ (1934), The overvaluation of love. *Psychoanal. Quart.*, 3:605–638.

Horowitz, L. C. (1998), Constructions of experience: A social constructivist approach for lesbians in psychoanalysis. Unpublished doctoral dissertation, University of Michigan, Ann Arbor.

_____ (2000), Resisting amnesia in the countertransference: A clinical strategy for working with the lesbian patient. *Clin. Soc. Work J.*, 1: 55–70.

Irigaray, L. (1985), *Speculum of the Other Woman*. Ithaca, NY: Cornell University Press.

Isay, R. A. (1989), *Being Homosexual: Gay Men and Their Development*. New York: Farrar, Straus & Giroux.

_____ (1996), *Becoming Gay: The Journey to Self-Acceptance*. New York: Pantheon Books.

Jones, E. (1927), The early development of female sexuality. *Internat. J. Psycho-Anal.*, 8:459–472.

Jones, M. A. & Gabriel, M. A. (1999), Utilization of psychotherapy by lesbians, gay men, and bisexuals: Findings from a nationwide study. *Amer. J. Orthopsychiat.*, 69:209–219.

Jordan, J. V., Kaplan, A. G., Miller, J. B., Stiver, I. P. & Surrey, J. L., eds. (1991), *Women's Growth in Connection: Writings from the Stone Center*. New York: Guilford Press.

Kennedy, H. C. (1980/1981), The "third sex" theory of Karl Heinrich Ulrichs. *J. Homosexual.*, 6:103–111.

Kertzner, R. & Sved, M. (1996), Midlife gay men and lesbians: Adult development and mental health. In: *Textbook of Homosexuality and Mental Health*, ed. R. P. Cabaj & T. S. Stein. Washington, DC: American Psychiatric Press, pp. 267–288.

Kimmel, D. C. & Sang, B. E. (1995), Lesbians and gay men in midlife. In: *Lesbian, Gay, and Bisexual Identities over the Life Span*, ed. A. R. D'Augelli & C. Patterson. New York: Oxford University Press, pp. 191–213.

Kinsey, A., Pomeroy, W. & Martin, C. (1948), *Sexual Behavior in the Human Male*. Philadelphia, PA: Saunders.

Kohut, H. (1971), *The Analysis of the Self*. New York: International Universities Press.

———— (1977), *The Restoration of the Self*. New York: International Universities Press.

———— (1984), *How Does Analysis Cure?* Chicago: University of Chicago Press.

———— & Wolf, E. (1978), The disorders of the self and their treatments: An outline. In: *Essential Papers on Narcissism*, ed. A. Morrison. New York: New York University Press, 1986, pp. 175–196.

Krajeski, J. (1996), Homosexuality and the mental health professions. In: *Textbook of Homosexuality and Mental Health*, ed. R. P. Cabaj & T. S. Stein. Washington, DC: American Psychiatric Press, pp. 17–32.

Lewes, K. (1988), *The Psychoanalytic Theory of Male Homosexuality*. New York: Simon & Schuster.

Lewis, L. A. (1984), The coming out process for lesbians: Integrating a stable identity. *Soc. Work*, 29:464–469.

Magee, M. & Miller, D. (1997), *Lesbians Lives: Psychoanalytic Narratives Old and New*. Hillsdale, NJ: The Analytic Press.

Malyon, A. K. (1982a), Biphasic aspects of homosexual identity formation. *Psychother. Theory Res. Pract.*, 19:335–340.

———— (1982b), Psychotherapeutic implications of internalized homophobia in gay men. In: *Homosexuality and Psychotherapy: A Practitioner's Handbook of Affirmative Models*, ed. J. C. Gonsiorek. New York: Haworth Press, pp. 59–70.

Maroda, K. J. (1994), *The Power of Countertransference: Innovations in Analytic Technique*. Northvale, NJ: Aronson.

———— (1999), *Seduction, Surrender, and Transformation: Emotional Engagement in the Analytic Process*. Hillsdale, NJ: The Analytic Press.

McDougall, J. (1979), The homosexual dilemma: A clinical and theoretical study of female homosexuality. In: *Sexual Deviation*, ed. I. Rosen. Oxford, England: Oxford University Press.

———— (1980), *Plea for a Measure of Abnormality*. New York: International Universities Press.

———— (1995), *The Many Faces of Eros: A Psychoanalytic Exploration of Human Sexuality*. New York: Norton.

Mereck, M. (1986), The train of thought in Freud's "Case of homosexuality in a woman." In: *Perversions: Deviant Readings*. New York: Routledge, 1993, pp. 13–32.

Miller, J. P. (1991). Can psychotherapy substitute for psychoanalysis? In: *The Evolution of Self Psychology: Progress in Self Psychology, Vol. 7*, ed. A. Goldberg. Hillsdale, NJ: The Analytic Press, pp. 45–58.

Mitchell, S. A. (1988), *Relational Concepts in Psychoanalysis: An Integration*. Cambridge, MA.: Harvard University Press.

————— (1993), *Hope and Dread in Psychoanalysis*. New York: Basic Books.

Moses, A. E. & Hawkins, R. O. (1982), *Counseling Lesbian and Gay Men*. St. Louis, MO: Mosby.

Natterson, M. & Friedman, J. (1995), *A Primer of Clinical Subjectivity*. Northvale, NJ: Aronson.

Nava, M. & Davidoff, R. (1994), *Created Equal: Why Gay Rights Matter to America*. New York: St. Martin's Press.

Nystrom, N. (1997), Mental health experiences of gay men and lesbians. Presented at American Association for the Advancement of Science symposium on assessing health needs of gay men and lesbians, Houston, TX.

O'Connor, N. & Ryan, J. (1993), *Wild Desires and Mistaken Identities: Lesbianism and Psychoanalysis*. New York: Columbia University Press.

Ornstein, E. D. & Ganzer, C. (1997), Mitchell's relational conflict model: An analysis of its usefulness in clinical social work. *Clin. Soc. Work J.*, 25:391–406.

Parks, C. A. (1999), Lesbian identity development: An examination of differences across generations. *Amer. J. Orthopsychiat.*, 69:347–361.

Ponse, B. (1978), *Identities in the Lesbian World: The Social Construction of the Self*. Westport, CT: Greenwood Press.

Potter, S. J. & Darty, T. E. (1981), Social work and the invisible minority: An exploration of lesbianism. *Soc. Work*, 26:187–192.

Racker, H. (1957). The meaning and uses of countertransference. *Psychoanal. Quart.*, 26:303–357.

Reiter, L. (1989), Sexual orientation, sexual identity, and the question of choice. *Clin. Soc. Work J.*, 17:138–150.

Renik, O. (1995), The ideal of the anonymous analyst and the problem of self-disclosure. *Psychoanal. Quart.*, 64:446–495.

Rich, A. (1980), Compulsory heterosexuality and lesbian existence. *Signs*, 5/4:631–660.

Riddle, D. I. & Morin, S. (1977), Removing the stigma: Data from individuals. *APA Monitor*, 11:16–28.

Rose, S. & Zand, D. (2000), Lesbian dating and courtship from young adulthood to midlife. *J. Gay & Lesb. Soc. Serv.*, 11:77–04.

Rudolph, J. (1988), Counselors' attitudes toward homosexuality: A selective review of the literature. *J. Counsel. Dev.*, 67:165–168.

Saghir, M. T. & Robbins, E. (1973), *Male and Female Homosexuality: A Comprehensive Investigation*. Baltimore, MD: Williams & Wilkins.

Schafer, R. (1959), Generative empathy in the treatment situation. *Psychoanal. Quart.*, 28:347–373.

Schafer, S. (1976), Sexual and social problems of lesbians. *J. Sex Res.*, 12:50–69.

Schatz, B. & O'Hanlan, K. (1994), *Anti-Gay Discrimination in Medicine: Results of a National Survey of Lesbian, Gay and Bisexual Physicians*. San Francisco: American Association of Physicians for Human Rights.

Schwaber, E. (1983), Psychoanalytic listening and psychic reality. *Internat. J. Psycho-Anal.*, 10:379–392.

Schwartz, A. E. (1998), *Sexual Subjects: Lesbians, Gender, and Psychoanalysis*. New York: Routledge.

Shane, M., Shane, E. & Gales, M. (1997), *Intimate Attachments*. New York: Guilford Press.

Siegel, E. V. (1988), *Female Homosexuality: Choice Without Volition*. Hillsdale, NJ: The Analytic Press.

Slater, S. (1994), Approaching and avoiding the work of the middle years: Affairs in committed lesbian relationships. *Women Ther.*, 15:19–34.

Socarides, C. (1988), *The Preoedipal Origin and Psychoanalytic Theory of Sexual Perversions*. New York: International Universities Press.

Spaulding, E. C. (1993), The inner world of objects and lesbian development. *J. Anal. Soc. Work*, 1:5–31.

Stoller, R. (1968), *Sex and Gender*. New York: Science House.

———— (1976), Primary femininity. *J. Amer. Psychoanal. Assn.*, 24:59–78.

———— (1985), *Presentations of Gender*. New Haven, CT: Yale University Press.

Stolorow, R. D. & Atwood, G. E. (1979), *Faces in a Cloud: Subjectivity in Personality Theory*. New York: Aronson.

———— & ———— (1992), *Contexts of Being: The Intersubjective Foundations of Psychological Life*. Hillsdale, NJ: The Analytic Press.

———— ———— & Brandchaft, B. (1994), *The Intersubjective Perspective*. Northvale, NJ: Aronson.

———— & Lachmann, F. M. (1980), *Psychoanalysis of Developmental Arrests*. New York: International Universities Press.

Suchet, M. (1995), "Having it both ways": Rethinking female sexuality. In: *Lesbians and Psychoanalysis*, ed. J. M. Glassgold & S. Iasenza. New York: Free Press, pp. 39–62.

Teicholz, J. G. (1999). *Kohut, Loewald, and the Postmoderns*. Hillsdale, NJ: The Analytic Press.

Thompson, C. (1942), Cultural pressures in the psychology of women. *Psychiatry*, 5:331–339.

———— (1947), Changing concepts of homosexuality in psychoanalysis. *Psychiatry*, 10:183–189.

Tully, C. T. (1992), Research on older lesbian women: What is known, what is not known, and how to learn more. In: *Gay and Lesbian Lifestyles: A Guide for Counseling and Education*, ed. N. J. Woodman. New York: Irvington Press, pp. 235–264.

———— (1995), In sickness and in health: Forty years of research on lesbians. In: *Lesbian Social Services: Research Issues*, ed. C. T. Tully. New York: Haworth Press, pp. 1–18.

Vetere, V. A. (1982), The role of friendship in the development and maintenance of lesbian love relationships. *J. Homosexual.*, 8:51–65.

Wallerstein, R. (1986), *Forty-Two Lives in Treatment*. New York: Guilford Press.

Weille, K. L. H. (1993), Reworking developmental theory: The case of lesbian identity formation. *Clin. Soc. Work J.*, 21:151–160.

Weinstock, J. S. (2000), Lesbian friendships at midlife: Patterns and possibilities for the 21st century. *J. Gay & Lesb. Soc. Serv.*, 11:1–32.

Westphal, K. F. O. (1869), Die kontrare Sexualempfindung: Sümptom eines Neuropathologischen (psychopathischen) Zustandes. *Arch. Psychiat. Nervenkrank.*, 2:73–108.

Whiston, S. C. & Sexton, T. L. (1993), An overview of psychotherapy outcome research: Implications for practice. *Psychother. Theory Res. Pract.*, 24:43–51.

Winnicott, D. F. (1947), Hate in the countertransference. *Internat. J. Psycho-Anal.*, 30:69–75.

———— (1971), *Playing and Reality*. London: Tavistock.

Wolf, E. S. (1998), *Treating the Self: Elements of Clinical Self Psychology*. New York: Guilford Press.

Woodman, N. J. & Lenna, H. R. (1980), *Counseling Gay Men and Women*. San Francisco: Jossey-Bass.

Index

197